The Godly Family

A series of essays
on the duties of
parents and children.

by
Samuel Davies, Philip Doddridge,
Arthur Hildersham, Thomas Houston,
Samuel Stennett, Henry Venn,
George Whitfield, and Samuel Worcester

With a foreword by Gary Ezzo

Soli Deo Gloria Publications
...for instruction in righteousness...

Soli Deo Gloria Publications
P.O. Box 451, Morgan, PA 15064
(412) 221-1901/FAX 221-1902

*

© 1993 by Soli Deo Gloria Publications.
All rights reserved. Printed in the
United States of America.

*

ISBN 1-877611-73-5

*

Second printing 1996

Contents

Section 3 - The Duties of Children

Section 4 - The Eternal Family

Foreword

This book is for your nightstand, not for gathering dust on the shelf in your guest bedroom. In the cacophony of recently published literature on parenting and family growth, this particular collection of 17th and 18th century works is spiritually refreshing. Soli Deo Gloria Publications brings the 20th century reader back to the basics - the Holy Spirit, the Holy Scriptures, and the duty of families to serve God. This volume contains the work of George Whitfield, Samuel Davies, Arthur Hildersham, Philip Doddridge, Thomas Houston, Samuel Stennett, Henry Venn and Samuel Worcester - venerable men whose theology on the family was bounded by the banks of divine definition and divine purpose of the family.

Those seeking benefit from these early orators, as it relates to family fidelity, are soon struck by the timelessness of their message. Men's hearts and needs have not changed with time. The emotions experienced by a young mother sitting in Arthur Hildersham's congregation in 1627 are the same shared by mothers today. Whitfield sternly warned fathers against secular pursuits at the expense of family leadership. Samuel Worcester told his congregation to get control of their children and exercise godly authority over their souls. Thomas Houston implored parents to seek early the conversion of their children so they would not live for themselves but for God. Philip Doddridge taught that family devotions and prayers are the stuff that strong,

God-loving families are made of. Henry Venn said your children will take seriously only what you take seriously. All this and much more. Whether it be sober-minded assessment, family leadership, exercise of authority, the need for conversion, family devotions, or parental example, this group of eight godly men knew God, knew His people, and knew their needs.

Late twentieth-century Westerners have sophisticated behavior schools of study, with millions of dollars of expenditure on family research. Yet, while information is up, morality is down. It has been said that those who ignore history are destined to repeat misjudgments of the past. Thus we would do well to listen to wisdom calling from the grave. Their views of the family started with a hierarchy of authority. They accepted the headship of the husband and father and proceeded to define the nature of that headship in response to God and the needs of their loved ones. They believed that the ebb and flow of cultural morality depended on what the family is, and what it will become through religious training. They knew that when families are under an ill discipline, all society will be ill disciplined. With that knowledge, they brought their urgent message.

In these pages, you will receive no man-made psychological theories. Whitfield, Davies, Hildersham, Doddridge, Worcester, Houston, Stennett, and Venn thundered forth the good Word of our Lord with power and conviction seldom presented in modern elocution. Different men, living in different places, at different times, sharing a single message. You may ask why a theology of the family is so important? The answer is that the family, not the individual, is the value-generated institution of every society. Once it becomes secular in its thinking, each subsequent generation suffers. Therefore, the cause of God must be maintained in the world, and the family must serve as God's primary mouthpiece. Your soul will feast on this wisdom.

Gary Ezzo
Growing Families International
PO Box 8073
Northridge, CA 91327

1

The Necessity and Excellency
of Family Religion
by Samuel Davies

"But if any provide not for his own, and especially
for those of his own house, he hath denied the faith,
and is worse than an infidel." 1 Timothy 5:8.

The great Author of our nature, who has made us
sociable creatures, has instituted various societies
among mankind, both civil and religious, and
joined them together by the various bonds of relation. The first and radical society is that of a family,
which is the nursery of the church and state. This
was the society instituted in Paradise in the state of
innocence, when the indulgent Creator, finding
that it was not good for man, a sociable creature, to
be alone, formed a helpmeet for him, and united
them in the endearing bonds of the conjugal relation. From thence, the human race was propagated;
and, when multiplied, it was formed into civil governments and ecclesiastical assemblies. Without
these associations, the worship of God could not be
publicly and socially performed, and liberty and
property could not be secured. Without these, men
would turn into savages and roam at large, destitute

of religion, insensible of the human passions, and disregarding each other's welfare. Civil and religious societies are, therefore, wisely continued in the world, and we enjoy the numerous advantages of them. But these do not exclude, but presuppose, domestic societies, which are the materials of which they are composed; and, as churches and kingdoms are formed out of families, they will be such as the materials of which they consist. It is, therefore, of the greatest importance to religion and civil society that families be under proper regulations that they may produce proper plants for church and state and, especially, for the eternal world in which all the temporary associations of mortals in this world finally terminate, and to which they ultimately refer.

Now, in families, as well as in all governments, there are superiors and inferiors. And, as it is the place of the latter to obey, so it belongs to the former both to rule and to provide. The heads of families are obliged not only to exercise their authority over their dependents, but also to provide for them a competency of the necessities of life, and, indeed, their right to rule is but a power to provide for themselves and their domestics.

This is implied in my text, where the apostle makes the omission of this duty utterly inconsistent with Christianity, and a crime so unnatural, that even infidels are free from it. "If any provide not for his own, and specially for those of his own house, he hath denied the faith, and is worse than an infidel."

The apostle, among other things in this chapter, is giving directions how widows should be treated in the church. If they were widows indeed, that is, wid-

owed and entirely destitute of relations to support
them, then he advises to maintain them at the public expense of the church (vss. 3, 9, 10). But if they
were such widows as had children or nephews, then
he orders that they should be maintained by those
their relatives, and that the charge should not fall
upon the church (vss. 4, 16).

He supposes that the relatives of some of them
might be unwilling to put themselves to this expense. And, to engage such to their duty, he exposes
the unnatural wickedness of neglecting it. "If any
provide not for his own, and specially for those of
his own house, he hath denied the faith, and is
worse than an infidel."

By a man's own are meant poor relatives who are
unable to support themselves, and by his house is
meant those that are his domestics and that live
with him, such as wife, children, servants. The former, a man is obliged to provide for, but especially
the latter; and, if he neglects it, he has denied the
faith. In fact, however much he may profess it in
words, he is no Christian, nor to be treated as such.
Nay, he is worse than an infidel, for many heathens
have had so much humanity and natural light as to
observe their duty, supporting their domestics and
such of their relatives as could not procure a subsistence for themselves.

In order to make provision for our families, we
must be careful or laborious, according to our circumstances, and see that all our domestics are so
too. "And him that will not work, neither let him
eat," 2 Thessalonians 3:10.

"This," some of you will say, "is excellent doctrine, and this is our favorite text, which we often descant upon to justify our eager pursuit of the world. This commandment have we kept from our youth up, and, as we exert ourselves to provide estates for our children, we are not chargeable with any guilt in this case."

But stay, sirs. Before you peremptorily conclude yourselves innocent, let me ask you, are your domestics, your wives, children, and servants nothing but material bodies? If so, I grant your duty is fulfilled by providing for their bodies. If they are only formed for this world and have no concern with a future, then it is enough for you to make provision for them in the present state. They are like your cattle, upon this hypothesis, and you may treat them as you do your beasts: fodder them well and make them work for you. But are you so absurd as to indulge such a thought? Are you not fully convinced that your domestics were made for eternity, endowed with immortal souls, and have the greatest concern with the eternal world? If so, can you think it sufficient that you provide for their bodies and their temporal subsistence? I appeal to you, is there not as much reason for your taking care of their immortal spirits as of their perishing bodies? Ought you not to be as regardful and as laborious for their comfortable subsistence in eternity as in time? Nay, is not your obligation to family religion as much more strong, as an immortal spirit is more important than a machine of animated clay, and the interests of eternity exceed those of this transitory world. If, then, he that does not provide for his domestics a competency of the necessities of life has denied the faith, and is worse than an infidel, what shall we say of him that neglects their souls, and takes no pains to form them for a happy immortality? Surely, he must be worse than one that is worse than an infidel, and how extremely bad then must he be! He has more than denied the faith, however confidently he may profess it.

You see that, though this text does not immediately refer to family religion, yet it will admit of a very natural accommodation to that purpose and, in this view, I intend to handle it.

Several of you, my hearers, I do not doubt, have long since formed and practised Joshua's resolution: "As for me and my house, we will serve the Lord," Joshua 24:15. While vanity laughs aloud, and impiety belches out its blasphemies in families around you, the voice of spiritual rejoicing and salvation is heard in your tabernacles, Psalm 118:15. I congratulate you, my dear brethren, and hope your families will be nurseries for religion in future times, and educate many for the heavenly state; nay, I hope you have seen some of the happy effects of it already in the early impressions that begin to appear upon the tender minds of your dear children, and the promising solemnity and reformation of some of your slaves. It were to be wished that all of you made conscience of this matter, and it would not at all seem extravagant to expect it; for, surely, it would not be extravagant to expect that you, who attend upon public worship and profess the religion of Jesus, should not so grossly deny the faith as to be worse than infidels. But, alas! my friends, though I do not affect to be spying into your families, "I am

jealous over you with a godly jealousy", lest some of
you habitually neglect this very important duty.
Though family religion is not the peculiarity of a
party, but owned to be obligatory by Christians in
general (and, therefore, Christians of all denominations should conscientiously observe it, if they
would act consistently with their own principles),
yet are there not several in this assembly who live
without religion in their houses? Conscience can
find out the guilty, and I need not be more particular.

It is certainly a most lamentable thing that any
who have enjoyed such opportunities for instruction, who have been solemnly and frequently
warned, exhorted, and persuaded, and who have
come under the strongest obligation to this duty
should, notwithstanding, live in the wilful and habitual neglect of it. For persons to omit it for want of
instruction about its obligation might be very consistent with a tender conscience, and nothing would
be necessary to bring such to the practice, but to
convince them it is their duty, which it is very easy to
do; but to omit family religion in our circumstances,
my brethren, reveals such a stupid indifference
about religion, or so inveterate an aversion to it, that
it is lamentably doubtful whether a conviction of the
duty will determine you to the practice of it. When
persons have long habituated themselves to sin
against light, it is hard to take any effectual measures to deal with them. All that the ministers of the
gospel can do is to convince their understandings,
to persuade, to exhort, to invite, to threaten; but
such are accustomed to resist these means, and now

they find it no great difficulty to master them. I, therefore, make this attempt with discouragement, and hardly hope to succeed with such of you as have hitherto obstinately fought against conviction; and the attempt is still the more melancholy, as I know that, if what shall be offered does not prevail upon you to make conscience of family religion, the additional light you may receive will but render you more inexcusable, increase your guilt and, consequently, your punishment. This is one of the tremendous consequences of the ministry of this neglected, disregarded gospel that may strike ministers and people with a solemn horror. However, I am not without hopes of success with some of you who have not yet been cursed with a horrid victory over your consciences. I hope that, when you are more fully convinced of this duty, you will immediately begin the practice of it. But though I had no expectation of success, I am still obliged to make the attempt. Though nothing can animate a minister more than the prospect of success, yet he is not to regulate his conduct wholly according to this prospect. He must labor to deliver his own soul by warning even such as may not regard it. He must declare the whole counsel of God whether they hear or whether they forbear. I shall, therefore, my dear brethren, endeavor honestly this day to bring you to Joshua's resolution, that you and your houses will serve the Lord; and let him who is hardy enough to despise it prepare to answer for it at the supreme tribunal, for he despises not man but God.

I would not have you perform anything as a duty till you have sufficient means to convince you that it is a duty; and I would not confine you to an over-frequent performance of the duty I am now to open to you. Therefore, when I have briefly mentioned the various parts of family religion, I shall:

I. Prove it to be a duty from the law of nature and Scripture revelation.

II. Show in what seasons or how frequently family religion should be statedly performed.

III. I shall consider what particular obligation the heads of families lie under, and what authority they are invested with to maintain religion in their houses.

IV. And lastly, I shall answer the usual objections made against this important duty.

As to the parts of family religion, they are prayer, praise, and instruction. We and our families stand in need of blessings in a domestic capacity; therefore, in that capacity, we should pray for them; in that capacity, too, we receive many blessings. Therefore, in that capacity, we should return thanks for them; and singing of psalms is the most proper method of thanksgiving. Further, our domestics need instruction about the great concerns of religion; therefore, we should teach them. But I need not stay to prove each of these branches to be a duty, because the following arguments for the whole of family religion will be equally conclusive for each part of it, and may be easily accommodated to it. Therefore:

I. I shall prove that family religion is a duty from the light of nature and of Scripture.

To prepare the way, I would observe that you

should hear what shall be offered with a mind in love with your duty when it appears. You would not willingly have a cause tried by one that is your enemy; now "the carnal mind is enmity against God" and, consequently, while you retain that carnal mind, you are very unfit to judge the force of those arguments that prove your duty towards him. If you hate the discovery, you will shut your eyes against the light and not receive the truth in love. Therefore, lie open to conviction and I doubt not but you shall receive it from the following arguments.

If family religion is due to the supreme Being, upon the account of His perfections and the relation He bears to us; if it is one great design of the institution of families; if it tends to the advantage of our domestics; if it is our privilege, then family religion appears to be our duty from the law of nature.

PROOFS FROM THE LAW OF NATURE

1. *If family religion is a just debt to the supreme Being, upon account of his perfections and the relation He sustains to us as families, then it must be our duty to maintain it according to the law of nature.* Now this is the case in fact.

God is the most excellent of beings and, therefore, worthy of homage in every capacity from His reasonable creatures. It is the supreme excellency of the Deity that renders Him the object of personal devotion, or the religion of individuals, and the same reason extends to family religion; for such is His excellency that He is entitled to all the worship which we can give Him: and, after all, "He is exalted above all our blessing and praise," Nehemiah 9:5. That is, He still deserves more blessing and praise than we can give Him. Hence, it follows that our capacity is the measure of our obligation to serve Him; that is, in whatever capacity we are that admits of service to Him, we are bound to perform all that service to Him because He justly deserves it all. Now, we are capable of worshipping Him as a family, for family devotion, you must admit, is a thing possible in itself. Therefore, we are bound to worship Him in that capacity. If any of you deny this, put your denial into plain words, and you must shudder at yourselves. It must stand thus, "I must admit that such is the excellency of the Deity that He has a right to all the homage which I can pay Him in every capacity; yet I owe Him none, I will pay Him none in the capacity of a head of a family. I admit I owe Him worship from myself as an individual, but my family as such shall have nothing to do with Him." Will you, sirs, rather run into such an impious absurdity as this than admit yourselves obliged to this duty?

Again, God is the Author of our sociable natures and, as such, claims social worship from us. He formed us capable of society and inclined us to it and, surely, this capacity ought to be improved for religious purposes. Is there any of you so hardy as to say, "Though God has made me a sociable creature, yet I owe Him no worship as such, and will pay Him none?" You may as well say, "Though He formed me a man, and endowed me with powers to serve Him, yet as a man or an individual I will not serve Him." And what is this but to renounce all obligations to

God, and to cut yourselves off from all connection with Him. Now if your social nature lays you under an obligation to social religion, then it must oblige you to family religion, for a family is the first society that ever was instituted. It is a radical society from which all others are derived; therefore, here social religion began (as it must have begun in families before it had place in other societies), and here it ought still to continue.

Again, God is the Proprietor, Supporter, and Benefactor of our families as well as of our persons and, therefore, our families as such should pay Him homage. He is the owner of your families, and where is the man that dares deny it? Dare any of you say, "God has nothing to do with my family; He has no right there, and I will acknowledge none!"? Unhappy creatures! Whose property are you, then? If not God's, you are helpless orphans, indeed, or rather, the voluntary avowed subjects of hell. But if your families are His property, must you not admit that you should worship Him as such? What! Pay no acknowledgment to your great Proprietor? How unjust! The apostle argues that, because our persons are His, therefore, we should serve Him, 1 Corinthians 6:19-20, and, surely, the argument is equally strong in this case. Further, are not your families entirely dependent upon God as their Supporter and Benefactor? Should He withdraw His supporting hand, you and your houses would sink into ruin together. Are you not, then, obliged in a family capacity to acknowledge and praise Him? You also receive numberless blessings from Him in a domestic capacity. Every evening and morning, every night and

day, you find His mercies flowing down upon your
houses, and shall no grateful acknowledgments ascend from them to Him? You also, every moment,
stand in need of numerous blessings not only for
yourselves, but for your families, and will you not
jointly with your families implore these blessings
from your divine Benefactor? Here again consider
the language of your refusal, and it must strike you
with horror: "I admit that God is the proprietor of
my family, that He is the constant support of my
family, that I and mine every moment receive mercies from Him, and depend entirely upon Him for
them; yet my family as such shall pay no worship,
shall serve Him no more than if we had no concern
with Him." Can you venture upon such a declaration
as this?

2. *If family religion was the principal design of the institution of families, then family religion is our indispensable duty.*

That families were founded by God may be in-
ferred from the creation of different sexes, the institution of marriage, the various relations among
mankind, and from the universal agency of his providence, Psalm 68:6 and 113:9.

And that family religion was the principal end of
the institution is evident, for can you think that God
would unite a number of immortals, heirs of the
eternal world together in the most intimate bonds,
in this state of trial without any reference to their future state? Were your families made for this world
only or for the next? If for the next, then religion
must be maintained in them, for that alone can
prepare you for eternity; or if you say your families

were formed for this world, pray, what was this world made for? To be the final residence, or to be only a stage along which to pass into your everlasting home, a place of probation for candidates for immortality? And must not religion, then, be maintained in your families? They should be nurseries for heaven, and that they cannot be if you banish devotion from them.

If the conjugal relation, which is the foundation of families, was first instituted for religious purposes, then, certainly, the worship of God ought to be maintained in them. But the former is true, "Did not He make one?" Malachi 2:15; that is, one of each sex that there might be one for one, and that the very creation of our nature might carry an intimation that polygamy was unnatural. "And wherefore one?" that is, wherefore did God make but one of each sex when He had the residue of the spirit and could have made more? Why, His design was that He might seek a godly seed; that is, that children might not only be procreated, but retain and convey down religion from age to age. But can this design be accomplished if you refuse to maintain religion in your families? Can you expect that godliness shall run on in the line of your posterity if you habitually neglect it in your houses? Can a godly seed be raised in so corrupt a soil? Therefore if you omit this duty, you live in families in direct opposition to the end of the institution and deny your domestics the greatest advantage they can enjoy as members of a family; a consideration which leads me to another argument.

3. If family religion tends to the greatest advantage of our families, then it is our duty; and to neglect it is wickedly to rob ourselves and ours of the greatest advantage.

If you deny that religion is advantageous, you may renounce the name of Christians; yes, and of men, too. Religion places its subjects under the blessing and guardianship of heaven; it restrains them from those practices which may be ruinous to them in time and eternity; it suppresses such dispositions and passions as are turbulent and self-tormenting, and affords the most refined and substantial joys.

Now I appeal to you whether it is not more probable that your family will be religious if you solemnly worship God with them and instruct them than it would be if you neglected these duties? How can you expect that your children and servants will become worshippers of the God of heaven if they have been educated in the neglect of family religion? Can prayerless parents expect to have praying children? If you neglect to instruct them, can you expect they will grow up in the knowledge of God and of themselves? If they see that you receive daily mercies from the God of heaven, and yet refuse Him the tribute of praise, is it not likely they will imitate your ingratitude and spend their days in a stupid insensibility of their obligations to their divine Benefactor? Is it as likely they will make it their principal business in life to secure the favor of God and prepare for eternity, when they see their parents and masters thoughtless about this important concern, as if they saw you every day devoutly worshipping God with them, and imploring His blessing

upon yourselves and your households? Their souls,
sirs, their immortal souls, are entrusted to your care,
and you must give a solemn account of your trust;
and can you think you faithfully discharge it while
you neglect to maintain your religion in your families? Will you not be accessory to their perdition,
and in your skirts will there not be found the blood
of your poor innocent children? What a dreadful
meeting may you expect to have with them at last?
Therefore, if you love your children; if you would
make some amends to your servants for all the service they do to you; if you would bring down the
blessing of heaven upon your families: if you would
have your children make their houses the recepta-
cles of religion when they set up in life for themselves, if you would have religion survive in this
place and be conveyed from age to age; if you would
deliver your own souls; I beseech, I entreat, I charge
you to begin and continue the worship of God in
your families from this day to the close of your lives.

4. *You are to consider family religion not merely as a duty
imposed by authority, but as your greatest privilege granted by
divine grace.* How great the privilege to hold a daily
intercourse with heaven in our dwellings! To have
our houses converted into temples for that adorable
Deity whom the heavens and the heaven of heavens
cannot contain! To mention our domestic wants before Him with the encouraging hope of a supply! To
vent the overflowings of gratitude! To spread the savor of His knowledge, and talk of Him whom angels
celebrate upon their golden harps and in anthems
of praise! To have our families devoted to Him while

others live estranged from the God of their life! If all this does not appear the highest privilege to you, it is because you are astonishingly disaffected to the best of Beings. And, since the Almighty conde-scends to allow you this privilege, will you wickedly deny it yourselves? If He had denied it to you, you would, no doubt, have cavilled at it as hard; you would have murmured had He laid a prohibition on your family and told you, "I will accept worship from other families; they shall converse with Me every day; but, as for yours, I will have nothing to do with them. I will accept no worship from them; you may not make mention of the name of the Lord." How would you tremble if God had marked your families with such a brand of reprobation? And will you put this brand upon them with your own hand? Will you deny that privilege to your families which would strike you with horror if God denied it? Will you af-fect such a horrid singularity that, when other fami-lies are admitted into a familiar audience with the Deity, you will keep from Him and pay Him no homage in yours?

These arguments are chiefly derived from the light of nature, and plainly show that family reli-gion is a duty of natural religion. Accordingly, hea-thens and idolaters have observed it. The heathens had their Lares, their Penates, or household gods. Such were Laban's gods which Rachel stole from him, Genesis 31:34; and such were those of Micah, Judges 17:4-5. These, indeed, were idols, but what did they stand instead of? Did they not stand instead of the true worship of the true God? What reformation was necessary in this case? The renouncing of these

idols and taking nothing in their room? Or the renouncing of them and taking the true God in their
place? Undoubtedly the latter. And will you not
blush that heathens should exceed you? That you
should be, according to the text, "worse than infidels?" And must you not tremble lest they should
rise up in judgment against you, and condemn you?

Proofs from Scripture Revelation

I now proceed to some arguments more purely
scriptural, which prove the necessity of family religion in general, or of some peculiar branch of it.

1. *We may argue from the examples of the saints, recorded
and commended in Scripture.* Good examples infer an
obligation upon us to imitate them; and when they
are transmitted down to posterity with honor in the
sacred records, they are proposed to our imitation,
and as really bind us to the duty as express precepts.

Now we are here surrounded with a bright cloud
of witnesses. Even before the introduction of the
clearer dispensations of the gospel, we find that the
saints carefully maintained family religion.

On this account Abraham was admitted into
such intimacy with God that He admits him into his
secrets. "Shall I hide from Abraham that thing
which I do; for I know him, that he will command
his children and his household after him, and they
shall keep the way of the Lord," Genesis 17:18.

We find that Isaac and Jacob, by the influence of
his good example and instructions, follow the same
practice. They, as well as he, built an altar to the

Lord wherever they pitched their tents; an altar, then, being a necessary utensil for divine worship. This you will find repeatedly in the short history we have of these patriarchs, particularly in Genesis 26:25; 28:18, and 33:20.

We find Job so intent upon family devotion that he rises up early in the morning and offers burnt-offerings; and this he did, we are told, not upon extraordinary occasions only, but continually, Job 1:5.

The devout king David, after he had spent the day in the glad solemnity of bringing the ark to its place, returned to bless his house, 2 Samuel 6:20. He had his hour for family devotion; and, when that is come, he leaves the solemnity of public worship and hastens home. This was agreeable to his resolution, "I will behave myself wisely in a perfect way. I will walk within my house with a perfect heart," Psalm 101:2.

Daniel ran the risk of his life rather than omit this duty, which some of you omit with hardly any temptation. When the royal edict prohibited him upon penalty of being cast into the lion's den, "he still prayed and gave thanks to God, as he did aforetime."

"As he did aforetime." This is added to show that he had always observed a stated course of devotion in his family, and that it was not a transient fit of zeal that now seized him. Daniel 6:10.

These illustrious patterns we find under the dark dispensations of the Old Testament. How much more zealous should we be, who enjoy the meridian light of the gospel, to keep the religion of Jesus in our families!

In the New Testament, we repeatedly find our blessed Lord in prayer with His family, the apostles. St. Paul thrice mentions a church in a private house, Romans 15:5, 1 Corinthians 6:19, and Colossians 4:15, by which he probably means the religious families of Nymphas and that pious pair Priscilla and Aquila. And Cornelius is an instance peculiarly observable, who, though a heathen and ignorant of the coming of Christ, feared God (an expression that often signifies to worship God) with all his house; and prayed unto God always; that is, at all proper seasons. And when a divine messenger was sent to him to direct him to send for Peter, we are told he was found praying in his house; that is, with his domestics, as the word often signifies, Acts 10:2 & 30.

If it might have any weight, after such authentic examples as these, I might add that, in every age, persons of piety have been exemplary in family religion. And, if you look around you, my brethren, you will find, that by how much the more religious persons are, by so much the more conscientious they are in this duty. What if some, like the Pharisees, use it as a cloak for their clandestine wickedness; this is no objection against the practice. Otherwise, there is hardly one branch of religion or morality but what must be rejected too; for every good thing has been abused by hypocrites to disguise their secret villany.

2. *We may argue from several Scripture precepts, which either directly or consequently refer to the whole, or to some branch of family religion.*

The apostle Paul, having given various directions about relative duties in families, subjoins, *Continue in prayer, and watch in the same with thanksgiving,* Colossians 4:1. Peter exhorts husbands to dwell with their wives according to knowledge, that their prayers might not be hindered, 1 Peter 3:7, which certainly implies that they should pray together. And here I may observe, by-the-by, what is, perhaps, immediately intended in this text, that beside the stated worship of God, common to all the family, it may be very proper for the husband and wife to retire for prayer at proper seasons by themselves together. As there is a peculiar intimacy between them, they ought to be peculiarly intimate in the duties of religion; and, when retired together, they may pour out their hearts with more freedom than before all the family and particularize those things that could not be prudently mentioned before others. But to return, we are enjoined to pray always with all prayer and supplication, Ephesians 6:18; and, surely, family prayer must be included in these comprehensive terms.

As to family instruction, it was expressly enjoined upon the Israelites. "These words which I command thee shall be in thy heart, and thou shalt teach them diligently unto thy children, and shalt talk of them when thou sittest in thy house," Deuteronomy 6:6-7, and 11:19. They were commanded to instruct their domestics in the nature and design of the ordinances of that dispensation, particularly the passover, Exodus 12:26-27. And the Psalmist mentions all the wonderful works of God as what ought to be taught by parents to children from age to age. And must not parents now be under even superior obligations to inform their children of the more glorious doctrines and ordinances of the gospel? Again, it is enjoined as a duty common to Christians in general, though they should not be united in one family, to exhort one another daily; Hebrews 3:13; and to teach and admonish one another, Colossians 3:16. How much more, then, is it our duty to teach, admonish, and exhort our families, which are more particularly entrusted to our care?

As to family praise, it is a duty because thanksgiving is so often joined with prayer in Scripture; Philippians 4:6; Colossians 4:2; 1 Thessalonians 5:17-18; and psalmody must be admitted to be the most proper method of expressing thankfulness by such as accept it a part of divine worship. "The voice of rejoicing and salvation is in the tabernacles of the righteous," Psalm 118:15; an expression that may properly signify praising God in psalms, and hymns, and spiritual songs, as we are commanded, Colossians 3:16.

And now, my brethren, I presume you are convinced that family religion is a duty, unless you shut your eyes against the light of nature and the light of Scripture; and, if convinced, you are reduced to this dilemma: either to set up the worship of God immediately in your families or sin wilfully against the knowledge of the truth. And which side will you choose? Oh, sirs, the case is so plain, you need no time to deliberate; it is as plain as whether you should choose life or death, heaven or hell!

If you, from henceforth, make conscience of this

important duty, it will be a most happy omen to your families and to this congregation. If the grateful incense of family devotion were ascending to heaven every morning and evening from every family among us, we might expect a rich return of divine blessings upon ourselves and ours. Our houses would become the temples of the Deity and our congregation feel his gracious influences. Our children would grow up in the knowledge and fear of God and transplant religion from our families into their own whenever they should be formed. Our servants and slaves would become the servants of righteousness and heirs with us of the grace of life. The animosities and contests that may now disturb our households, and render them like the dens of wild beasts, would cease. Vice would wither and die among us, and languishing religion would lift up its head and revive. This would certainly be the consequence in several instances if we were but to maintain family religion in a proper manner, for God has not commanded us to seek His face in vain; and, if this desirable success should not be granted universally, we shall still have the comfort to reflect that we have done our duty.

But how shocking is the prospect, if you are determined to resist conviction and live in the wilful neglect of this duty! Your families are like to be nurseries for hell; or, if there should be an Abijah in them, one "in whom some good thing is found towards the Lord God of Israel," 1 Kings 14:13, no thanks to you for it; you must be punished for your neglect of Him as though he had perished by your iniquity.

Remember, sirs, that the omission of a known, practical duty against the remonstrances of your conscience is a certain evidence that you are entirely destitute of all religion; and, therefore, I must discharge the artillery of heaven against you in that dreadful imprecation which, as dictated by inspiration, is equivalent to a prediction or denunciation. "Pour out Thy fury upon the heathen that know Thee not, and upon the families that call not on Thy name," Jeremiah 10:25. Observe here that you are ranked with heathens that know not God, and that the divine fury is imprecated upon you, and it shall fall; it shall fall speedily upon your devoted heads and your prayerless families unless you fly out of its reach by flying to the Lord in earnest supplications in your houses. Will you rather run the venture? Will you rather destroy yourselves and your domestics too, than spend a quarter or half an hour, morning and evening, in the most manly, noble, heavenly, evangelical exercises of devotion? Surely, you are not so hardy! Surely, you are not so averse to God and careless about your own welfare, and that of your dearest relatives and domestics! I request, I beg, I adjure you by your regard to the authority of God, by your concern for your own salvation and that of your families, by the regards you bear the interests of religion in this place and your poor minister, that this may be the happy evening from whence you may date the worship of God in your houses; that this may be the blessed era from which you and your houses will serve the Lord. I proceed:

II. To show in what seasons, or how frequently, family religion should be statedly performed.

Now it is more than intimated in Scripture that it should be performed every day and, particularly, morning and evening. Thus, the sacrifices under the law which were attended with prayer were offered daily, morning and evening. To this the Psalmist alludes, "Let my prayer be set forth before thee as incense," which was offered in the morning, "and the lifting up of my hands as the evening sacrifice," Psalm 141:2. Yea, his devotion was so extraordinary that he resolved, "Evening, and morning, and at noon, will I pray and cry aloud," Psalm 92:1-2.

Further, reason directs us to morning and evening as the proper season for family worship; for, pray, which would you omit? Dare you venture your families out into the world all the day without committing them to the care of Providence in the morning? Can you undertake your secular pursuits without imploring the divine blessing upon them? And, as to the evening, how can you venture to sleep without committing yourselves and yours to the divine protection, and returning thanks for the mercies of the day? Again, the very course of nature seems to direct us to these seasons. Our life is parcelled out into so many days; and every day is a kind of life and sleep a kind of death. And shall we enter upon life in the morning without acknowledging the Author of our life? Or shall we, as it were, die in the evening and not commend our departing spirits into His hands? Night is a kind of pause, a stop in the progress of life, and should kindle a devout temper in us towards our divine Preserver. I shall only add that the prophet hints that we should seek the Lord as the Author of the revolutions of night and day; "Seek Him that turneth the shadow of death into the morning, and maketh the day dark with night," Amos 5:8; that is, seek Him under that notion; and what time so proper for this as evening and morning? Therefore, my brethren, determine to begin and conclude the day with God.

III. I shall consider what particular obligation the heads of families lie under, and what authority they are invested with to maintain religion in their houses.

In all societies there must be a subordination, and particularly in families; and it is the place of the head of such societies to rule and direct. Particularly, it belongs to the head of a family, when there is no fitter person present to perform worship in it, to use proper means to cause all His domestics to attend upon it. The gentler means of persuasion ought to be used where they will succeed; but, when it is unavoidable, compulsive measures may be taken to oblige all our domestics to an attendance. The consciences of all, bond and free, are subject to God only, and no man ought to compel another to any thing as a duty that is against his conscience. But this is not the case here. Your domestics may plead a great many excuses for not joining in family worship, but they will hardly plead that it is against their conscience; that is, they will hardly say that they think they should sin against God in so doing. Here, then, you may use your authority; and perhaps some word they hear may touch their hearts. You should, in common cases, cause them all to attend morning and evening, unless your servants are scattered in different quarters and make conscience of praying together, which you should exhort them to do, and for which you should allow them convenient time.

That you are authorized and obliged to all this is evident from God's commending Abraham for commanding his children, etc.; from Joshua's resolving that not only he, but also his house, should serve the Lord; a resolution he could not perform unless he had authority over his house to compel them, at least externally, to serve the Lord, Joshua 24:15, and from the superiority which you have over your domestics, which enables you to command them in this case, as well as in your own affairs.

IV. And lastly, I come to answer the usual objections against this important duty of family religion.

It would be more honest for people frankly to admit that they have no heart to it, and that this is the real cause of their neglecting it, and not any valid objections they have against it; but, since they will torture their invention to discover some pleas to excuse themselves, we must answer them.

OBJECTION ONE. "I have no time, and my secular business would suffer by family religion."

Were you formed for this world only, there would be some force in this objection; but how strange such an objection sounds in the heir of an eternity! Pray, what is your time given to you for? And have you no time for what is the great business of your lives?

Again, why do you not plead, too, that you have

no time for your daily meals? Is food more necessary for your bodies than religion for your souls? If you think so, what is become of your understandings?

Further, what employment do you follow? Is it lawful or unlawful? If unlawful, then renounce it immediately; if lawful, then it will admit of the exercise of family religion, for God cannot command contradictions; and since He has commanded you to maintain His worship in your houses, that is demonstration that every calling which He allows you to follow will afford time for it.

Finally, may you not redeem as much time from idle conversation, from trifling, or even from your sleep, as may be sufficient for family religion? May you not order your family devotion so that your domestics may attend upon it, either before they go out to their work or when they come to their meals?

OBJECTION TWO. "I have no ability to pray; I am too ignorant."

If you had a proper sense of your wants, this plea would not hinder you. Did you ever hear a beggar, however ignorant, make this objection? A sense of his necessities is an unfailing fountain of his eloquence.

Further, how strange does this objection sound from you! What! Have you enjoyed preaching, Bibles, and good books so long, and yet do not know what to ask of God? Alas! What have you been doing?

Again, is neglecting prayer the way to improve in knowledge and qualify you to perform it?

Finally, may you not easily furnish yourselves

with forms of prayer, which you may use as persons weak in their limbs do their crutches, till you can lay them aside? It is bigotry only that will say that you should neglect the substance of the duty if you cannot perform every circumstance of it in the best manner.

OBJECTION THREE. "I am ashamed."
But is this shame well grounded? Is it really a shame to worship the God of heaven and share in the employment of angels? Are sinners ashamed to serve their Master. A little practice will easily free you from all this difficulty.

OBJECTION FOUR. "But, alas! I know not how to begin it."
Here, indeed, the difficulty lies; but why will you not own that you were hitherto mistaken, and that you would rather reform than persist obstinately in the omission of an evident duty?

OBJECTION FIVE. "But my family will not join with me."
How do you know? Have you tried? Are you not master of your own family? Exert that authority in this which you claim in other cases.

OBJECTION SIX. "But I shall be ridiculed and laughed at."
Are you then more afraid of a laugh or a jeer than the displeasure of God? Would you rather please men than Him?
Will you never become religious till you can ob-

tain the applause of the wicked for being so? Then you will never be religious at all.

Think how you will bear the contempt of the whole universe at last for the neglect of this duty!

Therefore, wherever you have your habitation, there let Jehovah, may I so speak, have an altar, and there let morning and evening prayers and praises be presented till you are called to worship Him in His temple above, where your prayers shall be swallowed up in everlasting praise. Amen.

2

The Great Duty of Family Religion
by George Whitfield

"As for me and my house, we will serve the Lord."
Joshua 24:15

These words contain the holy resolution of pious Joshua. In a most moving, affectionate discourse, he had recounted to the Israelites what great things God had done for them. In the verse immediately preceding the text, he drew a proper inference from what he had been delivering, and acquaints them in the most pressing terms that, since God had been so exceedingly gracious unto them, they could do no less than out of gratitude for such uncommon favors and mercies, dedicate both themselves and families to His service. "Now, therefore, fear the Lord and serve Him in sincerity and truth, and put away the gods which your fathers served on the other side of the flood." And by the same engaging motive, the prophet Samuel afterwards enforces their obedience to the command-ments of God, 1 Samuel 12:24, "Only fear the Lord and serve Him with all your heart; for consider how great things He hath done for you."

But then, that they might not excuse themselves (as too many might be apt to do) by his giving them a bad example, or think he was laying heavy burdens upon them while he himself touched them not with one of his fingers, he tells them in the text that whatever regard they might pay to the doctrine he had been preaching, yet he (as all ministers ought to do) was resolved to live up to and practice it himself: "Choose you therefore whom you will serve, whether the gods which your fathers served, or the gods of the Amorites, in whose land ye dwell; but as for me and my house, we will serve the Lord."

This resolution was worthy of Joshua, and no less becoming, no less necessary, for every true son of Joshua who is entrusted with the care and government of a family in our day; and, if it was ever seasonable for ministers to preach up, or people to put in practice, family religion, it was never more so than in the present age. It is greatly to be feared that out of those many hosueholds that call themselves Christians, there are but few that serve God in their respective families as they ought.

It is true indeed; visit our churches and you may perhaps see something of the form of godliness still subsisting among us; but even that is scarcely to be met with in private houses. So that were the blessed angels to come, as in the patriarchal age, and observe our spiritual economy at home, would they not be tempted to say, as Abraham said to Abimelech, "Surely the fear of God is not in this place," Genesis 20:11?

How such a general neglect of family religion first began to overspread the Christian world is difficult to determine. As for the primitive Christians, I am sure it was not so with them. No, they had not so learned Christ as falsely to imagine religion was to be confined solely to their assemblies for public worship; but, on the contrary, they behaved with such piety and exemplary holiness in their private families that St. Paul often calls their house a church. Salute such a one, says he, and the church which is in his house. And I believe we must forever despair of seeing a primitive spirit of piety revived in the world until we are so happy to see a revival of primitive family religion; and persons unanimously resolving with good old Joshua, in the words of the text, "As for me and my house, we will serve the Lord."

From which words I shall beg leave to insist on these three things.

I. It is the duty of every governor of a family to take care that not only he himself, but also that those committed to his charge, serve the Lord.

II. I shall endeavor to show after what a manner a governor and his household ought to serve the Lord.

III. I shall offer some motives in order to excite all governors, with their respective households, to serve the Lord in the manner that shall be recommended.

I. First, I am to show that it is the duty of every governor of a family to take care that not only he himself, but also those committed to his charge, should serve the Lord.

This will appear if we consider that every governor of a family ought to look upon himself as obliged to act in three capacities: as a prophet to instruct; as a priest to pray for and with; as a king to govern, direct, and provide for them. It is true, indeed, that the latter of these, their kingly office, they are not so frequently deficient in (nay, in this they are generally too solicitous);

but as for the former, their priestly and prophetic offices, like Gallio, they care for no such things. But
however indifferent some governors may be about it,
they may be assured that God will require a due discharge of these offices at their hands. For if, as the
apostle argues, he that does not provide for his own
house in temporal things has denied the faith and is
worse than an infidel, to what greater degree of apostasy must he have arrived who takes no thought to provide for the spiritual welfare of his family?

But further, persons are generally very liberal of
their invectives against the clergy, and think they justly
blame the conduct of that minister who does not take
heed to and watch over the flock of which the Holy
Ghost has made him an overseer; but may not every
governor of a family be in a lower degree liable to the
same censure who takes no thought for those souls
who are committed to his charge? For every house is,
as it were, a little parish, every governor (as was before
observed) a priest, every family a flock; and if any of
them perishes through the governor's neglect, their
blood will God require at his hands.

Were a minister to disregard teaching his people
publicly and from house to house, and to excuse himself by saying that he had enough to do to work out his
own salvation with fear and trembling, without concerning himself with that of others, would you not be
apt to think such a minister to be like the unjust judge
who neither feared God nor regarded man? And yet,
odious as such a character would be, it is no worse than
that governor of a family deserves who thinks himself
obliged only to save his own soul without paying any regard to the souls of his household. For (as was above

hinted) every house is, as it were, a parish, and every master is concerned to secure, as much as in him lies, the spiritual prosperity of everyone under his roof, as any minister whatever is obliged to look to the spiritual welfare of every individual person under his charge.

What precedents men who neglect their duty in this particular can plead for such omission, I cannot tell. Doubtless not the example of holy Job, who was so far from imagining that he had no concern as governor of a family with anyone's soul but his own, that the Scripture acquaints us, "When the days of his children's feasting were gone about, that Job sent and sanctified them, and offered burnt offerings, according to the number of them all; for Job said, It may be that my sons have sinned and cursed God in their hearts. Thus did Job continually." Nor can they plead the practice of good old Joshua whom, in the text, we find as much concerned for his household's welfare as his own. Nor lastly, that of Cornelius, who feared God not only himself, but with all his house. And were Christians but of the same spirit of Job, Joshua, and the Gentile centurion, they would act as Job, Joshua, and Cornelius did.

But alas! If this is the case, and all governors of families ought not only to serve the Lord themselves, but likewise to see that their respective households do so too, what will then become of those who not only neglect serving God themselves, but also make it their business to ridicule and scoff at any of their house that do? Who are not content with "not entering into the kingdom of heaven themselves, but those also that are willing to enter in, they hinder." Surely such men are factors for the devil indeed. Surely their damnation slumbers not. For although God, in His good providence, may suffer such stumbling blocks to be put in His children's way, and suffer their greatest enemies to be those of their own households, for a trial of their sincerity and improvement of their faith; yet we cannot but pronounce a woe against those masters by whom such offenses come. For if those that only take care of their own souls can scarcely be saved, where will such monstrous profane and wicked governors appear?

II. But hoping there are but few of this unhappy stamp, we proceed now to the second thing proposed: to show after what manner a governor and his household ought to serve the Lord.

1. *The first thing I shall mention is reading the Word of God.* This is a duty incumbent on every private person. "Search the Scriptures, for in them ye thnk ye have eternal life" is a precept given by our blessed Lord indifferently to all; but much more so ought every governor of a family to think it in a peculiar manner spoken to himself because (as has been already proved) he ought to look upon himself as a prophet, and therefore, agreeably to such a character, bound to instruct those under his charge in the knowledge of the Word of God.

This we find was the order God gave to His peculiar people Israel, for thus speaks His representative Moses, Deuteronomy 6:6-7, "These words (that is, the Scripture words) which I command thee this day, shall be in thy heart, and thou shalt teach them diligently unto thy children (that is, as it is generally explained, servants as well as children), and thou shalt talk of them when thou sittest in thy house." From whence we may infer that the only reason why so many neglect to read the words of Scripture diligently to their children is because the words of Scripture are not in their hearts; for if they were, out of the abundance of their heart their mouth would speak.

Besides, servants as well as children are, for the generality, very ignorant, and mere novices in the law of God. And how shall they know unless someone teaches them? And what more proper to teach them by than the lively oracles of God "which are able to make them wise unto salvation?" And who more proper to instruct them by these lively oracles than parents and masters who (as has been more than once observed) are as much concerned to feed them with spiritual as with bodily bread day by day.

But if these things are so, what a miserable condition are those unhappy governors in who are so far from feeding those committed to their care with the sincere milk of the Word, to the intent they may grow thereby, that they neither search the Scriptures themselves, nor are careful to explain them to others? Such families must be in a happy way indeed to do their Master's will who take such prodigious pains to know it! Would not one imagine that they had turned converts to the church of Rome, that they thought ignorance to be the mother of devotion, and that those were to be condemned as heretics who read their Bibles? And yet, how few families are there among us who do not act after this unseemly manner! "But shall I praise them in this? I praise them not; brethren, this thing ought not so to be."

2. *The second means whereby every governor and his*

household ought to serve the Lord is family prayer.

This is a duty though as much neglected, yet as absolutely necessary as the former. Reading is a good preparative for prayer, as prayer is an excellent means to render reading effectual. And the reason why every governor of a family should join both these exercises together is plain, because a governor of a family cannot perform his priestly office (which we before observed he is, in some degree, invested with) without performing this duty of family prayer.

We find it, therefore, remarked when mention is made of Cain and Abel offering sacrifices, that they brought them. But to whom did they bring them? Why, in all probability it was to their Father Adam, who as priest of the family was to offer sacrifice in their names. And so, likewise, ought every spiritual son of the second Adam, who is entrusted with the care of a household, to offer up the spiritual sacrifices of supplications and thanksgivings acceptable to God through Jesus Christ, in the presence and name of all who wait upon or eat meat at his table.

Thus we read our blessed Lord behaved when He tabernacled among us. For it is said often that He prayed with His twelve disciples, which was then His little family. And He Himself has promised a particular blessing to joint supplications: "Wheresoever two or three are gathered together in My name, there am I in the midst of them." And again, "If two or three are agreed touching anything they shall ask, it shall be given them." Add to this that we are commanded by the apostle to pray always, with all manner of supplication, which doubtless includes family prayer. And holy Joshua, when he set up the good resolution in the text, that he and his household would serve the Lord, certainly resolved to pray with his family, which is one of the best testimonies they could give of their serving him.

Besides, there are no families but what have some common blessings of which they have been all partakers to give thanks for; some common crosses and afflictions which they are to pray against; some common sins which they are all to lament and bewail. But how this can be done without joining together in one common act of humiliation, supplication, and thanksgiving is difficult to devise.

From all which considerations put together it is evident that family prayer is a great and necessary duty; and, consequently, those governors that neglect it are certainly without excuse. And it is much to be feared that, if they live without family prayer, they live without God in the world.

And yet, such a hateful character as this is, it is to be feared that, were God to send out an angel to destroy us as He once did to destroy the Egyptian firstborn, and withal give him a commision, as then, to spare no houses but where they saw the blood on the lintel, sprinkled on the door post, so now, to let no families escape but those that called upon him in morning and evening prayer, few would remain unhurt by his avenging sword. Shall I term such families Christians or heathens? Doubtless they do not deserve the name of Christians; and heathens will surely rise up in judgment against such profane families of this generation, for they had always their household gods whom they worshipped, and whose assistance they frequently invoked. And a pretty pass those families surely are arrived at who must be sent to school to Pagans. But will not the Lord be avenged on such profane households as these? Will He not pour out His fury on those that do not call upon His name?

3. *But it is time for me to hasten to the third and last means I shall recommend, whereby every governor ought, with his household, to serve the Lord: catechising and instructing their children and servants, and bringing them up in the nurture and admonition of the Lord.*

That this, as well as the two former, is a duty incumbent upon every governor of a house appears from that famous encomium or commendation God gives of Abraham, "I know that he will command his children and his household after him to keep the way of the Lord to do justice and judgment." And indeed scarcely any thing is more frequently pressed upon us in the holy writ than this duty of catechizing. Thus says God, in a passage before cited, "Thou shalt teach these words diligently to thy children." And parents are commanded in the New Testament to train up their children in the nurture and admonition of the Lord. The holy Psalmist acquaints us that one great end why God did such great wonders for His people was to the intent that when they grew up, they should show their children, or servants, the same. And in Deuteronomy 6, at the 20th and following verses, God strictly commands His people to instruct their children in the true nature of the ceremonial worship when they should inquire about it, as He supposed they would do in time to come. And if servants and children were to be instructed in the nature of the Jewish rites, much more ought they now to be initiated and grounded in the doctrines and first principles of the gospel of Christ; not only because it is a revelation which has brought life and immortality to a fuller and clearer light, but also because many seducers are gone abroad into the world who do their utmost endeavor to destroy not only the superstructure, but likewise to sap the very foundation of our most holy religion.

Would the present generation have their posterity be true lovers and honorers of God? Masters and parents must take Solomon's good advice and train up and catechize their respective households in the way wherein they should go.

I am aware of but one objection that can, with any show of reason, be urged against what has been advanced; which is that such a procedure as this will take up too much time, and hinder families too long from their worldly business. But it is much to be questioned whether persons that start such an objection are not of the same hypocritical spirit as the traitor Judas who had indignation against devout Mary for being so profuse of her ointment in anointing our blessed Lord, and asked why it might not be sold for two hundred pence and given to the poor. For has God given us so much time to work for ourselves, and shall we not allow some small pittance of it, morning and evening, to be devoted to His more immediate worship and service? Have not people read that it is God who gives men power to get wealth and, therefore, that the best way to prosper in the world is to secure His favor? And has not our blessed Lord Himself promised that if we seek first the kingdom of God and His righteousness, all outward gifts shall be added unto us?

Abraham, no doubt, was a man of as great business

as such objectors may be; but yet he would find time to command his household to serve the Lord. Nay, David was a king and, consequently, had a great deal of business upon his hands. Yet, notwithstanding, he professed that he would walk in his house with a perfect heart. And, to instance but one more, holy Joshua was a person certainly engaged very much in temporal affairs, and yet he solemnly declared before all Israel that as for him and his household they would serve the Lord. And if person would redeem their time, as Abraham, or David, or Joshua did, they would no longer complain that family duties kept them too long from the business of the world.

III. But my third and last general head, under which I was to offer some motives in order to excite all governors with their respective households to serve the Lord in the manner before recommended I hope will serve instead of a thousand arguments to prove the weakness and folly of any such objection.

1. *The first motive I shall mention is the duty of gratitude which you who are governors of families owe to God.* Your lot, everyone must confess, is cast in a fair ground; providence has given you a goodly heritage above many of your fellow creatures. And, therefore, out of a principle of gratitude, you ought to endeavor, as much as in you lies, to make every person of your respective households to call upon Him as long as they live; not to mention that the authority with which God has invested you as parents and governors of families is a talent committed to your trust, and which you are bound to improve to your Master's honor. In other things we find governors and parents can exercise lordship over

their children and servants readily, and frequently enough can say to one, "Go," and he goes; and to another, "Come," and he comes; to third, "Do this," and he does it. And shall this power be so often employed in your own affairs and never exerted in the things of God? Be astonished, O heavens, at this!

Faithful Abraham did not do this. No, God said that he knew Abraham would "command his servants and children after him." Joshua did not do this. No, he was resolved not only to walk with God himself, but to improve his authority in making all about him to do so too. "As for me and my household, we will serve the Lord." Let us go and do likewise.

2. *But, if gratitude to God will not move you, I think love and pity to your children should move you, with your respective families, to serve the Lord.*

Most people express a great fondness for their children; nay, so great that very often their own lives are wrapped up in those of their offspring. "Can a woman forget her sucking child, that she should not have compassion on the son of her womb?" says God by His prophet Isaiah. He speaks of it as a monstrous thing, and scarcely credible; but the words immediately following affirm it to be possible. Yes, they may forget, and experience also assures us they may. Father and mother may both forsake their children, for what greater degree of forgetfulness can they express towards them than to neglect the improvement of their better part, and not bring them up in the knowledge and fear of God.

It is true, indeed, parents seldom forget to provide for their children's bodies (though it is to be feared

that some men are so far sunk beneath the beasts that
perish as to neglect even that), but then how often do
they forget, or rather, when do they remember to secure the salvation of their immortal souls? But is this
their way of expressing their fondness for the fruit of
their bodies? Is this the best testimony they can give of
their affection to the darling of their hearts? Then was
Delilah fond of Samson when she delivered him up in
to the hands of the Philistines; then were those ruffians
well-affected to Daniel when they threw him into a den
of lions.

3. *But, if neither gratitude to God or love and pity to your*
children will prevail on you, yet let a principle of common
honesty and justice move you to set up the holy resolution in
the text.

This is a principle which all men would be thought
to act upon. But certainly, if any may be truly censured
for their injustice, none can be more liable to such
censure than those who think themselves injured if
their servants withdraw themselves from their bodily
work, and yet they in return take no care of their inestimable souls. For is it just that servants should spend
their time and strength in their master's service, and
masters not at the same time give them what is just and
equal for their service?

It is true, some men may think they have done
enough when they give unto their servants food and
raiment and say, "Did I not bargain with you for so
much a year?" But if they give them no other reward
than this, they are doing no more than they do for
their very beasts! But are not servants better than they?
Doubtless they are; and however masters may put off

their convictions for the present, they will find that a
time will come when they shall know they ought to
have given them some spiritual as well as temporal
wages; and the cry of those that have mowed down
their fields will enter into the ears of the Lord of
Sabaoth.

4. *But, if neither gratitude to God, pity to children, nor a
principle of common justice to servants are sufficient to balance all objections, yet let that darling, that prevailing motive
of self-interest turn the scale and engage you with your respective households to serve the Lord.*

This weighs greatly with you in other matters. Be
then persuaded to let it have a due and full influence
on you in this; and, if it has, if you have but faith as a
grain of mustard seed, how can you avoid believing
that promoting family religion would be the best
means to promote your own temporal as well as eternal
welfare? For "godliness has the promise of the life that
now is as well as that which is to come."

Besides, you all, doubtless, wish for honest servants
and pious children, and to have them prove otherwise
would be as great grief to you as it was to Elisha to have
a treacherous Gehazi or David to be troubled with a
rebellious Absalom. But how can it be expected they
should learn their duty unless those set over them take
care to teach it to them? Is it not as reasonable to expect you should reap where you had not sown, or
gather where you had not strewed?

If Christianity indeed gave any countenance to
children and servants to disregard their parents and
masters according to the flesh, or represent their duty
to them as inconsistent with entire obedience to their

Father and Master who is in heaven, there might then
be some pretense for neglecting to instruct them in
the principles of such a religion. But, since the precepts of this pure and undefiled religion are all of
them holy, just, and good, and the more they are
taught their duty to God, the better they will perform
their duties to you, I think to neglect the improvement
of their souls out of a dread of spending too much
time in religious duties is acting quite contrary to your
own interest as well as duty.

5. *Last, if neither gratitude to God, love to your children,
common justice to your servants, nor even that most prevailing motive, self–interest, will excite, yet let a consideration of
the terrors of the Lord persuade you to put into practice the pious resolution in the text.* Remember, the time will come,
and that perhaps very shortly, when we must all appear
before the judgment seat of Christ; where we must give
a solemn and strict account how we have had our conversation in our respective families in this world. How
will you endure to see your children and servants (who
ought to be your joy and crown of rejoicing in the day
of our Lord Jesus Christ) coming out as so many swift
witnesses against you, cursing the father that begot
them, the womb that bare them, the breasts which they
have sucked, and the day they ever entered into your
houses? Do you not think that the damnation which
men must endure for their own sins will be sufficient,
that they need to load themselves with the additional
guilt of being an accessory to the damnation of others
also? O consider this, all you who forget to serve the
Lord with your respective households, "lest He pluck
you away, and there be none to deliver you!"

But God forbid, brethren, that any such evil should befall you. No, rather I will hope that you have been, in some measure, convinced by what has been said of the great importance of family religion; and, therefore, are ready to cry out in the worlds immediately following the text, "God forbid that we should forsake the Lord;" and again in verse 21, "Nay, but we will (with our several households) serve the Lord."

And that there may be always such a heart in you, let me exhort all governors of families, in the name of our Lord Jesus Christ, often to reflect on the inestimable worth of their own souls and the infinite ransom, even the precious blood of Jesus Christ, which has been paid down for them. Remember that you are fallen creatures; that you are, by nature, lost and estranged from God; and that you can never be restored to your primitive happiness until, by being born again of the Holy Ghost, you arrive at your primitive state of purity and have the image of God re-stamped upon your souls and, thereby, are made meet to be partakers of the inheritance with the saints in light. Do, I say, but seriously and frequently reflect on and act as persons that believe such important truths, and you will no more neglect your family's spiritual welfare than your own.

No, the love of God which will then be shed abroad in your hearts will constrain you to do your utmost to preserve them. And the deep sense of God's free grace in Christ Jesus (which you will then have) in calling you, will excite you to do your utmost to save others, especially those of your own household. And, though, after all your pious endeavors, some may continue unreformed, yet you will have this comfortable reflection to make, that you did what you could to make your families religious. And, therefore, you may rest assured of setting down in the kingdom of heaven with Abraham, Joshua, and Cornelius, and all the godly householders who, in their several generations, shone forth as so many lights in their respective households upon earth. Amen.

3

A Plain and Serious Address to the Master of a Family on the Important Subject of Family Religion
by Philip Doddridge

Sir, you may easily apprehend that the many inter-ruptions to which personal visits are liable make it dif-ficult for ministers to find a convenient time in which they may apply themselves suitably and largely to those committed to their care; or, at least, they will necessar-ily make their progress through large congregations very slow. I, therefore, take this method of visiting you while alone, and of addressing you on the very impor-tant subject of family religion. For your own sake, and the sake of those dearest to you, I entreat you to give a calm, attentive hearing. And I would particularly desire that, if it is by any means practical (as with a little con-trivance and resolution I hope it may be), you would secure one hour on the morning of the Lord's Day af-ter you receive it, not merely to run over this letter in a cursory manner, but deliberately to weigh and con-sider it, and to come to some determination as in the sight of God that you will, or that you will not, comply with the petition which it brings; if I may not rather say, with the demand which, in His name, it makes upon you.

As I purpose to deliver it to every master of a family under my stated care, or to every mistress where there is no master (that no offense of any kind may be taken which it is in my power to prevent), I know it will come to many who have long been exemplary for their diligence and zeal in the duties I am recommending; to many whom their own experience has instructed in the pleasures and advantages which flow from them, and experience which will enforce them more effectually than anything which it is possible for me to say.

Such will, I hope, be confirmed by what they read in pursuing the good resolution they have taken and the good customs they have formed; and will also be excited more earnestly to endeavor to contribute towards introducing the like into other families over which they have any influence, and especially into those which may branch out from their own by the settlement of children and servants. In this view, as well as to awaken their thankfulness to divine grace, which has inclined them to the discharge of their duty in so great, yet so frequently neglected, an article of it, I hope the heads of praying families will not peruse this letter in vain. But it is intended as an address to those who have hitherto lived in the omission of it. And if there were but one such master of a family under my care, I would gladly submit to the labor in which I am now engaging myself for his sake alone. To such, therefore, I now turn myself, and O that divine grace might engage every one of such a character to hear me with attention, and might enforce upon his conscience the weight of reasons, the evidence of which the lowest may receive, and to which it is impossible that the highest should find anything solid to object!

Oh, my dear friend, whoever you are (for I know no one under my care to whom I may not address that appellation), give me leave to tell you plainly that, while I write this, I have that awakening Scripture before me, "Pour out Thy fury upon the heathen, that know Thee not, and upon the families that call not on Thy name," Jeremiah 10:25. I appeal to you whether this does not strongly imply that every family which is not a heathen family, which is not quite ignorant of the living and true God, will call upon His name. Well may it then pain my heart to think that there should be a professedly Christian family whom this dreadful character suits. Well may it pain my heart to think of the divine fury which may be poured out on the heads and on the members of it. And well may it make me desirous to do my utmost to secure you and yours from every appearance, from every possibility of such danger. Excuse the earnestness with which I may address you. I really fear lest, while you delay, the fire of the divine displeasure should fall upon you, Genesis 19:16-17. And as I adore the patience of God in having this long suspended the storm, I am anxious about every hour's delay, lest it should fall heavier.

I will, therefore, as plainly and seriously as I can, endeavor to convince you of your duty, if peradventure you are not already secretly convinced of it; as truly I believe, most who neglect it under the regular administration of gospel ordinances are. I will, then, touch on a few of those objections which have been pleaded to excuse, in some degree, so shameful an omission. And this will naturally lead me to conclude with a few hints which may serve by way of direction for the proper introduction and discharge of the services to which I am endeavoring to engage you.

I do not mean to handle the subject at large, which would afford abundant matter for a considerable volume; as indeed several volumes have been written upon it by divines of different denominations who, however various in other opinions, agree here. And what intelligent Christian can disagree? But I mean to suggest a few plain things which, it is evident, you have not sufficiently considered, and which, if duly weighed, may by the blessing of God answer my present purpose. No the arguments I propose will be such that, if you will not regard them little is to be hoped from any other. For surely the mind of man can discover none of greater and more universal importance, though I readily acknowledge that many others might enforce them with greater energy and address. Yet if the desire, the most earnest desire of succeeding can add any of the proper arts of persuasion, they will not be lacking here. And I would fain speak as one who considers how much of the glory of God, how much of your own happiness, and that of your dear children, for time and eternity, depends on the success of what I am now to lay before you.

What I desire and entreat of you is that you would honor and acknowledge God in your families by calling them together every day to hear some part of His Word read to them, and to join, for a few minutes at least, in your confessions, prayers, and praises to Him. And is this a cause that should need to be pleaded at large by a great variety of united motives? Truly the petition seems so reasonable, and a compliance with it from one who has not quite renounced religion might

seem so natural, that one would think the bare propos-
ing of it would suffice. Yet experience tells it is otherwise. This letter will come into the hands of some who,
though they maintain a public profession of religion,
have been again and again exhorted to it in vain, and
that for succeeding years. I might say a great deal to
upbraid such especially, on account of this neglect, but
I rather choose to entreat to the future performance of
the duty; humbly hoping that, criminal as former negligence has been, a gracious God will mercifully forgive
it to those who repent and desire to reform.

And O that I could engage you to this by presenting in the plainest, kindest, and most affectionate
manner, the reasonableness and advantage of this
duty! For if it is reasonable, if it is evidently advantageous, there are numberless general precepts of
Scripture which must comprehend and enforce it, if it
were less immediately supported than it is by particular
passages; which yet, as I shall presently show, do many
of them strongly recommend it us.

Consider, sir, for I address myself to every particular person, seriously consider the reasonableness of
family religion. Must not your conscience presently tell
you it is fit that persons who receive so many mercies
together should acknowledge them together? Can you,
in your own mind, be satisfied that you and your nearest relatives should pay no joint homage to that God
who has set you in your family, and who has given to
you, and to the several members of your family, so
many domestic enjoyments? Your Creator and theirs,
your Preserver and theirs, your daily Benefactor and
theirs? Can it be right, if you have any sense of these
things, each of you, in your own hearts, that the sense

of them should be concealed and smothered there, and that you should never join in your grateful acknowledgments to Him? Can you imagine it reasonable that when you have a constant dependence upon Him for so many mercies, without the recurrence of which your family would be a scene of misery, that you should never present yourselves together in His presence to ask them at His hand? Upon what principle is public worship to be recommended and urged, if not by such as have their proportional weight here?

Indeed, the force of these considerations has not only been known and acknowledged by the people of God in all ages (we have not only Noah and Abraham, Joshua and David, Job and Daniel, each under a much darker dispensation than ours, as examples of it); but we may venture to say, that wherever there has been a profession of any kind of religion, it has been brought into private houses as well as public temples. The poor heathens, as we certainly know from the remaining monuments of them, had their lares and penates, which were household images, some of them in private chapels and others about the common hearth, where the family used to worship them by frequent prayers and sacrifices. And the brass, wood, and stone of which they consisted shall, as it were, cry out against you, shall rise up against and condemn you if, while you call yourselves the worshippers of the one living and eternal God, and boast in the revelation you have received by His prophets and by His Son, you presume to omit an homage which the stupid worshippers of such vanities as these failed not to present to them while they called them their gods. Be persuaded then, I beseech you, to be consistent in your conduct. Either give up all pretenses to religion, or maintain a steady and uniform regard to it at home as well as abroad, in the family as well as in the closet or the church. But the reasonableness of this duty, and the obligations which bind you in conscience to the practice of it, will appear further if you consider the many advantages which will, by the divine blessing, attend a proper discharge of it. And here, I would more particularly represent the good influence which family devotions are likely to have upon the young persons committed to your care, upon your own hearts, upon the advancement of a general reformation, and the propagation of religion to those that are yet unborn.

ENTICEMENTS TO DUTY

1. *Consider in the first place what is most obvious, the happy influence which the duty I am recommending might have upon the young members of your family, the children and servants committed to your care.* For I now consider you as a parent and a master. "The father of a family" is a phrase that comprehends both these relations, and with great propriety, as humanity obliges us to endeavor to take a parental care of all under our roof. And indeed, you ought to consider your servants, in this view, with a tender regard. They are probably in the flower of life, for that is the age which is commonly spent in service; and you should recollect how possible it is that this may be, if rightly improved, the best opportunity their whole life may afford them for learning religion and being brought under the power of it. If your servants are already instructed in it, being

brought up in families where these duties have been maintained, let them not, if they should finally miscarry, have cause to impute it to you, and to testify to God in the day of their condemnation.

Let them not, if they should perish, have cause to testify before God in the day of their condemnation that under your roof they learned the neglect and forgetfulness of God, and all that their pious parents, perhaps in a much inferior station of life to you, had in earlier days been attempting to teach them. Or, if they come to you quite ignorant of religion, as, if they come from prayerless families it is very probable that they do, have compassion on them, I entreat you, and endeavor to give them those advantages which they never yet had, and which it is too probable, as things are generally managed, they never will have if you will not afford them.

But I would especially, if I might be allowed to borrow the pathetic words of Job, entreat you by the children of your own body, Job 19:17. I would now, as it were, present them all before you, and beseech you by the bowels of parental affection, that to all the other tokens of tenderness and love, you would not refuse to add this, without which many of the rest may be worse than in vain.

Give me leave to plead with you, as the instruments of introducing them into being. O remember, it is indeed a debased and corrupted nature that you have conveyed to them. Consider that the world into which you have been the means of bringing them is a place in which they are surrounded by many temptations, and in which, as they advance in life, they must expect many more. So that it is much to be feared that they

will remain ignorant and forgetful of God if they do
not learn from you to love and serve Him. For how can
it be expected that they should learn this at all if you
give them no advantages for receiving and practicing
the lesson at home?

And let me further urge and entreat you to remember that these dear children are committed to
your special care by God their Creator, who has made
them thus dependent upon you that you might have
an opportunity of forming their minds and of influenc-
ing them to a right temper and conduct. And can this,
by any means, be effectually done if you do not, at
proper times, call them together to attend to the instructions of the Word of God, and to join in solemn
prayers and supplications to Him? At least, is it possible
that it should be done any other way with equal advantage if this is not added to the rest?

Family worship is a most proper way of teaching
children religion, as you teach them language by insensible degrees – a little one day and a little another;
for to them, line must be upon line and precept upon
precept. They may learn to conceive aright of the divine perfections when they hear you daily acknowledging and adoring them. Their hearts may be touched
early with remorse for sin when they hear your confessions poured out before God. They will know what
mercies they are to ask for themselves by observing
what turn your petitions take. Your intercessions may
diffuse into their minds a spirit of love to mankind, a
concern for the interest of the church and of their
country; and what is not, I think, by any means to be
neglected, sentiments of loyalty towards those in authority over us, when they hear you daily invoking the

divine blessing upon them. And your solemn thanksgivings for the bounties of Providence, and for the
benefits of a spiritual nature, may affect their hearts
with those impressions towards the gracious Author of
all, which may excite in their little breasts love to Him,
the most noble and genuine principle of all true and
acceptable religion. Thus they may become Christians
by insensible degrees, and grow in the knowledge and
love of truth as they do in stature.

By observing your reverent and solemn deportment
(as reverent and solemn I hope it will always at such
seasons be), they may get some notion of an invisible
being before they are of age to understand the definition of the term "God;" and may feel their minds secretly impressed with a humble awe and veneration,
before they can explain to you their sense of it. And
whatever instructions you give them concerning His
nature and His will, and the way of obtaining His favor
by Jesus Christ, all your admonitions relating to the
importance of that invisible world we are going to, and
the necessary preparation for it will be greatly illustrated by the tenor of your daily devotions as well as by
those excellent lessons of the Word of God when
solemnly read to them morning and evening will afford. Nor is it by any means to be forgotten that while
they hear themselves and their own concerns mentioned before God in prayer, while they hear you
earnestly pleading for the divine blessing upon them
(especially if it is in expressions wisely varied, as some
particular occurrences in their lives and in yours may
require), it may very probably be a means of moving
their impressionable hearts; as it may powerfully convince them of the deep and tender concern for their

good, and may add great weight to the instructions you
may address to them. So that it may appear, even while
you are praying for them, that God hears. And indeed,
I have known some instances of excellent persons who
have dated their conversion to God even after they had
begun visibly to degenerate from their prayers, from
the serious and pathetic prayers, which they have
heard their pious fathers, perhaps I might add their
pious mothers, presenting before God on their account.

Indeed, were this duty properly attended to, it
might be expected that all Christian families would,
according to their respective sizes and circumstances,
become nurseries of piety; and you would see, in the
most convincing view, the wisdom of Providence in
making human infants so much more dependent on
their parents, and so much more incapable to shift for
themselves than the offspring of inferior creatures are.

Let me entreat you, then, my dear friend, to look
on your children the very next time you see them, and
ask your own heart how you can answer to God and to
them that you deprive them of such advantages as
these – advantages without which it is to be feared your
care of them in other respects will turn to but little account should they ever be so prosperous in life. For
what is prosperity in life without the knowledge, fear,
and love of God? What, but the poison of the soul
which swells and kills it? What, but the means of making it more certainly, more deeply, more intolerably
miserable; when all its transient and empty amusements are passed away, "like a dream when one
awaketh," Psalm 73:20? In short, not to mention the
happy influence which family devotion may have on

their temporal affairs by drawing down the divine blessing, and by forming their minds to those virtues which pave the way to wealth and reputation, health and contentment, which makes no enemies and attracts many friends. It is, with respect to the eternal world, the greatest cruelty to your children to neglect giving them those advantages which no other attentions in education, exclusive of these, can afford; and it is impossible that you should ever be able to give them any other equivalent. If you do your duty in this respect, they will have reason to bless you living and dying; and if you neglect it, take care that you and they come not, in consequence of that neglect, into a world where (horrid as the thought may seem) you will be forever cursing each other! And thus I am falling insensibly, because so naturally, from what I was saying of the concern and interest of those under your care, to your own, so far as it may be distinguished from theirs.

2. *Let me now press you to consider how much your own interest is concerned in this matter; the whole of your interest, both spiritual and temporal.*

Your spiritual interest is infinitely the greatest and, therefore, I will begin with that. Let me seriously ask you, do you not need those advantages for religion which the performance of family duty will give you, added to those of a more secret and a more public nature, if peradventure they are regarded by you? These instructions, these adorations, these confessions, these supplications, these intercessions, these thanksgivings, which may be so useful to your children and servants, may they not be useful to yourselves? May not your own heart have some peculiar advantage for being impressed, when you are the mouth of others in these domestic devotions beyond what, in a private station of life, it is otherwise possible that you should have? Oh, these lessons of religion to your own souls, every morning and evening, might be (if I may be allowed the expression) either the seed or foretaste of salvation to you. Nay, the remoter influence they may have on your conduct in other respects and at other times, when considered merely in the general as religious exercises performed by you in your family, is to be recollected as an argument of vast importance.

A sense of common decency would engage you, if you pray with your family, to avoid a great many evils which would appear doubly evil in a father or a master who kept up such religious exercises in his house. I will not now, sir, speak of yourself, for I would not offend by supposing anything grossly bad of you; but do you imagine that if reading the Scriptures and family prayer were introduced into the houses of some of your neighbors, drunkenness, lewdness, cursing and swearing, and profaning the Lord's Day would not, like so many evil demons, be quickly driven out? The master of a family would not, for shame, indulge them if he kept up nothing more than the form of duty; and his reformation, though only external and at first on a kind of constraint, would carry with it the reformation of many more who have such a dependence upon his favor that they would not sacrifice though, by a madness very prevalent among the children of men, they can venture to sacrifice their souls to every trifle.

And may it not, perhaps, be your more immediate concern to recollect that, if you prayed with your family, you would yourself be more careful to abstain from all appearance of evil, 1 Thessalonians 5:22? You would find out a way to suppress that turbulence of passion, which may now be ready to break out before you are aware, and other imprudences in which your own heart would check you by saying, "Does this become one who is by and by to kneel down with his domestics, his children and servants, and adore God with them, and pray against everything which displeases God and makes us unfit for the heavenly world?"

I will not say this will cure everything that is wrong, but I believe you are already persuaded that it would often have a very good influence. And I fear it is the secret desire of indulging some irregularities without such a restraint that, shameful as such conduct is, has driven out family prayer from several houses and has prevented its introduction into others. But if you have any secret disinclination of heart against it, in this view, it becomes you to be most seriously alarmed for, to speak plainly, I have hardly known a blacker symptom of damnation than a fear of being restrained in the commission of sin.

After this, it may seem a matter of small importance to urge the good influence which a proper discharge of family duty may have upon your own temporal affairs, both by restraining you from many evils, and engaging you to a proper conduct yourself, and also by impressing your children and servants with a sense of religion. And it is certain, the more careful they are of their duty to God, the more likely they will be to perform their duty to you. Nor can anything strengthen your natural authority among them more than your presiding in such solemnities, if supported by a suitable conduct. But, I would hope, more noble motives will have a superior weight. And therefore, waving this topic, I entreat you, as the last argument, to consider:

3. *The influence it may have on a general reformation, and on the propagation of religion to those who are yet unborn.* You ought to consider every child and servant in your family as one who may be a source not only of life, but (in some degree) of character and happiness to those who are hereafter to rise into being; yea, whose conduct may in part affect those that are to descend from them in a remote generation. If they grow up, while under your eye, ignorant of religion, they will certainly be much less capable of teaching it to others; for these are the years of discipline and, if they are neglected now, there is little probability of their receiving instruction afterwards. Nor is this all the evil consequence; for it is highly probable that they will think themselves sanctioned by your example in a like negligence, and so you may entail heathenism under the name of Christianity on your descendants and theirs for ages to come. Whereas your diligence and zeal might be remembered and imitated by them, perhaps, when you are in your grave; and the stock which they first received from you might, with rich improvements, be communicated to great numbers so that one generation after another might learn to fear and serve the Lord. On the whole, God only knows what a church may arise from one godly family; what a harvest may spring up from a single seed. On the other hand, it is impossible to say how many souls may, at length, perish by the treacherous neglect of a single person and, to speak plainly, by your own.

These, sir, are the arguments I have to plead with

you, and which I have selected out of many more. And now, give me leave seriously to ask you, as in the presence of God, whether there is not on the whole an unanswerable force in them? And if there is, what follows but that you immediately yield to that force and set up family worship this very day? For, I think, I would hardly thank you for a resolution to do it tomorrow; so little do I expect from that resolution. How can you excuse yourself in the continued omission? Bring the matter before God. He will be the final judge of it and, if you cannot debate the question as in His presence, it is the sign of a bad cause, and of a bad heart too, which is conscious of the badness of the cause and yet will not give it up, nor comply with a duty, of your obligation to which you are secretly convinced, while in effect you say, "I will go on in this sin and venture the consequence." O! It is a dreadful venture, and will be found provoking the Lord to jealousy as if you were stronger than He, 1 Corinthians 10:22.

OBJECTIONS

But, perhaps, there may arise in your mind some objections which may, in some degree, break the force of this conviction, and which, in that view, it may be expedient for me to discuss a little before I dismiss the subject and close my address to you. You may perhaps be ready to object:

OBJECTION ONE. "Family prayer is not, in so many words, commanded in Scripture and, therefore, however expedient in some cases, it cannot be so universal and so important a duty as we represent it."

ANSWER. I answer plainly that it is strongly recommended in Scripture, and consequentially commanded; as there are precepts which plainly include it,
though they do not particularly express it. And I appeal to yourself in this matter. When God is represented as giving this reason to His angels for a particular favor to be bestowed on Abraham. "I know that he
will command his children and household to keep the
way of the Lord, that he may obtain the blessing
promised," Genesis 18:19. Did He not hereby intend to
declare His approbation of the care which Abraham
took to support religion in his family? And can it be
supported in a total negligence of prayer? Again, do
you not, in your conscience, think that the Spirit of
God meant that we should take Joshua for an example
when he tells us that he resolved (and publicly declared the resolution) that he and his house would
serve the Lord, Joshua 24:15, which must express a religious care of his family too? Do you not believe that
the blessed Spirit meant it as a commendation of Job,
that he offered sacrifices for all his children, Job 1:5,
sacrifices undoubtedly attended with prayers, when he
feared lest the gaiety of their hearts, in their successive
feastings, might have betrayed them into some moral
evil? And was it not to do an honor to David that the
Scripture informs us that he went home to bless his
household, 2 Samuel 6:20, that is, to perform some
solemn act of domestic worship, when he had been
spending the whole day in public devotion? And do
you think when our blessed Lord, whose life was employed in religious services, so frequently took His disciples apart to pray with them that He did not intend
this as an example to us of praying with those under

our special care, or, in other words, with the members of our own family who are most immediately so? Or can you, by any imaginable artifice, delude yourself so far as to think that, when we are solemnly charged and commanded to pray with all prayer and supplication, Ephesians 6:18, this kind of prayer is not included with the apostolic injunction?

On the whole, the question lies in a very little room. Have I proved, by what I have said before, that family prayer is a reasonable thing? That it has a tendency to promote the honor of God, the interest of religion, and your own salvation, with that of those who are committed to your care? If you are really convinced of this, then all the general precepts which require the love of God and your neighbor, all that recommend a regard to the interest of Christ, and a concern for our own everlasting happiness bind it in this connection as certainly upon us as if it had been commanded in words as express as those in which we are required to enter in to our closets, and there to pray to our Father which is in secret, Matthew 6:6. This part of the argument is enforced with peculiar strength by that great and excellent writer, Mr. (John) Howe, in his posthumous sermon on the subject; which I earnestly recommend to every reader that can get an opportunity of perusing them.

And I will further add that if the care of family religion is (as I suppose every man's conscience will secretly testify that it is) a proper part of a religious education, then all those many passages of Scripture which recommend this must, in all reason, be understood as including that.

But perhaps you are ready to plead:

OBJECTION TWO. "It is generally neglected."

ANSWER. Yet scarcely can you have made or thought of this objection but you will see at the first glance that this must turn upon yourself, rather than on the whole appear favorable to your cause. It is the reproach of our age, if it is indeed generally neglected. And if it is generally excluded from the families of the rich and the great (who too frequently set the fashion where they are most apt to set it wrong), let it rather awaken a generous indignation in our breast to think that it is so excluded. At least let it awaken a holy zeal to exert ourselves so much the more, as it is certain that no association in vice can secure those that join in it. For it is expressly said, "though hand join in hand, the wicked shall not be unpunished," Proverbs 16:5. So will your obedience be more acceptable in proportion to the degree in which it is singular.

Were there not one praying family in the whole nation, in the whole world, I think it should instigate you to the practice rather than tempt you to neglect it, and you should press on, ambitious of the glory of leading the way. For what could be a nobler object of ambition than to be pointed out by the blessed God Himself as Job was, of whom He said, with a kind of triumph, "Hast thou considered My servant Job, that there is none like him in the land, or even on the earth?" Job 1:8. But, blessed be God, the neglect we have supposed is far from being universal. Let it, however, rejoice us if God might say, "There are such and such families, distinguishable from those in their neighborhood on this account; as prevalent as the neglect of family prayer is, they have the resolution to practice it and, like My servant Daniel, fear not the reproach and contempt which profane and ungodly men may cast upon them, if they may but honor Me and engage My favor. I know them. 'I hearken and hear, and a book of remembrance is written before Me for those who fear me and think on My name,' " Malachi 3:16.

Nor should you urge:

OBJECTION THREE. "I have so much business of another kind as not to be able to attend unto this."

ANSWER. I might cut the objection short at once by applying to your conscience whether you do not have time for many other things, which you know to be of much less importance. How many hours in a week do you spend for amusement, while you have none for devotion in your family? And do you indeed hold the blessing of God so very cheap, and think it a matter of so little importance, that you conclude your business must succeed the worse if a few minutes were taken daily to implore it before your family? Let me rather admonish you that the greater your business is, the more need you have to pray earnestly that your hearts may not be engrossed by it. And I would beg leave further to remind you that if your hurry of business were indeed so great as the objection supposes (which I believe is seldom the case), prudence alone might suggest that you should endeavor to contract it. For there are certain boundaries beyond which a wise and faithful care cannot extend; and as an attempt to go beyond these boundaries has generally its foundation in avarice, so it often has its end in poverty and ruin. But if you were ever so secure in succeeding for this world, how dear might you and your children pay for that success if all the blessed consequences of family religion, for time and eternity, were to be given up as the price of that very small part of your gains, which is owing to the minutes you take from these exercises that you may give them to the world? For you plainly perceive the question is only about them, and by no means about a strenuous application to the proper duties of your secular calling through the day. And if you will be rich upon such profane terms as are here supposed (for truly I can call them no better than profane), you will probably plunge yourself into final perdition and may, in the meantime, "pierce yourself through with many sorrows;" while religious families will learn, by happy experience, that the blessing of the Lord, which they are so often imploring together, "maketh rich, and addeth no sorrow with it," Proverbs 10:22, or that "a little with the fear of the Lord is better than great treasures," Proverbs 15:16, with that intermingled trouble in which the neglect of God must necessarily be expected.

But I conclude that yet more will be objecting:
OBJECTION FOUR. "I lack ability for this kind of work."

ANSWER. This I must reply, in the first place that, where the heart is rightly disposed, it does not require any uncommon abilities to discharge family worship in a decent and edifying manner. "The heart of a wise and good man, in this respect, teacheth his mouth and addeth knowledge to his lips," Proverbs 16:23, and out of the fullness of it, when it is indeed full of pious affections, the mouth will naturally speak, Luke 6:45. Plain, short sentences, uttered just as they rise in the mind, will be best understood by them that join with you; and they will be more pleasing to God than anything which should proceed from ostentation and parade.

I must also desire you to consider how many helps you may easily procure. The Scripture is a large and noble magazine of the most proper sentiments and most expressive language which, if you will attend to it with a becoming regard, will soon furnish you for this good work. And beside this, we have, in our language, a great variety of excellent forms of prayer for families as well as for private persons, which you may use, at least at first, with great profit. And if it is too laborious for you to learn them by heart, or if having learned them you are not able to trust your memory, what should forbid your reading them reverently and devoutly! I hope I shall give no offense to any good Christian by saying (but on this occasion I should offend my conscience by not saying) that I have long thought an irreconcilable aversion to forms of prayer, even of human composition as vain a superstition as a passionate attachment to them. And if any had rather that a family should be prayerless than that a well-chosen form should be gravely and solemnly read in it, I think he judges as absurdly as if he would rather see them starving to death than fed out of a dish whose materials or shape are disagreeable to him. The main thing is that God is reverently and sincerely adored; that suitable blessings, temporal and spiritual, be sought from Him for ourselves and for others, and cordial thanksgivings returned to Him for the various gifts of His continual bounty. And if this is done, the circumstances of doing it, though I cannot think them quite indifferent, are of comparatively small importance.

I know by sure experience, in a great variety of instances, that it is very possible for Christians of no extraordinary genius and with a very low education, to acquit themselves honorably in prayer without the assistance of forms. And they who, at first, need them may, and probably if they seriously set about it, would soon outgrow that need. But if they did not, God might be glorified, and families edified, by the continued use of such helps. And on the whole, if it indeed comes to this, that you would rather sacrifice all the benefits of family prayer than submit to the trouble of reading, or appointing another to read, a well-composed address which perhaps, with a small portion of Scripture before it, might not take up one quarter of an hour's time. Indeed, you must be condemned by God and your own conscience. In such a view, both must testify that it is neither lack of leisure nor lack of ability that prevents your discharging your duty, but a stupid indifference about it, or rather a wretched aversion to it; the natural consequence of which might, if a little reflected upon, be sufficient to throw the most careless and arrogant sinner into an awful alarm, if not a trembling condemnation.

I apprehend that the most plausible objections have now been canvassed; for I suppose few will be so weak and cowardly as to plead:

OBJECTION FIVE. "My domestics will not submit to the introduction of such orders as these."

ANSWER. But as this may be secretly thought of where it would not be pleaded, especially where these duties have unhappily been omitted when families were first formed, and in their most flexible and pliant state, I will bestow a few words on this head.

And here I must desire that you would not rashly conclude this to be the case with respect to your own. Do not think so unkindly of your domestics, if they are not extremely wicked indeed, as to imagine they would be secretly discontented with spending a little time daily in hearing the Word of God, and being present at your domestic devotion. Much less should you allow yourselves to think, until it appears in fact, that they will have the arrogance openly to dispute so reasonable a determination as this. Perhaps, on the contrary, they are even now secretly wishing that God would put it into your heart to make the attempt, and thinking with a kind of tender regret, "Why are we denied such a blessing when the members of this and that family in the neighborhood are favored with it?"

But if it is, indeed, as you suppose, that they would think of it with a secret aversion, and come into it with apparent reluctance, if they can be induced to come into it at all, you would do well to reflect whether this profaneness and perverseness may not, in a great measure at least, be owing to that very neglect which I am now pressing you to reform? Which, if it is, ought certainly to convince you in the most powerful and effectual manner, of the necessity of endeavoring to repair as soon as possible the mischief already done. And, if there is really an opposition made, you ought to let any in whom you discover it know that your measures are fixed and that you cannot, and will not, resign that just authority, which the laws of God and man give you in your own house, to their unhappy temper or daring impiety. Make the trial whether they will dare to break with you rather than submit to so easy a condition as that of being present at your hours of family worship. If it is a servant that disputes it, you will, no doubt, think it a great blessing to your family to rid it of so detestable a member, in that relation. And if it is a child, grown up to years that should be years of discretion, who sets himself against this reformation (and it is not possible that any others should oppose you), though it is certain that, wherever such a son of Belial is, he must be a great grief to your heart, you will be delivered from a great deal of distress which the sight of his wickedness must daily give you, by refusing him a place in your own family, which he would only disgrace and corrupt, and leaving him to practice those irregularities and scandals which always go along with such a presumptuous contempt of religion, anywhere else than under your own roof.

I can think of but one objection more, and that is:

OBJECTION SIX. "I do not know how to introduce a practice which I have so long neglected."

ANSWER. But this is an objection so very soon removed that, I hope, if nothing else lies in the way, your family will not continue another week in the unhappy circumstances in which your negligence has hitherto kept it. I would be unworthy of the name of a minister of the gospel if, whatever my other engagements were, I was not willing to give you my utmost assistance, as soon as possible, in so good a work as the reformation of this great and lamentable evil. Far from thinking it a trouble to visit you and spend an hour with you on such an occasion, who would not esteem it a refreshment and a blessing to come and inform your domestics, when gathered together for this purpose, how wise and happy a resolution you had taken to represent the reason they have to rejoice in it, and to bless God who had inspired you with it? And how sweet a work would it be to perform it as for the first time, imploring the blessings of Providence and grace on you and yours, and entreating those assistances of His Holy Spirit, which may qualify you more abundantly for discharging your peculiar part in it, and may render it the successful means of planting, or of supporting and animating, a principle of true religion in every soul under your care. Nor would the joy and delight be confined to the minutes spent with you at such a season. It would be carried home to the study and to the house of God. And the very remembrance of it would, for years to come, encourage you to other works of usefulness, and strengthen our hands in the work of the Lord.

And O my dear friend, whoever you are, do not be ashamed that a minister should, on this occasion, tell your children and servants that you are sensible of your former neglect, and are determined in the strength of God to practice such a duty, which it has indeed been criminal hitherto to omit. This is a mean and unworthy shame, and would prevent our reforming evils which are indeed shameful. It will be a glory to you to be willing and solicitous to revive languishing religion; a glory to give to other families an example which, if they have the wisdom and courage to follow, will undoubtedly bring down a rich variety of blessings on themselves and, if followed by considerable numbers, on the public. At least, it will be an honor to you in the sight of

men and, what is infinitely more, in the sight of God to
have made the generous effort, and not to make the
guilty neglect of former years an excuse for continuing
to neglect, when it should rather be a powerful argument immediately to practice.

But I would, by no means, insist that divine worship
should be introduced into your family in the particular
manner I have recommended. Use your own judgment
and pursue your own inclination so that it is effectually
and immediately done. You may, perhaps, think it convenient to call them together and read this letter to
them, telling them at the conclusion that you are, in
your conscience, convinced there is a reason in it
which cannot be answered and that, therefore, you are
resolved to act agreeably to it. You may then proceed
to read a portion of Scripture and to pray with them in
such a manner as you may think most expedient. But,
in whatever manner it is done, you will remember that
it must be with reverence and solemnity, and with that
unfeigned fervor of devotion as in the sight of the
heart-searching God. And you will further remember
that, when once introduced, it must be resolutely and
constantly carried on, for to cast out this heavenly
guest will, in some degree, be more shameful than not
to admit it. But, I hope, sweet experiences of the pleasure of these duties will be instead of a thousand arguments to engage our adherence to them.

May God give you resolution immediately to make
the attempt! And may He assist and accept you, and
scatter down every desirable blessing of Providence
and of grace on you and yours! So that this day may
become memorable in your lives as a season from
which you may date a prosperity and a joy hitherto un-

known, however happy you may have been in former
years; for very imperfect, I am sure, that domestic happiness must be in which domestic religion has no part.

How shall I congratulate myself if, in consequence
of the representation and address I have now been
making to you, I may be the blessed instrument in the
divine hand of inspiring you with such a resolution!
What an additional bond will then be added to our
friendship, while God continues us together in life!
Yea, what an everlasting bond of a nobler friendship in
a future life, where it will be before the throne of God,
my joy to have given such admonitions as these, and
yours, faithfully and obediently, to have received them!

But if, after all, you will not be persuaded, but will
hearken to the voice of cowardice, sloth, and irreligion
in defiance of so many awakening and affectioned reasons, you must answer it at last. If your children and
servants grow up in the neglect of God and pierce your
hearts with those sorrows which such servants, and especially such children, are likely to occasion. If they
raise profane and profligate families, if they prove the
curse of their country as well as the torment and ruin
of those most intimately related to them, the guilt is in
part yours and, I repeat it again, you must answer to
God for it at the great day, that you have omitted the
proper and appointed method of preventing such fatal
evils. In the meantime, you must answer the omission
to your own conscience, which probably has not been
easy in former days, and in future days may yet be
more unquiet. Yes, sir, the memory of this address may
continue to torment you if it cannot reform you. And if
you do not forsake the house of God, as well as exclude
God and His worship from your own house, you will

meet with new wounds; for new exhortations and admonitions will arm reflection with new reproaches.
And in this uncomfortable manner, you will probably
go on until what has been the grief and shame of your
life becomes the affliction of your dying bed.

Nor do I dare to presume to assure you that God
will answer your last cries for pardon. The best you can
expect, under the consciousness of this guilt, is to pass
trembling to your final doom. But whatever that doom
is, you must acquit your minister who has given you
faithful warning. and this letter, transcribed, as it were,
in the records of the divine omniscience, shall testify
that a matter of so great importance has not been
coldly and slightly urged by, dear sir, your affectionate
friend and faithful servant in our common Lord,

Philip Doddridge
December 20, 1740

4

Parental Duties Illustrated

A Sermon Preached at the Tabernacle
Salem, Massachusetts
October, 1811

by Samuel Worcester, D.D.
Late Pastor of Tabernacle Church

"But bring them up in the nurture and admonition of the Lord." Ephesians 6:4

One of the first and most important institutions of God was that of the family state. It was ordained from the beginning that a man should leave his father and his mother and cleave unto his wife, and that they two should become one flesh. But what was the great design of God in this institution? The prophet Malachi, at the 15th verse of his second chapter, answers the question. It was "that he might seek a godly seed." The institution of families, indeed, answers many important purposes, and is eminently conducive to the temporal as well as the spiritual interests of mankind. But the principal purpose in the view of Infinite Wisdom was evidently religious. Families were intended to be religious societies, in which the worship of God should be maintained, and in which means should be used for training up children from generation to generation in His fear and for His service. Accordingly, for about two thousand years, there were no churches, other than in families, and the cause of God was maintained in the world by means of family religion. And, since that period, both under the Mosaic and under the Christian dispensations, families have been distinctly recognized as constituent parts and nurseries of the Church. Correspondent with this great design of God are the instructions of His Word. The Scriptures abound with injunctions and directions to parents in regard to their religious care of their children. And as the Word of God, on this interesting subject, is line upon line and precept upon precept, so it is important that these injunctions and directions should be often and earnestly illustrated and enforced.

The Apostle having, in the former parts of this Epistle to the Ephesians, presented the great doctrines of the gospel in a clear and impressive light, proceeds, in the latter part, to make an application of them for practical Christian use. In this part, he gives very particular directions respecting the duties of husbands and wives, parents and children, masters and servants. Among these directions are the words of our text. The whole verse is as follows: "And ye fathers provoke not your children to wrath; but bring them up in the nurture and admonition of the Lord." By the nurture and admonition of the Lord, we are, doubtless, to understand the nurture and admonition which God has been pleased to prescribe. These, under several particulars, will now be considered:

DIRECTIONS TO PARENTS

1. *A very important part of the nurture and admonition which God prescribed consists in giving up our children to Him in the way which He has graciously appointed.*

God's gracious and everlasting covenant with His church presents to believing parents a promise of spiritual and saving blessings to their children. The promise is to be a God to them and to their seed after them. For parents to take hold on this promise by faith, and looking to the Lord for the blessings which it contains for their children, is of high and eternal importance. It is only in the way of a dutiful reliance, indeed, on the covenant for all needed grace, that parents can bring up their children, as they are required to do, in the nurture and admonition of the Lord. This duty is to be performed in faith, and for the right performance of it, as of every other duty, parents certainly need abundant grace. Without grace, they cannot walk before God and be perfect; neither can they without grace command their children and their households after them to keep the way of the Lord, to do justice and judgment. But how can they expect the requisite communications of grace unless they wait upon God for them in His instituted way? The grace promised in the covenant, to be received in a covenant way, is rich and sufficient. It is sufficient for parents, and it is sufficient for their children. It is sufficient to sanctify their hearts and to bring them to set their hope in God.

Were it not for the promises of the covenant, my brethren, would not believing parents sink under discouragements, and utterly despair of ever being able to train up their children for the holy service and king-

dom of God? But in a believing reliance on these
promises, have they not the greatest encouragement to
be faithful in duty, and to hope that of His rich and
covenanted mercy, God will, in due time, make them
to see that they have not labored in vain, but that they
are the seed of the blessed of the Lord, and their offspring with them.

But if we would obtain for our children the spiritual and saving blessings comprised in the gracious
promises of the covenant, we must believe, and be
faithfully obedient. We must believe, we must take hold
of the promises by faith; for, without faith, we have no
good title to any blessing of the covenant. We must
also be obedient, for it is only in the way of obedience
that we are to expect the favor of God and the communications of His grace.

If, then, God requires that we present our children
to Him in baptism, give them up to Him, take hold of
His promise, and thus publicly ratify and seal with Him
the everlasting covenant respecting our children, this
is certainly a momentous duty which ought to be performed in the lively exercise of faith, and in the faithful spirit of obedience. If we either neglect this duty altogether, or only attend upon it in a formal and unbelieving manner, we violate the covenant of our God,
and have occasion to fear that, unless we repent of this
sin, God, in His righteous sovereignty, will visit our iniquity upon our children.

2. *Faithfully to instruct our children in the principles of
religion is another important and instituted means of bringing them up in the nurture and admonition of the Lord.*

As soon as children come to an age and to a degree

of understanding to receive ideas on religious subjects, it becomes the bound duty of parents, with all parental tenderness, diligence, and fidelity, to instill divine knowledge into their opening minds. It is through the medium of divine truth that ordinarily God is pleased to convey His renewing and saving grace to the hearts of the children of men. But children are naturally destitute of knowledge. As they grow in age, they know nothing but what they learn. This is the case in respect to the things of this life, and especially is it the case in respect of the life to come. They know nothing of God or of Christ; nothing of heaven or hell; nothing of the great purpose for which they came into this world of trial, or of the future and eternal state to which they are hastening, any further than in some way or other they are instructed on these great and all-interesting subjects. If left to themselves, if no means are used for their religious instruction, they will remain and grow up in awful ignorance of God, and of all the great concerns of life and salvation.

Children should be taught early the important truths of God's Word. They should early be taught that there is a God; that He is a being of infinite power and wisdom, knowledge and goodness, justice, mercy and truth, one God in three persons; that He is to be loved with all the heart, and obeyed in all things with the most dutiful respect; that His law is holy, just, and good; that all mankind are by nature sinners, and are exposed to everlasting destruction; that God has freely given His own Son to die for sinners, and to bring in an everlasting righteousness for their justification; that every one ought immediately to repent and embrace the Savior; that all the unconverted reject the mercy of

God, and will continue to reject it to their eternal ruin, unless their hearts are renewed by divine grace; and that all who are thus renewed and made alive to God will be pardoned and sanctified, and finally received to honor, glory, and immortality.

These and other gospel truths connected with these should be taught to our children with great diligence and faithfulness. They are truths which concern their eternal salvation. Nor are we to say that our children cannot understand them; for it has been found by pleasing experience that, if proper means are used, children will very early get so much knowledge of divine truth as to be of the greatest benefit to them in all their future lives.

3. *The solemnities of public worship in the house of God, and wherever with propriety attended, is another important part of the divinely instituted means for bringing up children in the nurture and admonition of the Lord.*

The public worship of God is evidently designed as a very principal means for promoting divine knowledge in general, for keeping alive a sense of religious observation, for impressing the fear of the Lord, for preserving in view the solemn realities of eternity, and for imparting all the blessings of salvation, as well to the young as to the more advanced in age. It is especially by the preaching of the gospel that God is pleased to save them that believe. The Lord loves the gates of Zion more than all the dwellings of Jacob. It is in the places where His people meet together for the purpose of religious instruction and worship that He is wont to make the more special manifestations of His power and grace, not only for the quickening and edi-

fication of saints, but also for the conviction and conversion of sinners. It is, therefore, of high importance
that children should be early accustomed to the house
of God, and to attend upon all proper means of religious instruction. If they are early accustomed to this,
it is likely to become easy and pleasant to them; but if
they are not accustomed to it early, it is likely to be irksome and unpleasant.

It is a matter of common observation that young
people as well as old, who have from their early years
constantly and regularly attended on the more public
means of grace, are generally, in some good measure,
impressed with its importance and have a disposition
to attend, while those who have been but little accustomed to the house of God, or to any other place of religious worship and instruction, have too commonly
very little sense of the importance of attending, and
very little disposition to attend. Hence, it becomes the
duty of parents and heads of families to use great care
in respect to this matter. It is their duty to see that
their children, and those under their care, are brought
as early as is proper and convenient to the house of
God, and ever afterwards attend with all practicable
regularity upon the appointed and authorized means
of religious improvement. And it is their duty, in a
tender and affectionate manner, to explain the nature
of public worship, its design and its importance; to impress upon them the obligations of hearing as for their
eternal welfare, and of remembering and practicing
what they hear.

In ancient times, when the people of Israel went up
to the place where God had recorded His name to attend upon the reading of the law and the public and

solemn rites of His worship, they took with them their
children and their little ones. And in the primitive ages
of Christianity, Christians were very particular in requiring their children to accompany them to places of
religious instruction. And how proper, my brethren, is
it, how proper and how important, that our children,
the objects of our tenderest care and concern, should
be brought with us to our solemn meetings, that they
may learn to reverence the holy name and the sacred
institutions of the lord; that they may hear the counsels
and monitory instructions of the gospel; that we may
present them before the Lord and, with a lively interest
in their eternal welfare, supplicate for them the divine
favor and blessing.

4. *The proper exercise of parental authority is another important means of bringing up children in the nurture and
admonition of the Lord.*

As children naturally partake of the depraved nature of our depraved race, it is to be expected that, unless great care is used, they will wander away into the
paths of the destroyer and become accustomed to the
courses of impiety and dissipation. It is even to be expected that they will be impatient under the restraints
of a religious education, and manifest inclinations exceedingly trying to the feelings of their pious parents.
Their untoward inclinations are not to be indulged,
but to be checked and restrained. They are to be admonished, entreated, and corrected with all possible
faithfulness, tenderness, and perseverance. It is the indispensable duty of parents to guard their children, as
far as possible, from the baneful influence of vicious
company; to interpose their parental authority, when

necessary, to prevent their frequenting sense of dissipation and vice; to amend their irregularities of conduct, and to bring them to a habitual observance of the laws of morality and the institutions of our holy religion.

It is incumbent on parents to educate their children not only in the nurture, but in the admonition of the Lord; or, as Abraham did, to command their children and their households after them to keep the way of the Lord, and to do justice and judgment. It is doubtless a very difficult duty, and parents and heads of families need much wisdom and grace. While they are to command their children and their households after them to keep the way of the Lord, they are not to provoke them to wrath. They are carefully to avoid all unreasonable severity and harshness of treatment, and so to temper their authority with kindness and parental affection as to convince their children that in all the restraints imposed upon them, they have constantly and deeply at heart their highest good. They should aim and endeavor, as far as possible, to secure the affections of their children, so that they may delight in conforming to their requirements.

5. *Effectual fervent prayer is another important part of the means which God has instituted for the religious education of children.*

In the privilege of access to the throne of grace, the Christian parent enjoys a peculiar favor. There he may obtain mercy and find grace proportioned to his duty, and to all the difficulties of instructing his children in the fear of the Lord. Of the fullness of Christ, he may receive abundant fullness of wisdom, grace, and strength; and in answer to his fervent and persevering prayer, his children may also partake of the same fullness. Having solemnly dedicated his children to God in the way of divine appointment, and faithfully instructed them out of the divine Word, he may be greatly encouraged and animated in prayer by a believing view of God's gracious promise to be a God to him and to his seed after him; and, taking hold of the promise, he may humbly and importunately plead for the bestowment of His blessing on himself and on his children.

IMPROVEMENT

1. *It appears from what has been offered that true and eminent piety is of immense importance to parents and heads of families.*

In all the relations of life, we need much of the grace of God in order to a fulfillment of the various duties of our relations; but scarcely in any relation do we need more of divine grace than in that of parents and heads of families. To have children committed to our care, to have immortal souls entrusted to our charge to be brought up for God and for everlasting glory in His kingdom, is certainly a situation of high responsibility, the duties of which cannot be fulfilled without great wisdom, diligence, and piety. Surely, my brethren, to discharge our duty to our children with fidelity, we must have a lively faith in the gracious promises of the covenant that, in giving them up to God in baptism, we may make an entire surrender of them; and that ever afterwards, in our prayers for them, and in all our counsels and instructions, we may be sincere and faithful, and have an unwavering reliance on Him for a blessing.

This faith which is necessary, in respect to our children, is not a vain confidence that the Lord will renew and save them whether we are faithful or not but it is such a realizing view of His promise and faithfulness as will lead us constantly to look to Him, and humbly to depend upon Him, for all requisite grace. It is a faith which does honor to God, and gives all the glory of our salvation and the salvation of our children, to the riches of His mercy which, in His holy sovereignty, He has been pleased to reveal in His gracious covenant.

In proportion to our faith and piety, we shall be concerned for the salvation of our children, and shall be unceasing and abundant in our prayers, our instructions and admonitions, that they may be brought to renounce the vanities of the world and set their hope in God. But, my brethren, if we are not religious ourselves, how can we discharge our duty to our children? If we do not walk in our houses with a perfect heart, how can we command our children and our households after us to keep the way of the Lord? If we do not live habitually in the fear of the Lord, if we do not live, as the grace of God which brings salvation teaches, in the denial of ungodliness and worldly lusts, soberly, righteously, and devoutly in the world, how can we expect to train up our children in the way they should go, so that when they are old they will not depart from it? Oh, let us feel how important it is that we grow in grace and in the knowledge of our Lord and Savior, and be ever righteous before God, walking in all His statutes and ordinances blamelessly.

2. *It appears to be an important duty, incumbent on a Church of Christ, faithfully to watch over its members in respect to their duty to their children.*

Children who have been regularly given up to God in baptism have an important relation to the church, and are to be so far under the watch and care of the church as not to fail of enjoying a religious education. If the children of the church do not enjoy religious privileges, it is the duty of the church to rectify the error and to remove the evil. In other words, if parents in covenant are neglectful of their duty to their children, it is incumbent on their brethren in a faithful and Christian manner to tell them their faults and endeavor to bring them to repentance and to a performance of their duty.

3. *It behooves us, my brethren, to make solemn inquiry with ourselves in regard to the great duty inculcated in this discourse.*

Have we religiously given our children to God under the seal of the everlasting covenant? If indeed we have presented them at the baptismal font, have we done it in faith, sincerely giving them to God, and seeking His blessing, even life evermore? Have we since sacredly regarded them as set apart for God, and made it our care to bring them up for Him in the way He has prescribed? As they have become capable of receiving instruction, have we been faithful to instruct them in the things of religion with diligence and perseverance, answerable in any measure to the worth of their souls, the importance of their salvation, or the solemnity of our vows respecting them? Have we prayed with them and for them, bearing on their hearts constantly before God, and with deep concern for their eternal welfare, pleading in their behalf His covenant mercy, and imploring His grace to assist us in all our duty towards them? Have we made it our care to shield them from temptation, to restrain them from vice, and to command them after us to keep the way of the Lord? Ah! my brethren, why is it that we see our children so little attentive in general to their religious concerns? Why is it that they have so little knowledge of divine things and are so little affected with them? Why is it that so few of them appear to be subjects of divine grace and present partakers of covenant blessings? Why it is, in a word, that we do not see them under the influences of the Spirit, poured out from on high, springing up as willows by the water courses, subscribing with their own hands to the Lord, and surnaming themselves by the name of Israel? Is God unmindful of His covenant? Has He forgotten His promise to be gracious? Is He slack concerning His promise?

No, my brethren, "the Lord's arm is not shortened that He cannot save, neither is His ear heavy that it cannot hear; but our iniquities have separated between us and our God, and our sins have hid His face from us." Looking round upon our solemn assemblies, looking round upon our children, looking round upon one another and, above all, looking home upon ourselves, can we avoid the conviction, strong and painful, that we have greatly neglected our duty? Does it not, then, behoove us to humble ourselves before God, and resolve that wherein we have been negligent and unfaithful we will be so no more? Does it not behoove us to exhort one another daily while it is called today on this interesting subject, and to provoke one another to love and to good works? Does it not behoove us unitedly and fervently to call upon God, imploring His pardoning mercy, and earnestly beseeching Him not to visit our iniquities upon our children; but, according to His abundant grace, to pour out His Spirit upon our seed, and His blessing upon our offspring, and to give us one heart and one way that we may fear Him evermore, for the good of our selves and of our children after us. The Lord is very merciful, and will not turn away His ear from them that diligently seek Him.

Let us, then, my brethren, one and all, bring this subject home to our hearts, and meditate upon it in all its earnest and weight. Does God graciously propose to be a God to us and our seed after us? Is He ready not only to make us joint heirs with Christ to all the riches of his everlasting kingdom; but also to bestow the blessings of His covenant upon our children? And are not our hearts affected by His condescension and His goodness? Can we slight His grace? Can we despise His mercy? Can we be so ungrateful to God, so wanting in affectionate concern for the welfare of those who are our own flesh and blood?

Some of us, indeed, are under the most solemn vows. We have sworn to the Lord that we will be His people, and that we will educate our children for Him. Can we then go back? Can we prove faithless and false to our sacred engagements? Can we dishonor our God, bring reproach upon His covenant, and leave our children exposed to have our iniquities judicially visited upon them?

Our children, as well as ourselves, are born for eternity. This world shall pass away, the heavens shall be rolled together like a scroll, the fabric of the universe shall be dissolved; but our children will exist in happiness or in misery, in the realms of light or in the regions of darkness, when the earth and the heavens that now are shall be no more. They are committed to our care to be trained up with reference to their eternal state. As we are faithful or unfaithful, we may be instrumental to their eternal bliss or to their eternal woe! How glorious on the one hand, how dreadful on the other, is this thought!

O my brethren, can we trifle with concerns of this infinite moment? We must meet our children at the bar of God. We must appear with them in the presence of assembled worlds to give an account of the manner in which we have performed our duty to them, to our final Judge. Can we endure the thought of seeing them on the left hand? Of hearing their doom pronounced in that dreadful sentence, "Depart from Me, ye cursed?" Can we endure the thought of having it appear that, through our unfaithfulness, our children have perished forever? My brethren, by all that is tender in the name of parents, by all that is sacred in the vows of the covenant, by all that is interesting in the riches of divine grace, by the value of our children as immortal beings, by the joys of heaven and by the woes of hell, let us be incited, seriously and earnestly, to attend to this subject, and bring up our children in the nurture and admonition of the Lord.

Nor let it be thought that this is less important for those who are not in covenant with God and His people than for those who are. Your souls, my dear people, are all precious, the souls of your children are all precious, infinitely precious. The gracious language of God to you all is, "Incline your ear and come to Me, and I will make an everlasting covenant with you, even the sure mercies of David." Hear, then, every one of you. Come yourselves, bring your children with you into the covenant of our God. Come, parents; come children; and receive the blessing, even life forevermore. Amen.

5

The Duties of Parents Towards their Children

by Henry Venn
(from *The Whole Duty of Man*)

The nearest connection in life after the nuptial union is that which subsists between parents and their children. From this connection arises various duties, both of a temporal and a spiritual kind, to the discharge of which every Christian will conscientiously attend.

1. *It is a duty all parents owe their children to accustom them to early habits of industry, and to inspire them with a contempt and abhorrence of idleness as the great corrupter of the human mind and inlet to every vice.* The poor must strongly insist upon their children's giving themselves diligently to work, not only as necessary to procure themselves bread, but as the means of preventing temptations to pilfering and theft, and keeping them from infamy and the gallows. The children of the rich stand in no less need of being excited to industrious application of their time and talents. From their earliest years, they should hear that neither wealth nor a large estate, nor even nobility of birth, can preserve them from being despicable and noxious to society if they take no pains to acquire what will improve the

mind and give them ability to perform their duty; that
without love of employment suited to their station, like
truant schoolboys, they must seek men as idle as themselves for their companions; and, to kill time, they
must be eager in the pursuit of foolish and childish
amusements, and even be tempted to sink into meanness and the wickedness of a debauched life merely to
free themselves from the languor and misery of sloth.

On the contrary, by cultivating the love of study
and fine writers, by being active and useful, by improving their advantages of station, they will never feel time
a burden on their hands. They will always be doing
good and be honorable in their generation. These instructions, enforced by the example of the very conduct they inculcate, will work as a powerful antidote to
the intoxicating pride which wealth and grandeur naturally inspire; enforced, I say, by the example of the
conduct they inculcate; for, if the persons who give
these instructions violate them, they can have no effect. Children must necessarily believe that their parents judge that to be the way of happiness in which
they see them continually walk because they do it out
of choice; and, if they did not think it best, why should
they choose it? As it would, therefore, appear cruel in
parents to correct or reprove for tempers and practices
their children learn from themselves, so it would be
absured to expect that precept or reproof should
profit them when the persons from whom they come
are not themselves acting under their influence.

2. *It is the duty of parents to make a provision for their
children, sufficient, if they can, to enable them, by honest industry, or some liberal profession, to support themselves and be*

useful members of society. For what can be more contrary to the feelings of parental love than, by idleness or extravagance, to expose their offspring to poverty, or to force them to settle in a station of life much beneath that in which they were born - a cause frequently of much vexation to them, and a bitter disappointment which few are able to bear. But, with regard to what may properly be called a provision, reason, not fashion, the Word of God, not blind affection, must determine. When persons who were born to no estate think it incumbent on them to amass wealth sufficient to raise their children above the need of any employment or profession, scanty must be their charities and strong their love of money. And so far is opulence from being any real benefit to children that (a few instances excepted) it proves a corrupter of their hearts; it panders to their lusts, fixing in them habits of vanity, extravagance, and luxury.

3. *But the duty which, above all others, is incumbent upon parents is to provide, as far as lies within them, for the spiritual and everlasting welfare of their offspring.*
Here let me request the most serious attention of every parent. I am at a loss for words strong enough to describe the importance of this duty. Parents ought to consider themselves as chiefly living for the proper discharge of it, and as in the most solemn manner accountable to God for their conduct herein. Let them attend to the many and strong obligations by which they are bound to the performance of it.
This is clearly the command of God. He said, "These words which I command thee this day shall be in thine heart; and thou shalt teach them diligently

unto thy children, and shalt talk of them when thou sittest in thine house, and when thou walkest by the way, and when thou liest down, and when thou risest up," Deuteronomy 6:6-7. And Psalm 78:5-7, "He established a testimony in Jacob, and appointed a law in Israel, which He commanded our fathers that they should make known to their children, that the generation to come might know them, even the children which should be born; who should arise and declare them to their children, that they might set their hope in God, and not forget the works of God, but keep His commandments."

The New Testament enforces the same duty, and calls upon fathers to bring their children up in "the nurture and admonition of the Lord," Ephesians 6:4. The command of God thus to educate their children in the service of, and for the honor of, their Maker and Redeemer is universally acknowledged by pious parents.

Again, natural affection should influence Christian parents to be solicitous for the salvation of their children. That they know they have immortal souls is taken for granted; therefore, if they neglect the cultivation and improvement of them, anxious only to heap up wealth, to provide them with temporal subsistence, this is but a brutish fondness, not a rational, much less a Christian kind of love. A rational, a Christian affection for children must make parents reason thus with themselves: "These tender plants, sprung up from our own bodies, are endued with an immortal spirit; they possess a capacity of serving, loving, and enjoying the favor of the blessed God forever. And if they do not serve, love, and enjoy Him forever, their being instead of a blessing, will prove an insupportable curse. We, their parents, feel such love for them as impels us to think no pains too great to provide for their present comfort. But what does it avail to secure them, were we able, from the evils of transient sickness, pain, and poverty, if woes of endless duration are to be their final portion? What avails the most ardent affection, which reaches only to the mortal part, if all that lies in our power is not done, that after their passage through the present short-lived scene of things, they may enter into eternity in the favor of God?"

A small degree of natural affection, where there is any persuasion of the certainty of another world, must excite such reasonings as this in the breast of parents, and be followed with some correspondent care in the education of their offspring.

But, those parents who are in truth what they profess to be, Christians, have a clear view by faith of the realities of the invisible world. They feel their unspeakable importance; and such is their love to God that, were it in their power, there would not remain one rebel upon the face of the earth, one slave to sin. They are grieved to see any perishing while Jesus, mighty to save and merciful to pardon, stands ready, with open arms, to receive all who will come to Him for life. With what greater force, then, must these principles and sentiments work in them toward their own offspring. How solicitous, how active must they be, to secure their spiritual welfare!

Further, the aptitude of children to receive either good or bad impressions, which can scarcely be afterwards effaced, forms another powerful argument for instructing them with the utmost care in the knowl-

edge of God. Should this noble opportunity to season
their minds with excellent sentiments and to furnish
them with just notions be lost, all future methods of instruction or means of grace are likely to be without effect. For children very soon and justly conclude that
whatever their parents inculcate with seriousness and
frequency must be worthy of their remembrance; and,
on the contrary, that the things in which they have
never or very seldom been instructed, must be of little
or no advantage to their happiness. Hence, young
people who have never been taught at home the excellent majesty of the Lord our God, our absolute dependence upon Him, and His unwearied mercy towards
us, attend the public worship of His name with most
offensive levity and profaneness of carriage. What mere
babbling also must their secret prayers be (if they are
directed to pray at all) if they have never been taught
the worth of the soul or the weakness and depravity of
man on which is founded the necessity of prayer and
the aids of grace! What an invincible obstacle, humanly
speaking, to the success of the preacher of the gospel
must be found in the hearts of young people whose
natural ignorance, pride, and unbelief, like poisonous
plants, have been nourished by their parent's principles, or suffered to strengthen by their criminal neglect. Nay, even the calls of God in the voice of His
providence, by the death of relations, by misfortunes
and afflictions in the family, are likely to lose their intended benefit where no care has been taken to teach
children that these are monitors from God to lead
men to consider their ways and repent of their transgressions.

It is true (blessed be the free grace of God and the

power of His Spirit) that children who were utterly neglected and even became vicious through their parents' neglect have been, and are daily, brought to the knowledge of salvation by Christ. Nevertheless, it is certain that the prevalence both of empty formality and open profaneness is, in a great measure, owing to parents neglecting their duty to their children, and by them it must be answered for.

Another reason which should engage parents to care for the salvation of their children is that God takes particular notice of their behavior in this matter. Abraham, the father of the faithful and friend of God, stands greatly distinguished on this very account: "And the Lord said, Shall I hide from Abraham the thing which I do, seeing that Abraham shall surely become a great and mighty nation, and all the nations of the earth shall be blessed in him? For I know him, that he will command his children and his household after him." Other shining excellencies in Abraham might have been mentioned, but the Lord God, you observe, selects and holds forth to our notice as a peculiar excellency in which he delighted and names it in conjunction with the inestimable promise of the Savior, that Abraham would, above all things, regard the salvation of his children and the honor of God in his family.

On the other hand, how awful does the Scripture represent the indignation of the Almighty against the negligence of parents with respect to their children's spiritual welfare. Behold, He does a thing in Israel at which both the ears of every one that hears it tingle. The aged Eli, though piously disposed himself, yet, "because his sons made themselves vile and he restrained them not;" because he mildly admonished when he should have rebuked with all severity; expressed only his disapprobation of their conduct when he should have threatened them at their peril to persist and, upon their obstinacy, have delivered them up to the punishment of the law, for this neglect he is branded as, in some degree, an accessory to their iniquity. He is charged with "kicking at the sacrifice of God," and "honoring his sons above Him." He must hear the doom of his family that they should be cut off from the altar, and that the iniquity of his house should not be purged. "For them that honor Me I will honor, and they that despise Me shall be lightly esteemed", says He, 1 Samuel 2:30. From both these instances, judge how much it is the duty and interest of parents to be very diligent in training up their children in the knowledge and love of God.

The state of children, exposed to the most alarming dangers, also loudly calls upon parents to be solicitous for their salvation. Their case demands compassion, for they are wholly estranged from God. How much grief, anger, and vexation do you see them feel, even in their very childhood, from their natural stubbornness, passion, envy, pride, and selfishness. And do you not know what these disorders portend? What greater troubles, what severer conflicts, what more frequent vexations await them as their certain portion unless the strength of those baleful passions is subdued? Are you not conscious what latent seeds of various lusts are to be found in their hearts which will ripen by time and occasion to a terrible harvest of corruption unless prevented by you? Can you think of this and be negligent or dilatory in commending their case to the great Physician of souls, and teaching them how much they need and ought to seek for His power to heal them?

Were a parent to leave his child alone in paths beset with beasts of prey and full of covert precipices, would not his scandalous negligence or wanton barbarity shock every humane heart? But do you act a better part, O parent, if you leave your child to walk through this world filled with seducing objects, infested with a subtle, watchful adversary, and lying in wickedness, to walk through such a world without the light of faith, the defense of God, the influences of His Spirit; ignorant of the grounds of justice, truth, sobriety, chastisty, and a Christian life; with what strength they are to be practiced; why they are so absolutely required; and what the irreparable misery of violating these holy duties? A young man or woman entering upon the stage of life, ignorant of these things, is like a child deserted by its unnatural parent in the howling wilderness and is not more likely to escape destruction.

Again, were you content, O parent, to see your child hastening to poverty, to a jail and an infamous death, and used no methods to reclaim him, what words could express your guilt? Do not be deceived; you are, in effect, as guilty while you are negligent about their spiritual welfare. For go now and inquire of poor, imprisoned debtors about what deprived them of the sweets of liberty, and their family and society of the benefit of their labor. The answer in general from that place of wretchedness would be this: "Not the cruel rigor of our creditors towards us, not any unavoidable losses in trade, but early vice and headstrong passions never controlled in our education by religious instructions, never disciplines by the fear of God, brought us to this shameful house of our prison. Our parents were the first and the most effectual instruments of our ruin. Some of them live to see it and groan under the conviction of this heart-breaking truth. Amidst all the other instances of their affection, the grand one still was lacking, to give conscience authority by teaching us the Word of God. This would have made us tremble at those sins which have destroyed our possessions, our peace, and our character."

Consider, you parents, how such an accusation could be borne by any of you from the mouths of those who were entrusted by God to your care, that you might early instill into their minds the important principles of the Christian faith and guide them into the path of righteousness.

But, should there be any parents so hardened in profaneness as not to care what may become of their offspring hereafter, provided they escape poverty and prosper in this world, let them know and hear once more whether they will attend to the awful truth or not, that there is a day coming when they will see that their relation to their children was constituted for far higher purposes than to secure them advantages in this world or to keep them from its misfortunes. Then how insupportable will it be to them to hear their own children calling out for justice on them, imputing their damnation in a great measure to their cruelty. They kept the dreadful danger out of sight; they suffered their passions to rule; they joined in extolling pleasure, riches, honor, and power, but never exposed the mischief, infamy, and ruin inseparable from obstinate disobedience to God. How insufferable the anguish when children, with bitter imprecations, will rage against their father and mother, and curse the day in which they were born to them - born finally to aggravate their misery by perishing together with them.

The united force, therefore, of these various obligations, and these heart-affecting considerations, must make all Christian parents active and solicitous above everything, to do what lies in their power, as instruments to prepare their offspring to receive the truth of God to the saving of their souls, and to use those methods in which they may expect His grace to work with them and give them the desired efficacy.

6

Disciplining Children
by *Arthur Hildersham*
(From his lectures on Psalm 51 May 22,
May 29, and June 12, 1627)

This doctrine (that sin is passed from parents to children) serves to exhort and stir us up that are parents to do the uttermost of our endeavor to work grace in our children, and so cure that deadly wound that we have given them, and to preserve them from perishing by that poison and infection that we have conveyed upon them. Now, for the better enforcing of this so necessary an exhortation:

I will give you certain *motives* that may provoke us all to this care. The motives, are of three sorts:

Some of them respect our children, and our duty towards them.

Some of them respect ourselves and our own comfort.

Some of them concern our duty towards God and the respect we should have unto His glory.

I will also show you the *means* that we must use to this purpose.

THE MOTIVES

1. *Motives towards our children*

Of the first sort of motives, there are two principally.

First, our love to our children binds us to it. Nature moves us to love them, and has given bowels of pity and compassion towards them, when we see them in any misery. In so much as the Lord has been pleased to set forth his mercy and compassion towards His children by this. By the compassion of a mother, Isaiah 49:15, "Can a woman forget her suckling child, that she should not have compassion on the son of her womb? And by the compassion of a father," Psalm 103:13, "Like as a father pitieth his children, so the Lord pitieth them that fear Him." He is worse than a beast that does not love his children, and does not grieve to see them in misery, Lamentations 4:3, "Even the sea monsters draw out the breast, they give suck to their young ones."

And the Apostle teaches us, Romans 1:31, that they who are without this natural affection have extinguished in themselves the very light of nature, and are in God's just judgment given up unto a reprobate mind. And what love can we bear to our children if we have no care of their souls? The nature of true Christianity is to seek the good of their souls whom we love. "Charity edifieth," 1 Corinthians 8:1. See how Abraham expressed his love to Ishmael, Genesis 17:18, "O that Ishmael might live in Thy sight." Thus did Solomon's parents, Proverbs 4:3-4, "I was my father's son, tender and only beloved in the sight of my mother. He taught me and said unto me, Let thine heart retain my words, keep my commandments and live."

No, this is the only way to express true love to their bodies and their outward estate also. No lands or possessions that we can leave them can give us that assurance that they shall live comfortably in this life, as this will do, if we can be a means to breed saving grace in their hearts, 1 Timothy 4:8, "Godliness hath the promises even of this life."

Second, we admit that we are not bound to love them above others, yet we are bound in justice to make amends for the wrong we have done them. There is no man whom we have hurt in body, goods, or good name, but we are bound in conscience to do what we can to make satisfaction to him. See the equity of God's law in this point, Exodus 21:19, "He that smote him shall pay for the loss of his time, and shall cause him to be thoroughly healed." How much more are we bound to take care that our own children may be thoroughly healed of that wound that we have given them in our souls, of that filthy disease that we have infected them with?

2. *Motives concerning ourselves*
Now for the motives that concern ourselves and our own comfort. They are three, principally.

First, it will be a matter of singular comfort unto us to see the corruption of their nature healed, and saving grace wrought in them, especially if it is by our means. A great comfort to a minister is to see any of his people reformed and won to God by his labors. "Ye are our glory and our joy," said Paul in 1 Thessalonians 2:20. "I have no greater joy than to hear they my children walk in the truth," said the Apostle John in 3 John 4. But this must be much more comfort to a parent to see this in his own child. Solomon said, in Proverbs 10:1, "A wise son maketh a glad father." And, in 23:23-25, he says, "The father of the righteous shall greatly rejoice, and he that begetteth a wise child shall have joy of him, thy father and thy mother shall be glad, and she that bare thee shall rejoice."

Second, when grace is wrought in them (especially if it is by our means), they will be far more loving and dutiful unto us than otherwise they can be. "A wise son maketh a glad father," said Solomon in Proverbs 15:20. How? By his dutiful and respectful carriage towards him. This is his meaning there, as appears by the last words of the verse, "but a foolish son despiseth his mother." See this in the sons of Isaac. Esau did not care that he grieved his parents by mating with the daughters of Heth, but Jacob did, Genesis 26:34-35 and 27:46. See it also in the sons of Jacob. Of all his sons, Joseph, who had the most grace, was also the most loving and dutiful child to him, Genesis 45:11. This will make a man love him dearly who, otherwise, was a stranger unto him, if he were the means to win him to God. As we see in the affections of the Galatians towards Paul, Galatians 4:15, "I bear you record, that if it had been possible, you would have plucked out your own eyes to have done me good."

Third, and last, this will be a comfortable testimony unto us of the truth and soundness of that grace that is in ourselves, when we are careful to breed grace in all who belong to us, and especially to our own children. And, without this, we can have no such testimony and assurance of ourselves. Therefore, we shall find this oft

observed for a note of them that were soundly converted themselves; that their care was to reform their
families and make them religious also. There was
Abraham, Genesis 18:19; Joshua, Joshua 24:15;
Zaccheus, Luke 19:9; the nobleman of Capernaum,
John 4:53; Cornelius, Acts 10:2; Lydia, Acts 16:15; the
jailer, Acts 16:33-34; Crispus, the chief ruler of the syn-
agogue, Acts 18:8. Therefore, the Lord, in His law, for-
bade any proselyte to be admitted to the Passover
(though he was himself circumcised, and outwardly
professed the truth), unless all the males in the house
were circumcised also, and professed the faith as well
as himself, Exodus 12:48. And, in the condition of that
promise He made to His people for delivering them
out of the captivity, which He foretold He would bring
them for their sins, He requires not only that they
themselves should return to the Lord and obey His
voice, but their children also, Deuteronomy 30:2-3, "If
thou shalt return unto the Lord thy God, and shalt
obey His voice, thou and thy children, with all thy
heart, and with all thy soul, then the Lord thy God will
turn thy captivity."

It is as if He should say, "You do not turn to the
Lord yourself unfeignedly, with all your heart, unless
your care is that your children may do so also." But,
alas, if that law were not in force, that none should be
admitted to the Lord's Supper who had any in their
family that did not make at least an outward profession
of religion, how few communicants would we have? If
none may be accounted unfeignedly religious themselves whose children and servants do not live in an
outward conformity and obedience to the Word, how
few sound-hearted Christians will there be found in

this age?

3. *Motives concerning our duty to God*
The third and last sort of motives concern our duty to God, and the respect we should have unto His glory, and they are two principally.

First, the trust that the Lord has put us in, and the charge that He has given us concerning our children. For this we must know, that our children are not our own, but the Lord's (I speak to such as are God's people and members of His church). Thus did the Lord speak to His people, Ezekiel 16:20, "Thy sons and thy daughters, whom thou hast borne unto Me, thou hast taken and sacrificed." And as we have begotten and borne them for Him, so He has charged us to educate and bring them up for Him. And that is such a charge as the prophet tells Ahab in a parable, that he had received for the keeping of a man committed to his trust in the battle, 1 Kings 20:39, "If by any means he be missing, thy life shall be for his life."

If the child's soul perishes (through the parent's default, whom God put in trust to keep and look to it), the parent's soul must die for it. For this is the righteous sentence of God against them whom he has charged with the souls of others, Ezekiel 3:18, "He shall die in his iniquity, but his blood will I require at thy hand." If anyone objects that this is spoken of the charge God has given to prophets and ministers concerning their flocks, not of that which He has given to parents concerning their children, I answer this way. Every parent is as deeply charged by God with the souls of his children as any pastor is with the souls of his flock, and more deeply too.

You call our congregations that we are set over our "charge." And you say well, for so they are; and you can cry shame on us if we, either by idleness or worldliness, show ourselves careless of our charge, and you have indeed just cause to do so. But, in the meantime, you forget that your children and family are your charge also. You make no scruple of neglecting all duty, all care, of the souls of your own charge.

Know, therefore, for certain, that you are as much, yea much more, charged with the souls of your families, and of your children especially, than any pastor is with the souls of his flock. And hearken to your charge, I pray you.

You are as often, and as expressly, charged to use the means to save your children's souls, and to breed grace in them, as any minister is. Exodus 13:8, "Thou shalt show thy son" the meaning, the end, and use of the Sacrament of the Passover. Deuteronomy 6:6-7, "These words which I command thee this day, thou shalt teach them diligently to thy children." Psalm 78:5, "He established a testimony in Jacob, and appointed a Law in Israel, which He commanded our fathers, that they should make them known unto their children." Ephesians 6:4, "Ye fathers, bring up your children in the nurture and admonition of the Lord." No minister is more straitly charged of God to teach and catechize his flock than you are to instruct your children.

Parents stand obliged to their children by more and stronger bonds than any pastor can be to his flock, as we have heard in the first sort of motives.

Parents have more means and opportunities to prevail with their children than any pastor can have to do good upon his flock. The interest they have in their children's love and affection is a great matter; and so is the advantage they may take of their children's tender years, and so is their continual conversing with them, and so is their authority also. None have such opportunities to instruct and bring others to goodness as parents have.

This was what good Hezekiah meant in his prayer, Isaiah 38:18-19, "The grave cannot praise thee, death cannot celebrate thee; The living, the living he shall praise thee (and who among all the living?) the father to the children shall make known thy truth." In which respect we have seen, in those eight examples I mentioned unto you, how soon godly masters of families have prevailed with all that were under them to bring them unto an outward profession and conformity in religion.

Joshua is bold, Joshua 24:15, to undertake for himself and his house that they shall serve the Lord. Some might have said to him, "Soft, Joshua, speak this for yourself, and that is well too."

"No," said he, and that before all the people. "I will undertake this also for my whole house."

And in this respect also it is that the children's sins are said to be a blemish and reproach to the parents, Proverbs 28:7. Yes, the Lord often imputes the sins of the children unto the parents and lays them to their charge, 2 Chronicles 22:3. Ahaziah was a wicked man, for Athaliah was his mother. And the Apostle commands that such should only be admitted to the ministry who "govern well their own houses and keep their children in subjection," 1 Timothy 3:4-5; such "as have faithful children, not accused of riot or unruly," Titus

1:6, which he would not have done if parents were not chargeable with their children's sins, if they were not a chief cause of them, if it does not lay greatly in their power to prevent the ungraciousness of children. Let us all who are parents seriously think of this motive, namely, how God has charged us with our children's souls, and consider that it will be a most heavy reckoning that we must make unto God for them, if any of them shall perish through our default. And (on the other side) it will be a matter of unspeakable comfort to us at that day if we can be able to say of our children unto the Lord, as our blessed Savior speaks in John 17:12, "Those that Thou gavest me I have kept, and none of them is lost."

The second motive that concerns the Lord and His glory is that the hope of God's church, and the propagation of religion unto posterity, depends principally upon this, that parents take care to make their children religious. All who fear and love the Lord should unfeignedly desire and endeavor to provide for the continuance of religion, and for the deriving of it, unto posterity; especially that the true church and religion of God may continue in their own posterity. See a noble example of this care in the two tribes and the half, who had their possessions given them beyond Jordan, Joshua 22:24-25, "We have done it (set up this altar) for fear of this thing, saying, in time to come to your children might speak to our children, saying, What have you to do with the Lord God of Israel? So shall your children make our children cease from fearing the Lord." Concerning this you must understand that there is no man who desires to have a posterity, and to provide for a posterity, as much as the Lord does. And as it is counted a great honor to a man to have a great posterity, Proverbs 17:6, "Children's children are the crown of old men," so is this spoken of as a great honor to Christ, that he shall have a great posterity, Isaiah 53:8, "Who shall declare His generation?" And verse 10, "When thou shalt make His soul an offering for sin, He shall see His seed."

And surely this is the means whereby the Lord may have a seed and posterity raised and preserved. This is the means to derive religion unto posterity, when parents are not only religious themselves, but are careful to provide that their children may be also. This is the seminary of God's church. This was the cause of that commandment, Deuteronomy 4:9, "Take heed to thyself, and keep thy soul diligently, lest thou forget the things which thine eyes have seen, and lest they depart from thy heart, all the days of thy life, but teach them thy sons, and thy son's sons."

This is noted by the prophet, in Malachi 2:15, to have been the cause why the Lord at the first institution of marriage appointed but one woman for one man, and did so restrain promiscuous lust, "that he might seek a seed of God;" that is, that He might provide for the continuance of His church. And this is made by the prophet, Psalm 22:29-30, as one principal end God has respect unto in converting us Gentiles unto the gospel, and men of all sorts among us, poor and rich, "that our seed might serve Him and might be accounted unto the Lord for a generation;" that God might have a posterity and a people to serve Him when we are gone.

So, to conclude the motives, if we either respect our children, or our own comfort, or the glory of God, we must be careful to do our best endeavor that the corruption of nature that we have conveyed unto them may be healed, and that saving grace may be wrought in their hearts.

THE MEANS

Now it follows that we proceed unto the means that God has in His Word, directed parents to use for the saving of their children's souls. And those are five, principally.

1. *If we desire to save our children and heal their natures, we must be careful to maintain that authority and pre-eminence that God has given us over them.* We must take heed we do not lose that honor and reverence that is due us from our children. It is certain that, by the will of God, and even by the law of nature, there is an honor and inward reverence of heart due from the child to every parent, be the parent never so poor, never so full of weakness and infirmities. You know that in the fifth commandment, Exodus 20:12, this is made the sum of all the duties the child owes to his parents, "Honor thy father and thy mother," because this is the chief duty of all others. Yes, this is the root and fountain of all other duties a child can perform. If he does not, in his heart, honor and reverence them, he can do no duty to them well. "A son honoreth his father," said the Lord in Malachi 1:6. "If I be a father, where is Mine honor?" And Deuteronomy 27:16 says, "Cursed be he that setteth light by his father or mother." It is not sufficient for a child to love his parents, but he must also (out of this inward reverence and honor he bears them

in his heart) stand in awe of them and be afraid to offend them. Leviticus 19:3, "Ye shall fear every man his mother and his father." See how fearful Jacob was to grieve or offend his father, though he was an old, blind man, Genesis 27:12, "My father will peradventure feel me, and I shall seem to him as a deceiver, and I shall bring a curse upon me, and not a blessing."

And no marvel, though this honor and reverence is due to our parents; for our parents, by being the means and instruments of our being, are unto us in God's stead and (as His lieutenants) have had His power communicated unto them (for He only is properly and absolutely our Father, and the Author of our being, Matthew). And, in this respect, that which the Apostle speaks of husbands, in 1 Corinthians 11:7, and so of all superiors, may be said of them: they bear the image and glory of God. In honoring them, we honor God; in despising them, we despise the Lord.

Now this authority and pre-eminence that God has given us over our children, we must be careful to maintain. We must take heed that we do not lose this honor and inward reverence that is due unto us from them. That which the Lord requires of a minister towards his flock, Titus 2:15, that he should "speak, and exhort, and rebuke with all authority, and see that no man despise him," he should take heed that he does not, by his looseness, either in life or in doctrine, lose his honor and authority in the hearts of his people; for, if he does, there will be little hope that his doctrine shall ever do good, be his gifts never so excellent. That is every whit as much required of parents towards their children, and to every parent the Lord likewise says, "Maintain your authority, take heed that your children do not despise you."

We shall find it noted by the Apostle, 1 Timothy
3:4, to be a great blemish in a Christian, and such a
one as (be his gifts otherwise never so excellent) makes
him incapable of the honor of the ministry, "if he cannot rule in his own house, if he keep not his children
in subjection." Every father must be a ruler in his own
house, every child must be kept in subjection.

Our blessed Savior was subject unto His parents,
Luke 2:51. Yet His father, Joseph, was but a poor car-
penter, and his mother so poor that she could get no
better room in Bethlehem than a stable to be brought
to bed in. It is not sufficient for you who are parents to
advise and wish and admonish your children to leave
any lewd course you see them to hold. Eli did this
much, 1 Samuel 2:23-24, and yet we know God was
highly offended with him because he did not do
enough. Parents must do more than this; they must,
with authority, charge, command, and compel them to
do it. "I know," said the Lord of Abraham, Genesis
18:19, "that he will command his children to keep the
way of the Lord." And Deuteronomy 32:46, "Ye shall
command your children to observe, and do all the
words of this law," and "I charged every one of you,"
said the Apostle, 1 Thessalonians 2:11, "as a father
doth his children."

If parents do not maintain this authority, if they become hail-fellows with their children, as certainly many
have done nowadays, they shall dishonor their head, as
the Apostle speaks, 1 Corinthians 11:4. The dishonor
and contempt reaches unto God, whose image they
bear, whose person they represent, as we have heard.
They also undo their children and disable them from

profiting by any means they shall use for the reforming of them, or the saving of their souls.

"Surely this would be an excellent thing," you will say, "if parents could maintain their authority and honor in the hearts of their children; but how may this be done? This is such an age as there is little or no possibility of it."

I answer, it is true that this falls out sometimes through the just judgment of God, that parents do what they can, and yet children will be stubborn and rebellious, sons of Belial who will bear no yoke. It is foretold by the Holy Ghost, 2 Timothy 3:2, as one of the chief mischiefs and diseases that will reign and rage in these last days, and will make the times so perilous, that men will be disobedient to parents. It cannot be avoided, it must be so, so that the Scriptures may be fulfilled. And it is foretold as a sign and forerunner that presages the ruin of a state and nation, Isaiah 3:5, "The child shall behave himself proudly against the ancient, and the base against the honorable." Yet, it is also certain that parents themselves are, for the most part, the cause why they have no more honor and reverence in the hearts of their children, when they do not maintain, but rather lose, that authority that God has given them over His children, and that happens in two ways.

First, because they do not themselves honor and fear God, therefore, their children cannot honor nor fear them. Solomon, by the Spirit, tells us, Proverbs 11:16, "that a gracious woman retaineth honor," and that which is there said of a woman, even of a mother, may likewise be said of a gracious father, he retains honor. The true fear of God will procure reverence and esteem to a man, even in the hearts of such as have no grace in them, Mark 6:20, "Herod feared John, knowing that he was a just man, and an holy, and he observed him." For (1) this image of God carries such a majesty in it that a man cannot choose but to honor it in whomever he sees it. It is called, therefore, by the Apostle, "the spirit of glory," 1 Peter 4:14. (2) Besides, the Lord has bound Himself by promise to give honor to those that honor Him, 1 Samuel 2:30, "them that honor Me, I will honor." Our Savior said, John 12:26, "If any man serves Me, him will My Father honor." Certainly, if parents fear and honor God in their hearts, and express it in their whole conversation, their children must honor them. They could not despise them. On the other hand, if parents do not fear God themselves, their children cannot honor them.

If children see their parents as irreligious, malicious against religion, filthy and drunken persons, how can they honor them. I know they should be unwilling to see any such thing in their parents. They should, with Seth and Japheth, cast their mantle over them, but it is not possible for them to do it. That which is said of Jerusalem may be said of all men, Lamentations 1:8, "All that honored her, despise her, because they have seen her nakedness." They that thus see the nakedness of those who, by nature, they ought most to honor, cannot choose but to despise them. I told you, all parents bear the image of God, but these soul-sins deface it so that men can discern no glory in it, men cannot honor it. God has said, "They that despise Me shall be lightly esteemed," 1 Samuel 2:30; and, when God will have men to be despised, when He pours contempt upon them, when He says of any as He does of

Nineveh, Nahum 3:6, "I will cast abominable filth upon thee, and make thee vile," who can then honor them in their hearts? And this is one cause why most parents have no reverence in their children's hearts.

Second, another is this, because they neglected to keep their children in awe when they were young. They laid the reins upon their backs; they did not correct them, but pampered them in their tender years. "The fathers of our flesh corrected us, and we gave them reverence," said the Apostle in Hebrews 12:9. It is as if he had said, "If they had not corrected us, we would not have reverenced them so much." And it is expressly noted that this is the reason why David lost his honor in the heart of his son Adoniah, 1 Kings 1:6, "His father had not displeased him at any time, not so much as in saying, Why hast thou done so?"

I grant that those parents govern best who can maintain their authority, and keep their children in awe, with little or no sharpness or severity; and many parents are too apt to offend in too much rigor this way, otherwise the Apostle would not have given this charge twice unto parents, Ephesians 6:4 and Colossians 3:21, "Ye fathers, provoke not your children to wrath, exasperate them not." But this is also certain, that the best children, when they are young, are of a servile disposition, more moved with fear than love. The best man's heir, "as long as he is a child," says the Apostle in Galatians 4:1, "differeth nothing from a servant, though he be lord of all." And Solomon observes, Proverbs 29:19, that "a servant will not be corrected by words."

No parent may hope to weaken and destroy the corruption that is in his child's heart, though he teaches him never so well, and uses all the allurements he can to draw him to goodness, if he does not also correct him and use the rod sometimes. The Lord Himself, who is both the wisest and the best father, and who loves his children a thousand times more than any of us can love ours, takes this course with His children; yes, in this way He gives Himself as a model for all wise parents. Deuteronomy 8:5, "Consider in thine heart, that as a father chasteneth his son, so the Lord God chasteneth thee." And Hebrews 12:6-7, "Whom the Lord loveth, He chasteneth, and scourgeth every son whom He receiveth. If you endure chastening, God dealeth with you as sons, for what son is he whom the father chasteneth not?"

This is a special means commended unto us by the Holy Ghost, and sanctified to this end, even to abate the strength of natural corruption in children, and to make them capable of saving. And, therefore, it is to be observed in the law that no child was to be reputed graceless and past hope until he had showed himself not only unteachable, but incorrigible also; until his parents had used means to reform him not only by counsel, instruction, and reproof, but by correcting and chastisement also, and all in vain; who would not obey the voice of his father, nor the voice of his mother, and who, when they have chastened him, will not listen unto them, Deuteronomy 21:18. "He that spareth the rod hateth his son; but he that loveth him chasteneth him betimes," said Solomon in Proverbs 13:24.

You say, "It is nothing but love that makes me to bear with my child, and would you not have me love my child? Alas, who could find it in their heart to beat so sweet a child?"

But the Holy Ghost says that you lie! It is not love, indeed, it is hatred! We do not love our children, we hate them if we do not correct them speedily while they are such pretty young ones. Again, Proverbs 19:18, "Chasten thy son while there is hope." That is, while he is young, there is great hope of doing him good by it, and small hope afterwards if it is neglected then.

"O but," you will say, "I cannot endure to hear him cry!"

But what does the Holy Ghost say in the next words? "And let not thy soul spare for his crying." It is a strange thing to observe how the Holy Ghost speaks of the efficacy and fruits of this, and how He meets with all excuses that foolish parents are wont to pretend for the neglect of it. "Foolishness is bound in the heart of a child, but the rod of correction will drive it far from him," said Solomon in Proverbs 22:15.

"But would you have me be cruel to my own child?" you say.

No, says the Holy Ghost, this is no cruelty. You are unmerciful to your child if you do not correct him! Proverbs 23:13 says, "Withhold not correction from thy child, for if thou beatest him with the rod, he shall not die." He will die, he will perish, if you do not correct him; and are you not cruel if you will not do what you can to keep your child from perishing?

"O but," you will say, "alas, children's faults are nothing. Their stubbornness, lying, cursing swearing, and profanity are nothing!"

But what does the Holy Ghost say? Proverbs 23:14, "Thou shalt beat him with the rod and deliver his soul from hell." He will go to hell if you let him do what he wants to do. You may keep him from hell by correcting him.

"O, but this is the way to make my child hate me, yes, and to make him a dunce, so that I will never have comfort of him."

No, says the Holy Ghost, there is no such danger in it. Proverbs 29:17, "Correct thy son, and he shall give thee rest, yea, he shall give delight unto thy soul."

To conclude this first means, O that parents would see their sin in the neglect of this. (1) They lose that inward honor, reverence, and subjection also that their children owe unto them. (2) They spoil and undo their children, and make themselves the authors of all the ungraciousness. For the best-natured child in the world, if he is not kept in awe, if he is allowed to do what he will, must run to riot. Proverbs 29:15, "A child left to himself bringeth his mother to shame." Yes, and his father, too; though the mother only is there named, because she, usually, is most to blame for this kind. (3) They dishonor God and quite pervert His ordinance. For whereas, by God's ordinance, their children should honor them, they honor their children, as the Lord told Eli, 1 Samuel 2:29, "thou honorest thy sons above Me." And whereas, by God's ordinance, their children should fear them and be afraid to displease them, they are afraid to displease their children, as the Holy Ghost said of David, 1 Kings 1:6. He dared not displease his son Adoniah, not so much as with a cross word, or "by saying unto him, Why hast thou done so?"

2. *The second means all parents must use to destroy corruption of nature in their children, and to breed grace in*

them, is instruction. We heard in the motives that parents are as expressly and as often and as straitly
charged by God to teach their children as any minister
is to teach his flock. Yes, this domestic and parental instruction God has appointed, and sanctified for a special means to propagate religion, to restrain and
weaken the corruption of nature, and to prepare the
heart and make it more capable of grace. We heard
that speech of Hezekiah, Isaiah 38:19, "The living, the
living he shall praise thee, as I do this day, the father to
the children shall make known thy truth."

FOUR WAYS PARENTS MAKE GOD'S TRUTH KNOWN

There are four ways whereby you that are parents
may, yea must, do this.
1. Teach them soon to know God, to know what is
good and what is evil, teach them a few of the first and
easiest principles of religion while they are very young,
as soon as they discover any capacity or understanding,
as they will do if you observe it. Solomon said that,
when he was young and tender, "his father taught
him," Proverbs 4:3-4. His mother did too, Proverbs
31:1. And he often put God's people in mind not only
of the instruction and charge they received from their
fathers, but also of the law or doctrine of their mothers, Proverbs 1:8 and 6:20, which plainly shows that it
was the practice of God's church then that even mothers were teachers of their children. Even when they
were very young and under their government, they
were wont to teach them good things.
Yes, there is an expressed commandment for this,
not only that we should teach our children, but that we

should teach them even when they are very young. "Teach a child in his way," said Solomon, Proverbs 22:6; that is, by way that is fit for him, according to his capacity, according as he is able to receive it; a little at a time, as you pour liquor into narrow-mouthed bottles. As you do when you first begin to feed their bodies with a spoon, so you must do when you first begin to feed their soul with instruction.

2. You must quickly acquaint them with the practice of religion, like reading the Word, prayer, and giving thanks at their mealtimes, with singing of Psalms. We find, Matthew 21:15, that the little children had learned from their parents to sing Hosanna, part of Psalm 118, to the praise of Christ. Yes, more than this, parents should endeavor to restrain their children from evil and to breed in them a conscience of sin even while they are very young. You know the fourth commandment enjoins us that, not only ourselves, but also our children are to refrain from all work on the Sabbath, Exodus 20:10. Ezekiel professed unto God, Ezekiel 4:14, that from his childhood (from his infancy, as some read it) he had not eaten anything that God's law had forbidden. His parent taught him even then to make conscience of it. Parents, therefore, must join instruction with corrections, that they may breed in their children a knowledge and conscience of the sin for which they correct them. "Reproofs for instruction are the way of life," said Solomon in Proverbs 6:23. Without instruction, correction will do little good, and one fault amended by a child out of conscience, that it is a sin, is worth the amending of a hundred out of the rod only. That which David said of God's corrections may be fitly applied to this, Psalm 94:12, "Blessed is the

man who thou chastenest, O Lord, and teachest him out of Thy law." Few or none are the better even for the Lord's rods, if they are corrected only by Him, if they are not instructed also.

3. You must bring them with you to the church to the public worship of God quickly, even while they are very young, even as soon as they can come and be there without disturbing the congregation, so that they may be acquainted with God's worship and ordinances soon. Moses told Pharaoh, Exodus 10:9, that they must have their little ones with them to the solemn worship they were to do unto God in the wilderness, and would not accept liberty for all the rest, unless they might have their little ones with them. And when Joshua, according to God's commandment, read the law of God solemnly to the congregation of Israel, Joshua 8:35, they had their little ones with them in that solemn assembly. And when Christ was preaching in the congregation, the people brought their little children unto Him, Matthew 19:13, that their little ones might have the benefit of His prayers.

4. Last, you who are parents must examine your children as to how they profit by the means of grace. You must test them as to how they understand what they hear. Repeat it and make it more plain to them and, in repeating it, apply it also. Moses required the people, Deuteronomy 6:7, to teach that to their children which they heard from Him.

They might have objected, "What need is there for that, seeing they are present in the congregation, and heard what was taught as well as we did?"

Yes, but you must teach it to them again for all that, more plainly, more familiarly. "Teach these things dili-

gently to your children," he said. Yea, whet and
sharpen them upon your children (for so the word
signifies); that is, so repeat and make things plain to
them, so that you may apply them also and labor to
bring them to some feeling and conscience of that
which is taught to them.

O, how would religion flourish! How would knowledge and grace grow in your children, if you who are
parents would thus do your duty, if you would be
teachers as well as we, and lay your helping hand to
this work? And the best ministry in the world will do little good while you hang off and do nothing.

OBJECTIONS ANSWERED

There are two objections that some parents are apt
to make against this.

OBJECTION ONE. "It is an absurd thing," they say,
"to teach children religion, for them to meddle with
the Scriptures, or for them to be taught either to say
their catechism, or prayers, or grace. A parrot may as
well be taught these things as a little child. Alas, they
have no capacity to understand and be sensible of such
matters and, therefore, it is but a taking of God's name
in vain to teach them such things!"

Indeed, this has always been the thinking of carnal
men. Pharaoh could not abide to hear Moses say that
they must have their little ones with them to serve God,
Exodus 10:10. In Matthew 21:15, when the high priest
and scribes heard the little children meddle with the
Psalms, and sing Hosannas, "they were sore displeased." Yea, even the disciples themselves did not

understand, Mark 10:13. They were like carnal men in this, as appears by the rebuke they received for it from their Master, verse 14, "He was much displeased with them for it." When they saw men bringing their children to Christ, they rebuked them for it; but this is only a carnal conceit, as shall appear by three things that I have to answer to it.

First, children, when they are very young, are capable of the seeds and beginnings of regeneration and saving grace. See a notable proof for this in the example of John the Baptist, Luke 1:44, "As soon as the voice of thy salvation sounded in mine ears, the babe leaped in my womb for joy," said his mother to Mary. There were certainly in that baby the seeds and beginnings of saving knowledge, and faith, of saving grace both in his understanding, and in his will and affections also.

"But," you will say, "that case was extraordinary and miraculous."

I will grant that it was so, indeed, yet it is to the purpose for all that. For it shows that the youngest infant is not incapable of saving grace, but that God is able even to work it in them. And this should encourage us to use all the means we can to breed grace in them quickly, because we do not know how soon God may be pleased to work with the means and bless them unto them. According to Ecclesiastes 11:6, "In the morning sow thy seed, and in the evening withhold not thy hand, for thou knowest not whether shall prosper either this or that." But hear now some other examples to prove this that are not so extraordinary, as that of John the Baptist was.

For saving knowledge we have the Apostle's testi-

mony of Timothy, 2 Timothy 3:15, that he had known
the Holy Scriptures from his childhood; yea, from his
infancy, as the word properly signifies. And for the
seeds and beginnings of holy affections, see them in
the little children of God's people at Tyre, Acts 21:5.
They showed their love to the Apostle, and went with
their parents to bring him on his way to the seashore.
And for conscience of sin and a fear of offending God,
see it in Daniel 1:8, "He resolved with himself that he
would not defile himself with the portion of the king's
meat, nor with the wine that he drank." And if you
consider how long he lived after this (in the reign of
four kings - Nebuchadnezzar, Evilmerodach, Belshaz-
zar, and Darius), it will plainly appear that he was very
young when he made this conscience of sin.

Second, childhood is the fittest age of all to be
wrought upon this way. Children, of all others, are the
fittest to have the seeds and beginnings of saving grace
wrought in them. That which the prophet said by way
of exprobation to the Jews may be fitly applied to this
purpose, Isaiah 28:9, "Whom shall he teach knowledge? and whom shall he make to understand doctrine? Them that are weaned from the milk and drawn
from the breasts." They are not indeed fit to feed
themselves, nor capable of strong meat, but they are
the most fit of all others to be fed and dieted by others,
to be fed with milk. That is a comparison that the
Apostle uses twice, 1 Corinthians 3:2 and Hebrews
5:12.

Your children, while they are young, are like soft
wax: soft enough to receive any impression. They are
like little twigs, which you may bend and bow any
which way you want to. There is not in them that stub-

bornness, that spirit of contradiction, neither in their reason or will, to oppose and reason against good things, as you shall find in them of more years. In which respect our Savior tells us, Mark 10:15, we must all be like unto them, "Verily, I say unto you, whosoever shall not receive the kingdom of God as a little child, he shall not enter therein."

Third, and last, I answer this. Admit that your children have no understanding at all, no feeling of the good things you teach them while they are so young, admit no seeds, no beginnings of grace are wrought in them thereby. Will that which you teach them do them good afterwards and prepare, and make them more fit to receive good by the ordinary means of grace afterwards, when they shall come to more understanding and discretion? We baptize our children when they are infants, though they have, for the present, no feeling nor understanding of it. It is twice noted of our Savior's disciples, John 2:22 and 12:16, that the things which they understood never a whit at the first when Christ taught them, did them a great deal of good afterwards. And the same is noted also of the disciples of John, John 10:41. And parents may well think they have not lost their labor, but done a good and blessed work, if they have by their teaching prepared their children to receive good by the public ministry of the Word. And thus I have answered the first objection.

OBJECTION TWO. The second objection they make is this. Admit that children, by the teaching they have, may attain to some beginnings of knowledge and grace, yet no heed is to be taken of the good things that are in children, for they will quickly lose all again.

Many a young saint has proved to be an old devil.

But to these I object this way. I answer with the words of our Savior to the Sadducees (for they are certainly little better than Sadducees and atheists who say or think this way), Matthew 22:29, "Ye do err, not knowing the Scriptures, and the power of God." For:

First, the Scripture teaches us that a great guess may be made what our children will prove when they grow in years, by observing well their disposition when they are young. Proverbs 20:11, "Even a child is known by his doings, whether his work be pure, or whether it be right." For then they cannot dissemble, but will more freely discover their inclinations, and then they will do this when they are grown in years. And as experience has proved in a number of lewd men our old proverb to be true, "soon it pricks, that thorn will be," they discovered, when they were young, a most ungracious disposition; so it has also proved this true of many worthy men that the great towardness and inclinations unto good that appeared in them, while they were very young, presaged what they would prove afterwards. And parents shall do well to observe this, not only that they may know thereby what callings to fit and prepare their children for, but also what vices they should chiefly labor to prevent in them, and what good things above others they should principally nourish in them.

Second, Scripture teaches us that by teaching our children good things while they are young they will be made the better while they live. Proverbs 22:6, "Teach a child in his way, and when he is old, he will not depart from it." And experience in all ages has confirmed this, that as a vessel will long keep the savor of that liquor it was first seasoned with, so men keep the instructions they have learned in their childhood. The seeds of knowledge and grace which were sown in Moses' heart by his mother while she nursed him, Exodus 2:9-10, could never be gotten out of him by all the pleasures, honors, and examples he had in Pharaoh's court.

Third, the Scripture teaches us that, though some who have been negligent in their childhood have proved most lewd (and so it has been with men, too, as well as children), yet the worthiest men, and such as have done God most excellent service, began to be gracious and good quickly, even in their childhood. Many such examples we have as Joseph, and Moses, and Obadiah, 1 Kings 18:12, and Jeremiah, and Daniel, and John the Baptist, and Timothy, and many more. Those that proved to be such excellent saints when they were old were saints when they were young. And, on the other hand, as of all that we read and were possessed with evil spirits, the devil was most hardly gotten out of him whom he had possessed from his childhood, Mark 9:21 and 29. So we find by experience that the most of them who are old devils in their age were also young devils in their childhood, and showed much ungraciousness, even when they were very young. And thus I have finished the second means that you who are parents must use to heal your children's natures and breed grace in them. You must instruct them early, even while they are very young.

3. *The third means is a good example.* You who are parents must be careful to give a good example to your children. Cause it to appear to them in your whole

conversation that you unfeignedly fear God and love
good things. See three notable principles and examples of this care. (1) In Abraham, of whom God gives
this testimony, Genesis 18:19, that "He knew him, that
he would command his sons, and his house after him,
to keep the way of the Lord." He would go before
them himself in that way. (2) In Joshua: "Me and my
house," he said in Joshua 24:15, "will serve the Lord."
(3) In David, Psalm 101:2, "I will walk in the upright-
ness of mine heart, in the midst of mine house."
Without this, neither your commandments, nor correction, nor instruction will do them any good.

Therefore, Paul requires this even of Timothy and
Titus, men of such rare and extraordinary gifts, to see
that they gave good example as well as good teaching.
It is as if he had said, "You shall hardly do good upon
the people by your doctrine if they do not discern in
your lives that you believe and make conscience of that
which you teach, and then persuade others to it."

On the other hand, there is a great force in example to draw others either to do good or evil. See the
force of a good example, even in an inferior, especially
such a one as we love. The Apostle says in 1 Peter 3:1
"They that obey not the word may without the word be
won by the good conversation of their wives." And the
example of a superior, of one whom we not only love,
but reverence in our hearts, is of more force than any
inferiors can be. The Apostle says in Galatians 2:14 that
Peter, by his example, "compelled the Gentiles to do as
the Jews did." But domestic examples, especially the
example of parents, is of more force with their children to do them either good or harm than all other
examples are.

See the force it has to draw our children to good-ness, at least in outward conformity in three notable examples. It is said of Amaziah, King of Judah, 2 Kings 14:3, "He did that which was right in the sight of the Lord, yet not like David his father, he did according to all things as Joash his father did." And it is said of Azariah (or Uzziah) his son, 2 Kings 15:3, "He did that which was right in the sight of the Lord, according to all that Amaziah his father had done." And it is said of Jotham, his son, 2 Kings 15:34, "He did that which was right in the sight of the Lord, according to all that Uzziah his father had done."

And, on the other hand, see the force that the parent's example has to corrupt their children in three other examples. The first is of Zachariah, the king of Israel, of whom it is said, 2 Kings 15:9, "He did evil in the sight of the Lord, as his father had done, he departed not from the sins of Jeroboam." He would be of his father's religion. The second is that of the Samaritans, of whom it is said, 2 Kings 17:41, "These nations feared the Lord (made some profession of the true religion as the ten tribes had done) and served their graven images too, both their children, and their children's children" did this; "as did their fathers, so do they unto this day." The example of their fathers drew them into idolatry, and rooted them in it. The third is of the kingdom and church of Judah, of which we read in Jeremiah 17:1-2 that the main reason why they were so settled in their idolatry, so that there was no hope of reclaiming them, is that it was "graven upon the table of their heart, as with a pen of iron, or with the point of a diamond." The reason of it, I say, is rendered to be this, that "their children remembered

their altars, and their groves by the green trees upon
the high hills."

And certainly it is so in these days. A chief cause
why profaneness and impiety so cleaves to the hearts of
most men, so that no means are powerful enough to
reclaim them, is the evil example of their parents. O
think of this, you who are parents, and if nothing else
will reclaim you from lewdness, and make you careful
to take heed to your ways, let your love to your children do it, so that you may not corrupt them by your
evil example. Is it not wrong enough that you have
done unto them, in conveying into them so corrupt
and cursed a nature, but will you also, by your evil example, make them two fold more the children of hell
than they were by nature?

4. *The fourth means parents must use for the saving of
their children's souls is this. They must take heed how they
dispose of them when they place them abroad from them.* And,
as every true Christian will be careful of placing himself, that however he does for other commodities and
conveniences, he will not live where he shall lack the
means of grace, but resolves with David, Psalm 23:6, "I
will dwell in the house of the Lord all the days of my
life." So will he, in placing his children, be careful that
they may do so also.

They must take heed what schoolmasters and tutors
they sent them to, what service and what marriages
they place them in. (1) The Apostle Paul reports, Acts
22:3, that he was sent by his parents to Jerusalem, the
best school, the best university, the best college, and to
Gamaliel, the best teacher, the best tutor there, where
he was "taught according to the perfect manner of the

law of the fathers," and learned to be zealous towards God. (2) As for services, it is threatened as a great curse to God's people that their children should serve the greatest nobleman, yea, the greatest prince in the world, if he is a wicked man and enemy to God, yes, though they serve him in the highest offices that may be. The Lord said to Hezekiah, Isaiah 39:7, "Thy sons that shall issue from thee shall be eunuchs in the palace of the king of Babylon." (3) For marriages, we see the care of Abraham first, Genesis 24:3-4, and of Rebecca afterwards, Genesis 27:46, that their children might, by no means, match with the Canaanites.

Certainly, in this point, most parents evidently betray that they have no care at all of their children's souls. In placing their children in any of these three things, they aim at nothing but this, that they may get that which may make them able to live, and live in credit; but as for living under the means of grace, for living so that they may live eternally, they have no respect at all unto this. Whereby they show themselves to be "wholly sensual, not having the Spirit," as the Apostle speaks in Jude 19.

5. *The fifth and last means, without which all the former are to no purpose, is prayer.* Parents must be earnest with God in prayer for their children. Solomon's mother called him the "son of her vows," Proverbs 31:2. She had been wont to pray much for him. They should not only use these means, but pray earnestly to God to give them wisdom, to know what they may do to destroy corruption and breed grace in their children. They should pray as Manoah did, Judges 13:8, "Lord, teach me what I shall do to the child that Thou hast given

me." We should do as the woman of Canaan did, complain to God of the corruption that is in our children's natures, and desire Him to heal it. "Have mercy on me, O Lord," she said in Matthew 15:22, "my child is miserably vexed with a devil." And as Job offered sacrifice daily for them, Job 1:5, we should pray daily for them, that God would forgive them their sins.

Now, to conclude all this that I have said touching the means that parents are to use for the restraining and weakening of that corruption in their children which they have infected them with, and breed grace in them. I cannot assure you that, if you use these means, you shall see the effect and fruit of them in every one of your children; for you may justly object that many parents who have been as careful as is possible in the use of these means have had as ungracious children as any others (for the Lord is the God of all grace, and the only Author of it, 1 Peter 5:10, and He gives success and fruit to all means thereof, 1 Corinthians 3:6, and He works herein most freely, according to the good purpose of His own will, "as the wind bloweth where it listeth," John 3:8, and Romans 9:18, "He hath mercy on whom He will, and whom He will He hardeneth"). Yet I have two things to say for your encouragement and comfort who are Christian parents.

1. None have more cause to expect and, with patience, to wait for a blessing from God in the use of the means of grace towards any, than you have towards your children because of the promises God made to you concerning your children, Genesis 17:7, Psalm 22:29-30, Isaiah 44:3. And the fruit of your labor may appear hereafter, though it does not yet, as experience

has proved in many good men's children that, for a long time, lived most ungraciously.

2. Admit that, though God may never be pleased to vouchsafe a blessing to you in your labors, in your children, yet shall your labors, and the fruit of them, rebound into your own bosom, Psalm 35:13. For (1) you highly please God in doing your duty, and He accepts your work nevertheless, Isaiah 49:4 and 2 Corinthians 8:12, which will yield you unspeakable comfort, 2 Corinthians 1:12. (2) You have hereby delivered your own souls, so that the sins and damnation of your ungracious children shall never be imputed to you.

7

The Relative Duties on the Method of Instructing Children
by Henry Venn

The duty of Christian parents to instruct their children in the knowledge of God and of Christ has been laid before you. But, as the condition and capacities of men are very different, it is accordingly the duty of some, and what God will undoubtedly require at their hands, to bestow much more pains in this matter and to use a greater variety of methods with their children than others.

The poor will discharge their duty to their children by correcting them from their early childhood for lying, for pilfering, even in the smallest degree; for swearing, for quarrelling, and for every mark of a cruel disposition; by frequently declaring to them that it is a good and gracious God who gives their parents strength to provide good for their offspring; that He is their Maker, whose eyes are ever over all; that He will give unto every one according to His doings when He shall call the whole world before His tribunal; that this glorious God will ever bless, love, and comfort those that fear and love Him, but that He will punish with inconceivable pain all wicked and ungodly persons who do the things and indulge the tempers which He hates.

The poor who fear God themselves have it further in their power to guide their children to pray morning and evening; to tell them that the Bible is the Word of God which they must believe and love; to carry them to the sanctuary on the Lord's day, and to keep them from profaning it. And, when these things are enforced by a good example accompanied by prayer, there is little doubt but that their children will be greatly blessed and, generally speaking, tread in the steps of their godly and excellent parents. And, where so much time must be employed in hard labor, and the understanding can be so little improved, such a course as this may, I apprehend, be deemed a conscientious discharge of their duty towards their children while they are young.

But, when years have opened the minds of their offspring, all that believe in Jesus, however poor, will delight to enlarge their instructions. They will tell them that their own guilty consciences never found peace till they depended on the atoning blood of Jesus shed on the cross, and pleaded that alone for their pardon before God; that they obtained deliverance from their strongest sins only by praying for the power and indwelling presence of God's Spirit; that they have been kept in peace from worldly fears and from anxiety for a subsistence by casting all their care upon God, reconciled to them in His dear Son.

In the middle ranks of life, where superior education has better qualified parents, and leisure has made them capable of taking more pains with their children, it is certainly their duty to go far beyond the poor in this important matter. They must, therefore, not only use the same care as the poor in all the things already mentioned, by impressing them with a regard for truth, justice, and mercy, but study also the most probable methods of making divine knowledge pleasant to the souls of their children. A successful method of doing this, I apprehend, will be to watch the opportunities for giving life to religious instruction by an appeal to outward things and particular providences. Now, by a proper attention, this may be done by parents in so great a variety of instances as to take in all the particular branches of divine knowledge in which children should be established.

THE THINGS IN WHICH CHILDREN SHOULD BE INSTRUCTED

1. *The first thing in which all children should be thoroughly instructed is that God is good and gracious, and that the earth is full of His goodness.* To give force to this truth, which you must be often telling to your children, point out to them in the spring, when the whole country is arrayed in all its beauty, what their eyes attest: the wide-extended bounty of God; tell them that they are His clouds which drop fatness; that it is His sun which imparts its genial warmth to make the ground fruitful; that He causes the grass to grow for the cattle, herbs for the service of man, bread to strengthen man's heart, and oil and wine to make him of a cheerful countenance; that, could they see the extent of God's bounty, they would see

innumerable millions of creatures in heaven above, in earth beneath, and in the waters under the earth, sustained by His daily incessant communications of good.

In autumn, when the fields stand thick with shocks of corn, and the trees bend under their load of fruit, amidst this delightful scene draw aside the veil of ignorance and fix their attention upon God as the invisible, yet only, cause of all the plenty and beneficence around them.

In winter, you will have frequent opportunities of bringing the elements to bear witness to the glory of their Maker. In this dreary season of the year, when frost has made the earth as iron and congealed the flowing streams into solid ice, lead your children to observe how passive the whole creation is in the hand of its eternal Maker. When the cold is so intense as to become, in some degree, distressing, and its continuance would prove hurtful, then observe to them how instantly He changes the scene; He blows with His wind and the waters flow again. At another time, when the deep snow falls and covers every object with its fleeces, teach them how suddenly at His word it totally disappears, having answered the purpose for which it was sent.

Pursuing the same method, when you have told your children of the power of God, and what a dreadful thing it is to have Him for their enemy, repeat the instruction just after His thunder has shaken your dwelling, and the arrows of His lightening have glared before their eyes; or just after the tempestuous wind has left in the neighborhood some traces of its fury. That is the time to assure that fire and vapor, snow and hail, storm and tempest, wild and outrageous as they seem to us, move only as and where God appoints their course, with infinitely more exactness than the best disciplined troops obey the signals of their leader; and that, though the earth should be moved and the hills be carried into the midst of the sea, the Lord of hosts is with His obedient people and is their refuge and trust.

Thus, by pointing out to your children the invisible God as working in all these most sensible changes, and by furnishing their minds with those sublime Scriptures in which He asserts His immediate and absolute dominion over all the elements of fire and water, earth and air, you will make the creation a school of instruction to them. By this manner of teaching, you will give a body and substance to the truth, which, otherwise, is too abstract for their clear apprehension. Lectures of this kind, repeated not too frequently, lest they should surfeit children, a thing greatly to be guarded against, but at such intervals as these various appearances occur, will early form your children to adore their great Creator, and impress them with a sense of His presence and agency in every place. Thus, in the most rational manner, and in obedience to your Maker's command, you will talk of Him and His works and truth, when you go out and when you come in, when you sit down and when you rise up.

2. *Another truth of great importance which young children are capable of being taught is that health and strength are the gifts of God.* This, you must frequently assure them, is the truth. But more effectually to realize this truth,

watch some opportunity, and regard it as the noblest employ to carry them to the bed of a brother, a sister, or play-fellow, who is sick and in pain. Immediately after the visit, take them aside to tell them you waited for this opportunity to persuade them of the truth of what you have often taught them: that it is God who makes sick and makes well; that it is owing to His sovereign and infinitely wise appointment that some are on a bed of languishing, crying out through strong pain, others decked with health and smiling with joy; and conclude with observing how thankful you are to God that *they* are still preserved by Him in strength. The very same instruction may also be brought to their remembrance with a still more powerful application when they themselves feel the blessing of ease after the smart of pain.

It is of great benefit early to teach your children also that life and death, as well as sickness and pain, are at the supreme disposal of God. The proper season to rivet this instruction is when a domestic, a friend or neighbor, known to your children, has just expired and the awful report is brought to their ears. Then tell them the circumstances of the deceased immediately before death, the medicines used, the help of physicians, the sorrows, sighs and tears of friends and relations; these are to be urged as sensible proofs that it is God that takes away our breath in infancy, youth, or riper years, just as He sees fit, and that none can deliver out of His hand.

At the same time, especially, you should be careful to instruct your children what is meant by the news just brought to their ears. Such a one is dead.

Then assure them that to die is to pass out of a changing world into one unchangeable; that it is the removal of an immortal soul out of a corruptible body to be happy or miserable in an extreme degree, according to what it has done in this life; that to every proud, every wicked, every unbelieving man or woman, whether rich or poor, a king or a beggar, death is the beginning of endless sorrow; but that to every one who has loved God, and lived and believed in the Lord Jesus Christ, death is the door to endless joys and the perfection of glory.

And, if it should please God ever to bring your own children into extreme danger of death, and yet restore them again to your arms, it would be a very criminal neglect in you to omit telling them that you hung over their bed with tears, and felt for their pains, but could give them no ease; that you made your prayer to God and, by His power alone, they were relieved and made whole. Suppose, also, that either of you, their parents, have been recovered from the borders of the grave and brought again with joy to see your offspring; then is the season to impress them with the truth that God is the Lord of life and death; that it is He who has spared you in tender mercy to be still the guide of their youth and a place of refuge for them.

All these methods of instruction should be used; all these religious truths you ought to inculcate upon your children in their early childhood. As they advance to the period of youth, they are capable of being reasoned with, capable of perceiving the force of all those capital arguments upon which a godly and Christian life is supported, against all opposition from without or within. Now their faculties are strong enough to receive those important doctrines which before they were scarcely able to understand. The duty of parents, therefore, now requires them to proceed in more fully inculcating Christian principles; in representing to them the excellency and absolute necessity of loving God and delighting in His Word and service; the sin of being peevish and discontented, passionate and proud, envious or revengeful, unchaste, worldly or covetous.

By this time, your children will have committed so many faults, have been so often corrected or reproved for them, and only restrained, contrary to natural inclination, from committing many more and greater; that you will have various striking proofs to convince them that they are creatures corrupted in their nature, disaffected to the government and will of the glorious God, and full of vile propensities. Now show them the Scripture character of fallen man. Produce that awful passage, "Yea, also the heart of the sons of men is full of evil, and madness is in their heart while they live," Ecclesiastes 9:3. And that parallel to it, "We all like sheep have gone astray, we have turned every one to his own way," Isaiah 53:6. In full confirmation that they themselves are included in those Scriptures, and that their depravity is such as is here set forth, you may tell them what pains, what correction, what restraints you have been using with them from their very infancy, on account of their faults, to conquer their evil tempers and inspire them with love to God and man; and then appeal to their consciences, whether they do not find contrary tempers still rising and getting the mastery within, though they dare not suffer them to break out. While you are thus unanswerably proving their innate corruption, it is, however, your duty to do it with tender expressions of love lest, by seeming to upbraid, pride and prejudice should be excited.

The use you are immediately to make of this discovery is to prove to them the great need of the Redeemer's interposition and merits. For, after having fixed a conviction upon their consciences that they have often knowingly done what God has forbidden, what their own hearts condemned them for, and that they have taken pleasure therein, having proved that there has been a complication of injustice, ingratitude and rebellion in their conduct towards God, you may draw, with great force, this important conclusion, that it did not become Him, "by whom are all things," to pardon and receive into His favor such sinful creatures without an atonement, without some sufficient and everlasting demonstration of His infinite abhorrence of their sin, while He shows an astonishing degree of love for their persons; that without shedding of blood there can be no remission, nor any other way than through Christ Jesus, for the wisdom, justice, and mercy of God to act harmoniously in the salvation of sinners; and that it is upon account of what Jesus did and suffered that they have been spared, and never yet punished as their provocations deserved.

Now, also, is the time to bring to their mind the great doctrines which the Scriptures reveal; that the Redeemer who was in the form of God, and thought it not robbery to be equal with God, took upon Him the form of a servant and died on the cross, that all who believe in Him might be pardoned, sanctified, and saved. From this it will be easy to observe further to your children that no morality, no religion, can be acceptable to Him, however applauded and extolled by men, but that which is exercised in an entire dependence upon Jesus Christ; which proceeds out of a believing, humble heart, and which consists in a constant exercise of all those tempers towards the world, our fellow-creatures and our God, which were in Christ Jesus.

3. *One point more with respect to Scripture doctrines which your children are now very capable of being taught is their weakness and inability, unaided from on high, to live up to what the law of God justly requires.* You may observe to them how often they have been breaking their resolutions, acting against their convictions, sorry for doing amiss, wishing and striving in their own fancied power to make themselves better, yet still defeated, still only the more entangled vexed and guilty in their own eyes. Tell them that this must ever be the case if they ask not for the Spirit of God, if they place not their trust wholly in His power and influence; that God, knowing our weakness, has promised this Spirit, and commanded us to implore His continual aid and guidance. Desire them to make the experiment for themselves; to have done with placing confidence in their vows, promises, and good resolutions; to rely alone on Christ, and to pray, as creatures ruined by sin and utterly depraved, for the Spirit of God to work effectually in them; and conclude with assuring them that, in this very man-

ner, you yourselves make application for strength to
lead a Christian life, and that whatever conformity
to the will of God they see in your own behavior towards themselves or others is wholly owing not to
any goodness of yours, but to the grace of God
which is in you.

Other methods of forming children after the
Scripture model may be used by parents who have
much leisure and a good understanding, when their
offspring grow up to a state of manhood. At this season of life, it will be of excellent use to inform them
that the unhappy creatures whose crimes are made
public, and whose person are doomed to an igno-
minious death, were very early the despisers of God's
Word, His Son and His grace; wherefore they were
left to themselves, and this sin soon grew to such a
horrid size. Help them to trace the gay pleasure-
loving young woman from her first contempt of serious godliness and Scripture to the loss of her
honor, the disgrace of her friends, the irreparable
ruin of her character, perhaps to the imbruing her
hands in the blood of her own offspring. Point out
to them the robber, the thief, perhaps the assassin,
in the young man of spirit, infected with the plague
of uncleanness, the love of gaming, or the proud desire of appearing above his circumstances. Mark out
to them the course and issue of ungovernable passion and revenge, from its impatience of the control
of God's Word and the meek religion of Jesus, till it
presents itself unmasked, delivering up the man of
sense, of education, perhaps of noble birth, into the
hands of the common hangman. It is your duty, in
this alarming manner, not only to warn your chil-

dren against licentiousness, extravagance, passion
and revenge, but, above all things, to labor to persuade them that those persons, and those alone, can
be absolutely safe from the tyranny of sin who live by
faith on the Son of God. In full confirmation of this
truth, your own knowledge of the world will enable
you to point out to them many examples where fine
parts are utterly disgraced, where every shining accomplishment which nature and education can give
are rendered pernicious, even in a high degree, by a
union with unchastity or intemperance, avarice, or a
proud impatient spirit; which abominable tempers,
be most careful to assure your offspring, maintain
their tyranny because the principles of the Gospel
and the truths of God are set at nought.

Tell them that the Christian alone is freed from
the dominion of sin. This will gradually inspire
them with the highest veneration for the knowledge
of God in His Word and Son as the only bulwark,
which in fact it is, against all the wickedness of the
human heart; because only a knowledge of Christ
and a belief in the Bible can create a jealousy of the
first workings of corruption, and excite a fervent application to God for power to control and subdue it.

4. *The last method in instruction I shall mention, which is
of equal benefit with those already stated, is to remark to your
children, now capable of observation, the amiable behavior of
real Christians.* I suppose you to be acquainted with
some who justify their title to this glorious appellation. Remark the tranquillity of their countenance
and the modest of their conversation; observe how
free they are from passion and positiveness, from ill-

natured wit or ostentation; how far from despising those who lack their advantages, either of education, birth, or riches; how careful to give no pain or uneasiness to anyone. In further commendation of true Christianity, it will be of peculiar benefit to let your children, when grown up, see the behavior of sincere believers in the midst of their severest trials.

If you are a Christian yourself in spirit and in truth, it is most probable you will know persons of the same character. When they are in affliction or tribulation of any kind, carry your children to hear for themselves the meek, patient sufferers blessing God for all their afflictions; not fainting nor discouraged, but quietly enduring chastisement. Their discourse, their very countenance, will edify. This will irresistibly convince them of the value and substance of the knowledge of Christ, and open their eyes to see that it is as much to be desired for present support and consolation in a trying hour as to secure salvation in the eternal world. Then assure them that true faith in Jesus, showing itself in unfeigned subjection to His Gospel, leads all to the same blessed acquaintance with God, and cheerful submission to His holy will.

And, if an opportunity could be found of bringing your son or daughter to the bed-side of a departing saint, it will infinitely exceed the force of all instruction to let them see with their own eyes and hear with their own ears, the faithful servant of God speaking good of His name, declaring how true the Lord his strength is, proclaiming the peace of his own mind under the pains of approaching dissolution, while he is looking for the mercy of God through our Lord Jesus Christ unto eternal life.

Persons of rank or of easy fortune, those also of the ministerial and various other professions, with merchants and tradesmen of wealth, have opportunity of using these and many other methods of the same kind with their dear children before they arrive at man's estate. And if, in their own hearts, they infinitely prefer the favor of God before the praise of men, the happiness of eternity before the poor satisfaction of time, if they know there is no other way of salvation for their offspring than that which is marked out by the Spirit of God in His Word, then such attention to the everlasting welfare of their children will not be irksome, but delightful. Their reward, generally speaking, will be with them in their labors of love, and their hearts gladdened by seeing considerable impressions made upon their children.

But if, instead of this attention, custom and fashion are taken for the rule and measure of what you, O parents, will account a sufficient care of your children's education; if hours upon hours, from day to day, are consumed in amusements and mere sensual gratification, hurtful to yourselves and others, while your children hear from you no wholesome lectures, and see in you no prevailing concern for the honor of God and the salvation of their souls; your conduct is dreadful indeed. Your regard to Scripture is worthless, whatever you profess, and your ignorance of the excellency of God and the only way of true happiness is as gross as that of an Indian savage. Examine, therefore, and prove your Christian faith by your works. The care you take for the salvation of your offspring, or your neglect of them, is the surest test of what you esteem your supreme good, God or the world.

I shall only add farther on this head of the duty of Christian parents towards their childre, that it is absolutely necessary that the pains to instruct should be accompanied by constant prayer to God in their behalf. Without His grace, their best concerted efforts will be ineffectual and all their counsels vain; for it is God who gives the increase. You may take as much pains as it is possible to make your offspring Christians altogether, but still those who receive the Lord Jesus Christ are born not of blood, nor of the flesh, nor of the will of man, but of God. Therefore, you are the more earnestly, humbly, and incessantly to pray unto God to implant early in them His grace, and give power and success to your attempts; that as by them the inhabitants of the world are increased, an addition also may be made by their names to the church of the living God and the inhabitants of heaven.

8

Four Sermons on the Religious Education of Children

by Philip Doddridge

Dedication

To the Church of Christ, in Northampton, under my ministerial care.

My dear friends,

As I reckon the providence which fixed me with you in the pastoral relation among the most singular blessings of my life, I would always retain a sense of those engagements which it brings me under, to labor to the utmost for your spiritual improvement. And, through the divine goodness, I find it a delightful work; as your candid and serious temper adds a freedom and pleasure both to my public ministrations and private converses with you.

I take this opportunity of renewing the assurances I have often given you, that I could gladly converse with you more frequently at home did not the other work in which I am engaged as a tutor demand so large a share of my time. I heartily thank you that you so kindly consider it, and make all the allowances for it I could reasonably desire.

I trust, God is my witness, that it is a sincere concern for His glory and the interest of a Redeemer in the rising age that has determined me to undertake the additional labor of such an employment; and, as you voluntarily chose to sacrifice something of your private satisfaction to these great and important views, I hope you will have the pleasure to see them answered, and that you yourselves will not, on the whole, be losers by them. You know it is my desire that, as my pupils advance in the course of their preparatory studies, they would endeavor by their religious visits, conversation, and prayer to supply in part that lack of service to you which my care for them must necessarily occasion; and it is as a further supply of it that I now offer you these sermons on "The Religious Education of Children," which you heard from the pulpit some months ago.

The indulgence and thankfulness with which you then received them is one instance, among many others, of your relish for plain and practical preaching. When some of you expressed your desire that they might be made more public, I confess I knew not well how to deny you; and I was the more willing to comply with your request because it is a subject which cannot be often handled so largely in the course of preaching.

That tender concern of yours which led me to treat of education engaged me also to manage it in such a manner, as I apprehended might be most for your advantage and for theirs; that is, to make it, as far as I could, a warm and serious address to you. I have, likewise, for the same reason, retained that form in transcribing them for the press, though I am sensible it might have appeared more fashionable and polite to have cast them into a different mold, and to have proposed my remarks in a more cool and general way.

It is indeed my deliberate judgment that there is an important difference between popular discourses and philosophical essays. The more I converse with the most celebrated speakers of antiquity, the more I am confirmed in that thought; and I will take the liberty to add that, for the sake of common Christians, I could wish it were more generally considered. But whether in this respect I am in the right or the wrong, I must say with the Apostle to the Corinthians, "Brethren, it is for your sakes."

I would not willingly disgust persons of elevated genius and refined education, but, I must confess, the great labor of my life is to bring down my discourses to common apprehensions, and to impress the consciences of men by them in subserviency to the momentous design of their eternal salvation. And, as I am your shepherd, and you in a peculiar manner the people of my care whom God has committed to my hand, and of whom He will require an account from me, I would always cherish a peculiar concern for you and desire that, whenever I appear among you, my heart may overflow with a kind of paternal tenderness for you. There are, perhaps, some traces of this in these discourses, which a severe critic may censure and a profane wit may deride; nevertheless, I have a cheerful hope that they will be accepted by God and approved by you. If divine grace renders them useful to others, I would own it as an additional favor; and, that they might be so, I have diligently avoided whatever might offend any serious reader; yet they are yours by a peculiar claim. For you I composed them; for you I published them; and to you I now present them, humbly commending them and you to the blessing of God, and entreating your continued prayers that it may attend all the labors of your very affectionate brother and obliged servant in our common Lord,

Philip Doddridge
July 14, 1732

9

Sermon 1

"Train up a child in the way he should go, and when he is old he will not depart from it." Proverbs 22:6

It is a most amiable and instructive part of the character which Isaiah draws of the great Shepherd of the church that He should gather the lambs with His arm and carry them in His bosom, a representation abundantly answered by the tender care which our Redeemer expressed for the weakest of His disciples, and beautifully illustrated by the endearing condescension with which He embraced and blessed little infants. Nor is it foreign to the present purpose to observe that, when He recommends to Peter the care of His flock as the most important and acceptable evidence of His sincere affection to His person, He varies the phrase, in one place saying, "Feed My sheep," and in the other, "Feed My lambs." Perhaps it might be in part intended to intimate that the care of a gospel minister who would, in the most agreeable manner approve his love to his Master, should extend itself to the rising generation as well as to those of a maturer age and more considerable standing in the church. It is in obedience to His authority, and from a regard to His interest, that I am now entering on the work of catechizing; which I shall introduce with some practical discourses on the education of children, the subject which is now before us.

I persuade myself that you, my friends, will not be displeased to hear that I intend to handle it at large, and to make it the employment of more than a single sabbath. A little reflection may convince you that I could hardly offer any thing to your consideration of greater importance, and that, humanly speaking, there is nothing in which the comfort of families, the prosperity of nations, the salvation of souls, the interest of a Redeemer, and the glory of God, is more apparently and intimately concerned.

I very readily allow that no human endeavors, either of ministers or parents, can ever be effectual to bring one soul to the saving knowledge of God in Christ without the cooperating and transforming influences of the blessed Spirit. Yet you well know, and I hope you seriously consider, that this does not in the least weaken our obligation to the most diligent use of proper means. The great God has stated rules of operation in the world of grace as well as of nature; and, though He is not limited to them, it is arrogant, and may be destructive, to expect that He should deviate from them in favor of us or ours.

We live not by bread alone, but by every word that proceeds out of the mouth of God; and were He determined to continue your lives, or the lives of your children, He could, no doubt, feed or support you by miracles. Yet you think yourselves obligated to a prudent care for your daily bread, and justly conclude that, were you to neglect to administer it to your infant offspring, you would be chargeable with their murder before God and man; nor could you think of pleading it as any excuse that you referred them to a miraculous divine care while you left them destitute of any human supplies. Such a plea would only add impiety to cruelty, and greatly aggravate the crime it attempted to palliate. As absurd would it be for us to flatter ourselves with a hope that our children should be taught of God, and regenerated and sanctified by the influences of His grace, if we neglect that prudent and religious care in their education which it is my business this day to describe and recommend, and which Solomon urges in the words of my text: "Train up a child in the way he should go; and when he is old, he will not depart from it."

I need not offer you many critical remarks on so plain and intelligible a passage. You will easily observe that it consists of an important advice, addressed to the parents and governors of children, "Train up a child in the way he should go;" and also of a weighty reason by which it is enforced, "and when he is old he will not depart from it."

The general sense is undoubtedly retained in our translation, as it commonly is, but here, as in many other places, something of the original energy and beauty is lost.

The Hebrew word which we render "train up" sometimes signifies, in general, to initiate into some science or discipline; and, very frequently, to apply any new thing to the use for which it was intended. It is especially used of sacred things which were solemnly dedicated, or set apart, to the service of God. And, perhaps, it may here be intended to intimate that a due care is to be taken in the education of children from a principle of religion, as well as of prudence and humanity; and that our instructions should lead them to the knowledge of God, and be adapted to form them for His service, as well as to engage them to personal and social virtue.

It is added that a child should be trained up in the way in which he should go, which seems to be more exactly rendered by others at the entrance, or from the beginning of his way, to express the early care which ought to be taken to prevent the prevalency of irregular habits by endeavoring, from the first dawning reason, to direct it aright, and to infuse into the tender unpracticed mind the important maxims of wisdom and goodness.

To encourage us to this care, the wise man assures us that we may reasonably expect the most happy consequence from it; that, if the young traveller is thus directed to set out well in the journey of life, there is a fair prospect that he will go on to its most distant stages with increasing honor and happiness. "Train up a child in the way he should go; and when he is old, he will not depart from it."

I shall endeavor to illustrate and enforce this important advice in the following method, which appears to me the most natural and, for that reason, the most eligible. Each point will require a sermon all its own.

I. I shall more particularly mark out the way in which children are to be trained up.

II. Offer some plain and serious considerations to awaken you to this pious and necessary care.

III. Direct to the manner in which the attempt is to be made, and the precautions which are to be used in order to render it effectual. And then,

IV. I will conclude with a more particular application suited to your different characters, relations, and circumstances of life.

I am very sensible that it is a very delicate, as well as important, subject which is now before me; I have, therefore, thought myself obliged more attentively to weigh what has occurred to my own meditations more diligently to consult the sentiments of others and, above all, more earnestly to seek those Divine influences without which, I know, I am unequal to the easiest task but, in dependence on which, I cheerfully attempt one of the most difficult. The result of the whole I humbly offer to your candid examination, not pretending at any time to dictate in an authoritative manner, and least of all on such an occasion as this; but rather speaking as to wise men who are themselves to judge what I say. May the divine assistance and blessing attend us in all.

I. I am to describe the way in which children are to be trained up.

Our translation, as I have told you, though not very literal, is agreeable to the sense of the original; the way in which the child should go. And undoubtedly this is not other than the good old way, the way of serious, practical religion, the way which God has in His Word marked out for us, the way which all the children of God have trodden in every succeeding age, the way, the only way, in which we and ours can find rest to our souls.

But it is not proper to leave the matter thus generally explained. I would, therefore, more particu-

larly observe that it is the way of piety towards God,
and of faith in our Lord Jesus Christ; the way of obedience to parents and of benevolence to all; the way
of diligence and of integrity; the way of humility and
of self-denial. I am persuaded that each of these particulars will deserve your serious attention and regard.

1. *Children should undoubtedly be trained up in the way
of piety and devotion towards God.*

This, as you well know, is the sum and foundation of every thing truly good. "The fear of the Lord
is the beginning of wisdom." The Psalmist, therefore, invites children to him with the promise of instructing them in it; "Come, ye children, hearken
unto me, and I will teach you the fear of the Lord."
And, it is certain, some right notions of the
Supreme Being must be implanted in the minds of
children before there can be a reasonable foundation for teaching them those doctrines which peculiarly relate to Christ under the character of the
Mediator; for he that comes unto God by Him must
believe that He is, and that He is the rewarder of
them that diligently seek Him.

The proof of the being of God, and some of
those attributes of the divine nature in which we are
most concerned, depends on such easy principles
that I cannot but think the weakest mind might enter into it. A child will easily apprehend that, as every house is built by some man, and there can be no
work without an author, so He that built all things is
God. And from this obvious idea of God as the
Maker of all, we may naturally represent Him as very
great and very good, that they may be taught at once

to reverence and love Him.

It is of great importance that children early imbibe an awe of God, and a humble veneration for His perfections and glories. He ought, therefore, to be represented to them as the great Lord of all; and, when we take occasion to mention to them other invisible agents, whether angels or devils, we should, as Dr. Watts has most judiciously observed, always represent them as entirely under the government and control of God; that no sentiments of admiration of good spirits, or terror of the bad, may distract their tender minds or infringe on those regards which are the incommunicable prerogative of the Great Supreme.

There should be a peculiar caution that, when we teach these infant tongues to pronounce that great and terrible name, The Lord our God, they may not learn to take it in vain, but may use it with a becoming solemnity, remembering that we and they are but dust and ashes before Him. When I hear the little creatures speaking of "the great God, the blessed God, the glorious God," as I sometimes do, it gives me a sensible pleasure, and I consider it as a probable proof of great wisdom and piety in those who have the charge of their education.

Yet, great care should be taken not to confine our discourses to these awful views lest the dread of God should so fall upon them that His excellencies should make them afraid to approach Him. We should describe Him as not only the greatest, but the best of beings. We should teach them to know Him by the most encouraging name of "The Lord, the Lord God, merciful and gracious, longsuffering, and abundant in goodness and truth, keeping mercy for thousands, and forgiving iniquity, transgression, and sin." We should represent Him as the universal, kind, indulgent parent who loves His creatures and, by all proper methods, provides for their happiness. And we should particularly represent His goodness to them; with what more than paternal tenderness He watched round their cradles; with what compassion He heard their feeble cries before their infant thoughts could form themselves into prayer. We should tell them that they live every moment on God, and that all our affection for them is no more than He puts into our hearts, and all our power to help them is no more than He lodges in our hands.

We should also solemnly remind them that, in a very little while, their spirits are to return to this God; that as He is now always with them, and knows everything they do, speak, or think, so He will bring every work into judgment, and make them forever happy or miserable, as they, on the whole, are found obedient or rebellious. And here the most lively and pathetic descriptions which the Scriptures gives us of heaven and hell, should be laid before them, and urged on their consideration.

When such a foundation is laid in the belief of the being and providence of God, and of a future state both of rewards and punishments, children should be instructed in the duty they owe to God, and should be particularly taught to pray to Him and to praise Him. It would be best of all if, from a deep sense of His perfections and their own necessities, they could be engaged to breathe out their souls before Him in words of their own, were they ever so weak and broken. Yet you will readily allow that, till this can be expected, it may be very proper to teach them some forms of prayer and thanksgiving, consisting of such plain Scriptures, or other familiar expressions as may best suit their circumstances and understandings. If the Lord's Prayer is taught them as a form, I hope you will consider how comprehensive the expressions are; how fast the ideas rise and vary; and, consequently, how necessary it is that it is frequently and largely explained to them, lest the repetition of it degenerate into a mere ceremony, as I fear it does among many who are, perhaps, most zealous for its use.

But what I have said on this head, of piety and devotion, must be considered in an inseparable connection with what I am to add under the next.

2. *Children must be trained up in the way of faith in the Lord Jesus Christ.*

You know, my friends, and I hope many of you know it to the daily joy of your souls, that Christ is the way, the truth, and the life; and that it is by Him we have boldness and access with confidence to a God who might otherwise appear as a consuming fire. It is, therefore, of great importance to lead children quickly into the knowledge of Christ, which is, no doubt, a considerable part of the nurture and admonition of the Lord which the Apostle recommends, and was, perhaps, what he principally intended by those words.

We should, therefore, teach them quickly that the first parents of the human race most ungratefully rebelled against God and subjected themselves, and all their offspring, to His wrath and curse. The awful consequences of this should be opened at large, and we should labor to convince them that they have made themselves liable to the divine displeasure (that dreadful thing!) by their own personal guilt; and thus, by the knowledge of the law, should we make way for the gospel, the joyful news of deliverance by Christ.

In unfolding this, great care ought to be taken that we do not fill their minds with an aversion to one sacred person while we endeavor to attract their regards to another. The Father is not to be represented as severe and almost inexorable, hardly prevailed upon by the intercession of His compassionate Son to entertain thoughts of mercy and forgiveness. Far from that, we should speak of Him as the overflowing fountain of goodness, whose eye pitied us in our helpless distress, whose almighty arm was stretched out for our rescue, whose eternal counsels of wisdom and love formed that important scheme to which we owe all our hopes. I have had occasion to show you at large that this is the Scripture doctrine; our children should be early taught it, and taught what that scheme was, as far as their understanding can receive it and ours can explain it. We should often repeat to them that God is so holy, and yet so gracious that, rather than He would on the one hand destroy man, or, on the other, leave sin unpunished, He made His own Son a sacrifice for it, appointing Him to be humbled that we might be exalted; to die that we might live.

We should also represent to them (with holy

wonder and joy) how readily the Lord Jesus Christ consented to procure our deliverance in so expensive a way. How cheerfully He said, "Lo, I come; I delight to do Thy will, O My God!" To enhance the value of this amazing love, we should endeavor, according to our weak capacities, to teach them who this compassionate Redeemer is; to represent something of His glories as the eternal Son of God, and the great Lord of angels and men. We should instruct them in His amazing condescension in laying aside these glories that He might become a little weak helpless child and, afterwards, an afflicted, sorrowful man. We should lead them into the knowledge of those circumstances of the history of Jesus, which may have the greatest tendency to strike their minds, and to impress them with an early sense of gratitude and love to Him. We should tell them how poor He made Himself that He might enrich us, how diligently He went about doing good, how willingly He preached the gospel to the lowest of the people. And we should especially tell them how kind He was to little children and how He chided His disciples when they would have hindered them from being brought to Him. It is expressly said that Jesus was much displeased and said, "Suffer little children to come unto Me, and forbid them not, for of such is the kingdom of God." A tender circumstance! which perhaps was recorded (in part at least) for this very reason, that children in succeeding ages might be impressed and affected with it.

Through these scenes of His life, we should lead them on to His death; we should show how easily He could have delivered Himself (of which He gave so sensible an evidence in striking down by one word those who came to apprehend Him), and yet how patiently He submitted to the most cruel injuries, to be scourged and spit upon, to be crowned with thorns, and to bear His cross. We should show them how this innocent, holy, and divine Person was brought as a lamb to the slaughter; and, while they were piercing Him with nails, instead of loading them with curses, He prayed for them, saying, "Father, forgive them, for they know not what they do." And when their little hearts are awed and melted with so strange a story, we should tell them it was thus He groaned, bled, and died for us, and often remind them of their own concern in what was then transacted.

We should lead on their thoughts to the glorious views of Christ's resurrection and ascension, and tell them with what adorable goodness He still remembers His people in the midst of His exaltation, pleading the cause of sinful creatures, and employing His interest in the court of heaven to procure life and glory for all that believe in Him and love Him.

We should then go on to instruct them in those particulars of obedience by which the sincerity of our faith and our love is to be approved; at the same time reminding them of their own weakness, and telling them how God helps us by sending His Holy Spirit to dwell in our hearts to furnish us for every good word and work. An important lesson, without attending to which, our instruction will be vain, and their hearing will likewise be vain!

3. *Children should be trained up in the way of obedience to their parents.*

This is a command which God recommended from Mount Sinai by annexing to it a peculiar promise of long life; a blessing which young persons greatly desire. The Apostle, therefore, observed that it is the first commandment with promise; namely, a command eminently remarkable for the manner in which the promise is adjoined. And it is certainly a wise constitution of Providence that gives so much to parental authority, especially while children are in their younger years, their minds being then incapable of judging and acting for themselves in matters of importance. Children should, therefore, be early taught and convinced by Scripture that God has committed them into the hands of their parents; and, consequently, that reverence and obedience to their parents is a part of the duty they owe to God, and disobedience to them is rebellion against Him. And parents should, by no means, indulge their children in a direct and resolute opposition to their will in matters of greater or smaller moment; remembering that a child, left to himself, brings his parents to shame and himself to ruin; and with regard to subjection, as well as affection, it is good for a man to bear the yoke in his youth.

4. *Children should be trained in the way of benevolence and kindness to all.*

The great Apostle tells us that love is the fulfilling of the law, and that all those branches of it which relate to our neighbor are comprehended in that one word "love." This love, therefore, we should endeavor to teach them; and we shall find that, in many instances, it will be a law to itself, and guide them right in many particular actions, the obligations to which may depend on principles of equity which lie far beyond the reach of their feeble understandings. There is hardly an instruction relating to our duty more happily adapted to the capacity of children than that golden law (so important to all of the maturest age), "Whatsoever ye would that others should do unto you, do ye so unto them." This rule we should teach them and, by this, should examine their actions. From their cradles, we should often inculcate it upon them that a great deal of religion consists in doing good; that the wisdom from above is full of mercy and good fruits, and that every Christian should do good unto all as he has opportunity.

That such instructions may be welcome to them, we should endeavor, by all prudent methods, to soften their hearts to sentiments of humanity and tenderness, and guard against everything that would have a contrary tendency. We should remove from them, as much as possible, all kinds of cruel and bloody spectacles, and should carefully discourage any thing barbarous in their treatment of brute creatures; by no means allowing them to sport themselves in the death or pain of domestic animals, but rather teaching them to treat the poor creatures kindly and take care of them; the contrary to which is a most detestable sign of a savage and malignant disposition. "The merciful man regardeth the life of his beast."

We should, likewise, take care to teach them the

odiousness and folly of a selfish temper, and encourage them in a willingness to impart to others, what is agreeable and entertaining to themselves. Especially we should endeavor to form them to sentiments of compassion for the poor. We should show them where God has said, "Blessed is the man that considereth the poor, the Lord will remember him in the day of trouble." He that has pity upon the poor lends to the Lord, and that which he has given will He pay him again. And we should show them, by our own practice, that we verily believe these promises to be true and important. It might not be improper, sometimes, to make our children the messengers by which we send some small supply to the indigent and distressed; and, if they discover a disposition to give something out of the little stock we allow them to call their own, we should joyfully encourage it, and should take care that they never lose by their charity, but that in a prudent manner we abundantly repay it. It is hardly to be imagined that children thus brought up should, in the advance of life, prove injurious and oppressive; they will rather be the ornaments of religion and blessings to the world, and probably will be in the number of the last whom Providence will suffer to want.

5. *Children should be trained up in the way of diligence.*
This should undoubtedly be our care, if we have any regard to the welfare, either of their bodies or their souls. In whatever station of life they may at length be fixed, it is certain there is little prospect of their acquitting themselves with usefulness, honor, and advantage without a close and resolute applica-

tion; whereas the wisest of princes and of men has said, "Seest thou a man diligent in his business; he shall stand before kings, he shall not stand before mean men." And it is evident that a diligent prosecution of business keeps one out of the way of a thousand temptations which idleness seem to invite, leading a man into numberless instances of vice and folly because he has nothing else to do.

A prudent and religious parent will, therefore, be concerned that his children may not early contract so pernicious a habit, nor enter upon life like persons that have no business in it, but to crowd the stage and stand in the way of those who are better employed. Instead of suffering them to saunter about from place to place (as abundance of young people do to no imaginable purpose of usefulness, or even of entertainment), he will quickly assign them some employment for their time; an employment so moderated and so diversified as not to overwhelm and fatigue their tender spirits, yet sufficient to keep them wakeful and active. Nor is this so difficult as some may imagine; for children are a busy kind of creatures, naturally fond of learning new things, and trying and showing what they can do. So that, I am persuaded, were perfect inactivity to be imposed upon them as a penance, but for one hour, they would be heartily weary of it, and would be glad to seek their refuge from it in almost any business you would think fit to employ them about.

Thus should they be disciplined in their infant years, should early be taught the value of time, and early accustomed to improve it, till they grow fit for some calling in life in which they would, at length,

be placed with this important maxim deeply en-
graven upon their minds, "That full employ, in
whatever service they are fixed, is a thing by no
means to be dreaded, but, on the contrary, greatly to
be desired."

I shall conclude this head with the mention of a
very remarkable law among the Athenians which
ordained that those who had been brought up to no
employment by their parents should not be obliged
to keep them, if they came to want in their old age,
which all other (legitimate) children were.

6. *Children should be trained up in the way of integrity.*

Simplicity and godly sincerity is not only a very
amiable, but an essential, part of the Christian character; and we are, every one of us, indispensably
obliged to approve ourselves Israelites indeed in
whom there is no allowed guile. And this is a circumstance that will peculiarly require our regard in
the education of our children, and of all young persons under our care.

It is very melancholy to observe how soon the artifices and deceits of corrupt nature begin to reveal
themselves. In this respect, we are transgressors
from the womb, and go astray almost as soon as we
are born, speaking lies. Great care, therefore, should
be taken to form the minds of children to a love for
truth and candor, and a sense of the meanness as
well as the guilt of a lie. We should be cautious that
we do not expose them to any temptations of this
kind, either by unreasonable severities, on account
of little faults, or by hasty surprises, when inquiring
into any matter of fact, which it may seem their in-

terest to disguise by a falsehood; and, when we find
them guilty of a known and deliberate lie, we should
express our horror of it not only by an immediate
reproof or correction, but by such a conduct towards
them for some time afterwards as may plainly show
them how greatly we are amazed, grieved, and displeased. When so solemn a business is made of the
first faults of this kind, it may be a means of preventing many more.

I will further add that we ought not, only thus
severely, to critically remark upon a direct lie, but
likewise, in a proper degree, to discourage all kinds
of equivocations and double meanings, and those
little tricks and artifices by which they may endeavor
to impose on each other, or on those that are older
than themselves. We should often inculcate upon
them that excellent Scripture, "He that walketh up-
rightly, walketh surely, but he that perverteth his way
(that twists and distorts it with the perplexities of artifices and deceit) shall at length be known." Be
showing them every day how easy, how pleasant, how
honorable, and how advantageous it is to maintain a
fair, open, and honest temper; and, on the other
hand, what folly there is in cunning and dishonesty
in all its forms; and how certain it is that, by study-
ing and practicing it, they take the readiest way to
make themselves noxious and useless, infamous and
odious. Above all, should we remind them that the
righteous Lord loves righteousness, and His favorable countenance beholds the upright; but lying
lips are such an abomination to Him that He expressly declared, "All liars shall have their part in
the lake which burneth with fire and brimstone."

7. Children should be trained up in the way of humility.

This is a grace which our Lord particularly invites us to learn of Him, and most frequently recommends to us, well knowing that, without it, so humbling a scheme as He came to introduce would never meet with a welcome reception. And, with regard to the present life, it is a most lovely ornament which engages universal esteem and affection; so that before honor is humility. On the whole, we find he that exalts himself is abased, and he that humbles himself is exalted, both by God and man.

A regard, therefore, to the ease, honor, and happiness of our children should engage us to an early endeavor of checking that pride which was the first sin and the ruin of our natures; and diffuses itself so wide and sinks so deep into all that draw their original from degenerate Adam. We should teach them to express humility and modesty in their converse with all.

They should be taught to treat their superiors with peculiar respect, and should, at proper seasons, be accustomed to silence and reserve before them. Hence they will learn, in some degree, the government of the tongue; a branch of wisdom which, in the advance of life, will be of great importance to the quiet of others, and to their own comfort and reputation.

Nor should they be allowed to assume airs of insolence towards their equals, but rather be taught to yield, to oblige, and to give up their right for the sake of peace. To this purpose, I cannot but think it desirable that they should be generally accustomed to treat each other with those forms of civility and complaisance which are usual among well-bred people in their rank of life. I know those things are mere trifles in themselves, yet they are the out-guards of humanity and friendship, and effectually prevent many a rude attack which, taking its rise from some little circumstance, may nevertheless be attended with fatal consequences. I thought it proper to mention this here because, as Scougal very justly and elegantly expresses it, "These modes are the shadows of humility, and seem intended to show our regard for others, and the low thoughts we have of ourselves."

I shall only add further that it is great imprudence and unkindness to children to indulge them in a haughty and imperious behavior towards those who are most their inferiors. They should be made to understand that the servants of the family are not their servants, nor to be under their government and control. I rather insist upon this because I have generally observed that where young people have been permitted to tyrannize over persons in the lowest circumstances of life, the honor has shamefully grown upon them till it has diffused insolence and arrogance through their behavior to all about them.

8. *Last, children should be trained up in the way of self-denial.*

As without something of this temper we can never follow Christ or expect to be owned by Him as His disciples, so neither indeed can we pass comfortably through the world. For, whatever inexperienced youth may dream, a great many distasteful and mortifying circumstances will occur in life which will unhinge our minds almost every hour if we cannot manage and, in many instances, deny our appetites, our passions, and our humors. We should, therefore, endeavor to teach our children this important lesson quickly; and, if we succeed in our care, we shall leave them abundantly richer and happier in this rule and possession of their own spirits than the most plentiful estates, or the most unlimited power over others, could make them.

When a rational creature becomes the slave of appetite, he sinks beneath the dignity of the human nature, as well as the sanctity of the Christian profession. It is, therefore, observable that when the Apostle mentions the three grand branches of practical religion, he puts sobriety in the front; perhaps to intimate that, where that is neglected, the other cannot be suitably regarded. The grace of God, namely the Gospel, teaches us, to live soberly, righteously, and godly. Children therefore, as well as young men, should be exhorted to be sober-minded; and they should be taught it by early self-denial. It is certain that if their own appetite and taste were to determine the kind and quantity of their food, many of them would quickly destroy their constitution and, perhaps, their lives, since they have often the greatest desire for those things which are the most improper. And it seems justly observed by a very wise man (who was himself a melancholy instance of it), that the fondness of mothers for their children, in letting them eat and drink what they will, lays a foundation for most of those calamities in human life which proceed from bodily indisposition. Nay, I will add that it is the part of wisdom and love not only to deny what would be unwholesome, but to guard against indulging them in too great a nicety, either of food or dress. People of sense cannot but see, if they would please to consider it, that to know how to fare plainly, and sometimes a little hardly, carries a man with ease and pleasure through many circumstances of life which, to luxury and delicacy, would be almost intolerable.

The government of the passions is another branch of self-denial to which children should early be habituated; and so much the rather because, in an age when reason is so weak, the passions are apt to appear with peculiar force and violence. A prudent care should, therefore, be taken to repress the exorbitances of them. For which purpose it is of great importance that they never be suffered to carry any point by obstinacy, noise, and clamor, which is indeed to bestow a reward on a fault that deserves a severe reprimand. Nay, I will venture to add that, though it is very inhuman to take pleasure in making them uneasy by needless mortifications, yet when they are eagerly and intemperately desirous of a trifle, they ought, for that very reason, sometimes to be denied it to teach them more moderation for the future. And if, by such methods, they gradually learn to conquer their little humors and fancies, they learn no inconsiderable branch of true fortitude and wisdom. I cannot express this better than in the words of Mr. Locke, in his excellent treatise on the subject before us, "He that has found out the way to keep a child's spirit easy, active, and free, and yet at the same time to restrain him from many things which he has a mind to, and draw him to things uneasy to him, has got the true secret of education."

I have sometimes been surprised to see how far a sense of honor and praise has carried some children of a generous temper in a long and resolute course of self-denial. But, undoubtedly, the noblest principle of all is a sense of religion. Happy would it indeed be if they were led to see that there is but very little in this kind of gratifications and indulgences; that the world itself is but a poor empty trifle, and that the great thing a rational creature should be concerned about is to please God and get well to heaven. May divine grace teach us this important lesson for ourselves that we may transmit it with greater advantage to our children! Amen.

10

Sermon 2

"Train up a child in the way he should go, and when he is old, he will not depart from it." Proverbs 22:6

It is certainly a very pleasing reflection to every faithful minister of the gospel that the cause in which he is engaged is the most benevolent, as well as the most religious, subserving the glory of God by promoting the happiness of mankind. It must be a great satisfaction to a man of integrity and humanity to think that it is not his business to dazzle and confound his hearers with the artifices of speech, to give the appearances of truth to falsehood, and importance to trifles, but to teach them to weigh things in an impartial balance and, by the words of truth and soberness, to lead them into the paths of wisdom and of goodness.

This is a satisfaction which I peculiarly find this day while I am urging you to that religious care in the education of children, which I have at large opened in the former discourse. And it is a circumstance of additional pleasure that I am pleading the cause of the weak and the helpless, of little tender creatures who are incapable of pleading for themselves, and know not how much their interest is concerned. Nor am I without a secret hope that, if the Divine Spirit favors us with His assistance, some who are yet unborn may have eternal reason to rejoice in the fruits of what you are now to hear. Amen.

II. Having already endeavored to describe the way in which children are to be trained up, I now proceed to propose some arguments to engage parents to this pious care.

And here I would entreat you distinctly to consider that the attempt itself is pleasant; you have great reason to hope it may be successful and that success is of the highest importance.

1. The attempt itself is pleasant.

I speak not merely of the pleasure arising from the consciousness of discharging present duty and a probable view of future success; such a satisfaction may attend those actions which are, in themselves, most painful and mortifying. But I refer to the entertainment immediately flowing from the employment itself when rightly managed. This is, undoubtedly, one of those ways of wisdom which are ways of pleasantness, as well as a path which, in its consequences, is peace and happiness; it is a commandment, in keeping of which there is great reward.

The God of nature has wisely annexed a secret unutterable delight to all our regular cares for the improvement of our rising offspring. We rejoice to see our tender plants flourish, to observe how the stock strengthens, and the blossoms and the leaves successively unfold. We trace with a gradually advancing pleasure their easy smiles, the first effects of speech on their stammering tongues, and the dawnings of reason in their feeble minds. It is a delightful office to cultivate and assist opening nature, to lead the young strangers into a new world, and to infuse the principles of any useful kind of knowledge which their age may admit and their circumstances require. But when we attempt to raise their thoughts to the great Father of spirits, to present them, as in the arms of faith, to Jesus the compassionate Shepherd, and teach them to inquire after Him; when we endeavor to instruct them in the principles of divine truth, and form them to sentiments of prudence superior to what any other labor for their improvement can give.

On this occasion, my friends, I persuade myself I may appeal to the repeated experience of many among you. Do you not find that the sweetest truths of Christianity, which are your hope and your joy in this house of your pilgrimage, are peculiarly sweet when you talk them over with your children? Do you not find that your instructions and admonitions to them return into your own bosom with a rich increase of edification and refreshment? Thus, while you are watering these domestic plantations, you are watering also yourselves; and, from these holy converses with your children, you rise to more endearing communion with your heavenly Father: God, by His Spirit, visiting your souls in the midst of those pious cares, and giving you immediate comfort and strength as a token of His gracious acceptance and, perhaps, as a pledge of future success. This leads me to the following:

2. *I urge the religious education of children by the probability there is that it will be tended with such success as to be the*

means of making them wise and good.

This is the argument urged by Solomon in the text, "Train up a child in the way in which he should go, and when he is old he will not depart from it." Being early initiated into the right way, he will pursue it with increasing pleasure; so that, with regard to the prosperity of the soul, as well as of the body, his path will be like the morning light which shines more and more unto the perfect day.

It is true, this assertion is to be understood with some limitation as expressing the probability rather than the certainty of the success; otherwise, experience would contradict it in some melancholy instances. Would to God there were none untractable under the most pious and prudent methods of education; none who, like deaf adders, stop their ears against the voice of the most skillful charmers, and have been accustomed to do so from their infancy! Would to God there were none of those who appeared to set out well, and seemed eager in inquiring the way to Zion with their faces thitherward, who have forgotten the guides of their youth and the covenant of their God, and are, to this day, wandering in the paths of the destroyer, if they are not already fallen in them! But do you throw by every medicine which some have used without being recovered by it; or decline every profession of which there are some who do not thrive? What remedy must you then take? What calling must you then pursue? The application is obvious. It would be folly to pretend to maintain that religious education will certainly obtain its end; but let me entreat you to consider that it is, in its own nature, a very rational

method; that it is the method which God has appointed, and a method which, in many instances,
has been found successful. Attend seriously to these
remarks and then judge whether prudence and conscience will not oblige you to pursue it.

CONSIDER THESE REMARKS

1. The religious education of children is a very
rational method of engaging them to walk in the
way in which they should go.

There is this most evident advantage attending
our early attempts of this kind, that we shall find the
mind more open and disengaged, not tainted with
all those corrupt principles, nor enslaved to those
irregular habits which they would probably imbibe
and contract in the advance of age. Though the pa-
per on which we would write the knowledge of God
is not entirely fair, it is clear of many a foul inscription and deep blot with which it would soon be cov-
ered. Though the garden in which we would plant
the fruits of holiness is not free from weeds, yet
many of them are but, as it were, in the invisible
seed, and the rest are not grown up to that luxuriant
size which we must expect if due cultivation is omitted or delayed.

It is a further advantage which deserves to be
mentioned here that infancy and childhood is the
most impressionable age; and, as principles are
then most easily admitted, so they are most firmly retained. The ancients, those judicious observers of
human nature, as well as many modern writers, are
full of this remark in their discourses on education,

and illustrate it by a great many beautiful allusions which are well known.

The new vessel takes a lasting tincture from the liquor which is first poured. The soft clay is easily fashioned into what form you please. The young plant may be bent with a gentle hand; and the characters, engraved on the tender bark, grow deeper and larger with the advancing tree. It will be our wisdom, then, to seize these golden opportunities; and so much the rather, as it is certain they will either be improved or perverted; and that, if they are not pressed into the service of religion, they will be employed as dangerous artillery against it.

But you will say, "With all these advantageous circumstances, we cannot infuse grace into the hearts of our children; and, after all our precautions, corrupt nature will prevent us and fix a wrong bias on the mind before we can attempt to direct it aright." A mournful, but too evident, truth! which, far from denying or suppressing, I would often declare and inculcate; and the rather, now, as it greatly confirms my argument. Are the influences of a degenerate nature unavoidably so strong, and will you suffer them to be confirmed by these additional advantages? Do you apprehend that, running with the footmen, you shall be in danger of fainting? And do you, for that very reason, choose to contend with the horsemen? You cannot surely, in the face of so much reason and Scripture, urge this as an excuse against making any attempts at all of this kind; and how, then, is it an apology for the neglect of those which are (other things being equal) the most rational and easy? But the trifling plea is more evidently silenced by observing:

2. The religious education of children is a method which God has appointed; and this greatly increases the probability of its success.

I assuredly know, and may God more deeply engrave it on our hearts, that with regard to your labors, as well as ours, "neither is he that planteth anything, nor he that watereth, but God that giveth the increase." But consider, I beseech you, how that increase is to be hoped for; is it in the omission, or in the use, of prescribed means? I urge it on your consciences, my friends, that religious education is an ordinance of God which, therefore, you may reasonably hope He will honor with a blessing. And you might as justly expect that your soul should flourish in an unnecessary absence from the table and house of the Lord, or a habitual neglect of reading and prayer, as that your children should grow up for God while you fail in your endeavors to engage them in His service. I repeat it again, religious education is an ordinance of God. And is it a work of labor and difficulty to prove the assertion? Which of you does not know that Christian parents are solemnly charged to bring up their children in the nurture and admonition of the Lord; and that, even under the Mosaic economy, God urged it on His people in a very affecting manner? Surely you must have observed how strictly God charged it upon the Jews to take all opportunities to this purpose, occasional, as well as stated. "These words, says He, which I command thee this day, shall be in thine heart; and thou shalt teach them diligently to thy children, and shalt talk of them when thou risest up." And elsewhere, "Thou shalt teach them to thy sons and thy sons' sons," plainly recommending a care of more remote, as well as immediate, descendants, of grandchildren as well as children. Thus, when God established a testimony in Jacob, and appointed a law in Israel, He commanded the fathers that they should make them known unto their children; that the generation to come might know them, even the children that should be born; that they should arise and declare them unto their children so that religion might be transmitted to every rising age. You cannot be ignorant of such passages as these, which need no comment to explain them, and, consequently, you cannot but know that the religious education of children is a divine institution as well as, in itself, a most rational attempt, after which you will not wonder to hear:

3. That it has, in fact, been attended with a very happy success.

We acknowledge that the great God does not confine Himself to work by this way, and that He sometimes displays His sovereignty in visibly turning out of it. We acknowledge that He sometimes leaves those who had been, as it were, born and brought up in His family to forsake it in a very scandalous manner, while He seems to go into the very territories of Satan, into ignorant, carnal, and profane families, and takes from thence persons, whom He erects as trophies of free, surprising, and, as Mr. Howe justly expresses it, "unaccountable grace." But you well know that these are more rare and uncommon cases; and, though some of you, my friends, are, and I hope you will never forget it, happy instances of the singular divine goodness; yet most of you, as I apprehend, were from your childhood trained up in the knowledge of God, and are living monuments of the success which has attended the care of parents or masters in this particular. The greater part of those who have of late been admitted to your communion have, to my certain knowledge, mentioned it with thankfulness; and I rejoice to think how many of the rising generation among us, if even a child may be known by his doings, are likely to increase the number, and give us an encouraging hope that they will at length be set as olive-plants around the Lord's table as well as yours. I persuade myself it is so elsewhere, and think I may pronounce it with some confidence that the families of God's children are, generally speaking, the nurseries of His church. Solomon, no doubt, had observed that a good education had generally been successful, or we could by no means account for the remark in the text; and a very accurate writer of our own age and nation has carried it so far as to say that "of all the men we meet with, nine parts in ten are what they are, good or bad, useful or not, according to their education."

I hope you are, by this time, convinced that, humanly speaking, there is a great probability that religious education may be the effectual means of promoting serious piety in the rising age; which was the second argument by which I was to recommend it.

3. *This second argument may be greatly strengthened by observing that the success which we may so reasonably expect*

is a matter of very high importance.

It is of evident importance to the honor of God and the support of religion, to the present and future happiness of your children, and to your own comfort both in life and death. Let me give you some weighty and comprehensive thoughts; which I shall briefly touch, and to which I beg you will renew your attention.

First, the honor of God, and the interest of a Redeemer, is greatly concerned in the behavior of your children; and, consequently, in your care of their education, which is likely to have so great an influence upon it.

We live in a dying world. Our fathers, where are they? Sleeping in the dust, as we must shortly be. We are sure that in a little while, a very little while, these places must know us no more; and, when we are moldering in the house of silence, who must fill our places in the house of God? Who must rise up in our stead for the support of religion among those that succeed us? From whom can it be expected but from our children? Yet how can we expect it from these in the neglect of a method which comes recommended by so many advantageous circumstances? "Yes," you will perhaps be ready to say, "God will take care of His own cause, and almighty grace will do what we have not attempted, because we knew that we could not accomplish it." Almighty grace can indeed do it; and almighty power can, of these stones on which we tread, raise up children to Abraham. But show me your warrant from the Word of God for expecting it, either in one case or in the other. You will possibly answer, "He has promised to be ever with His church, and that the gates of hell shall not prevail against it; but that one generation shall arise and declare His mighty works unto another, and that the kingdom of His Son shall continue as long as the sun and the moon endure." Blessed be His name for these encouraging promises which shall, no doubt, be accomplished. But where has He engaged that this kingdom shall always continue among us? Such passages as these will no more prove that the gospel shall never be removed from Great Britain than they would one have proved that it should never be taken away from Pergamos or Thyartira, or any other of the Asian churches which have, so many ages ago, been given up to desolation.

Now let me entreat you for a few moments to dwell upon that thought. What if the gospel should be lost from among your descendants? What if in the age of the these little ones, or the next that shall succeed to theirs, the house of the Lord should be forsaken and His table abandoned? What if the ministry should be grown into disuse, or the servants of Christ in it should have nothing to do but to bear a fruitless testimony against an unbelieving generation till, when their hearts are broken with so sad an office, the gospel here dies with them and religion is buried in their graves? Is it a thought easily to be supported by a true Israelite that the ark of the Lord should thus be lost, and God should write upon us "Ichabod," the sad memorials of a departed glory?

It would surely be peculiarly melancholy that religion should die in the hands of those who were the children of the kingdom. And were not yours so? In this respect, my friends, permit me to say that

I am witness against some of you. When you have offered your children to baptism, you have delivered them into my hands with an express declaration of your desire, that they might be devoted to God; and have received them again with a solemn charge and promise to bring them up for Him, if their lives should be continued. And as for those of you who do not practice this institution, I doubt not but many of you are equally faithful in dedicating your infant offspring to God. Is it not then reasonable to expect from both that they should be brought up as a seed to serve Him? And from whom may we hope it, if not from you? If you have experienced the power of divine grace upon your own souls, and have tasted that the Lord is gracious, I think it should awaken a holy zeal to spread the sweet savor of His name and Word wherever you come. You should labor to the utmost for the advancement of His gospel among all your acquaintances, and even among strangers; how much more in your own families, among those whom you have received from Him, among those whom you have so solemnly given back to Him.

Second, the character of your children and, consequently, your care in their education is of the most evident importance to their present and future happiness.

I need not surely employ a great deal of time in proving the truth of the assertion. As Christians, you must undoubtedly admit that godliness is profitable to all things, having the promise of the life which now is, as well as of that which is to come. If your children, through the divine blessing on your holy care, become truly religious, they will not only be

preserved from those follies and crimes which stain
the honor and ruin the substance of families, but
they will secure a fair reputation; they will take the
most probable method to make life truly comfortable; they will be entitled to the paternal care and
blessings of God; and, to crown all, will be heirs of
eternal glory with Him. And what could your most
prudent, faithful, tender love wish for them as a
greater, or indeed as a comparable, good? On the
other hand, if they prove vicious and profane
(which, in so dangerous an age, it is very probable
they may, if they have no religious principle to secure them), what can you expect but their infamy
and misery in this world, and their eternal destruction in the next?

One would imagine that such considerations as
these should very deeply impress the heart of a parent; and, if they were alone, should be sufficient to
gain the cause. You who have so tender a regard to
all their temporal concerns; you that rise early and
sit up late that you may advance their fortunes, that
you may furnish them with those dubious and un-
certain possessions which may be blessings or
curses, as they are improved or abused; can you bear
to think that they may be forever poor and miserable? Surely, it should cut you to the heart to look on
a child and reflect, "Here is an heir of eternal misery. Alas! what am I doing for him? Preparing an estate? Contriving for his present convenience or
grandeur!" Vain, wretched preposterous care which,
to use a very plain simile, is like employing yourselves in trimming and adorning its clothes while
the child itself were fallen into the fire, and would

be in danger of being destroyed, if not immediately plucked out. Hasten to do it with an earnestness answerable to the extremity of the case, and so much the rather as the danger is, in part, owing to you.

I will not now say how far your personal mistakes in conduct may have been a snare and a temptation to your children; nor can I pretend to determine it. But I am confident of this, that they have derived from you a corrupt and degenerate nature. Through your veins, the original infection which tainted the first authors of our race has flowed down to them. And is not this an affecting thought? And ought it not to quicken you to attempt their relief?

Dr. Tillotson sets this in a very moving light: "When a man has, by treason, tainted his blood and forfeited his estate, with what grief and regret does he look on his children, and think of the injury he has done to them by his fault; and how solicitous is he before he tries to petition the king for favor to his children! How earnestly does he charge his friends to be careful of them, and kind to them!" We are those traitors. Our children have derived from us a tainted blood, a forfeited inheritance. How tenderly should we pity them! How solicitously should we expect ourselves to prevent their ruin! Mr. Flavel expresses the thought still more pathetically: "Should I bring the plague into my family, and live to see all my poor children lie dying by the walls of my house; if I had not the heart of a tiger, such a sight would melt my very soul." And surely, I may add, were there a sovereign antidote at hand, perhaps an antidote I had myself used, should I not direct them to it and urge them to try it, I should be still more savage and criminal. The application is easy: may the Lord deeply impress it on your souls that your dear children may not die eternally of the malignant plague they have taken from you!

This is one consideration which should certainly add a great deal of weight to the argument I am upon. I will conclude the head with the mention of another; I mean, the peculiar advantages which you, their parents have for addressing yourselves to them. You who have known them from their infancy are best acquainted with their temper and manner of thinking; you who are daily with them may watch their most tender moments, the most favorable opportunities of pleading with them; your melting affection for them will suggest the most endearing sentiments and words on such occasions. Their obligations to you, and love for you, will probably dispose them to attend with the greatest pleasure to what you say; or your authority over them, your power of correction, and a sense of their dependence upon you in life, may prevent much of that opposition and contempt which, from perverse tempers, others might expect; especially if they were not supported by your concurrence in their attempts to instruct and reform your children.

On the whole, then, since your obligations and your encouragements to attempt the work are so peculiar, I may reasonably hope you will allow its due weight to this second consideration, that the character and conduct of your children and, consequently, your care in their education, is of the highest importance to their present and future happiness. I add, once more:

Third, it is of great moment to your own comfort, both in life and death.

Solomon often repeats the substance of that remark; "A wise son make a glad father, but a foolish son is the heaviness to his mother." And the justice of it in both its branches is very apparent. Let me engage you seriously to reflect upon it as a most awakening inducement to the discharge of the important duty I am recommending.

If you have reason to hope that your labors are not in vain, but that your children have become truly religious, it must greatly increase your satisfaction in them that they are dear to you, not only in the bands of the flesh, but in those of the Lord. You will not only be secure of their dutiful and grateful behavior to you, but will have the pleasure of seeing them grow up, in their different stations, to prospects of usefulness in the church and in the world. Should Providence spare you to the advance of age, they will be a comfort and honor to your declining years. You will, as it were, enjoy a second youth in their vigor and usefulness; nay, a sense of their piety and goodness will undoubtedly be a reviving cordial to you in your dying moments. A delightful thought will it indeed be! "I am going to take my leave of the world, and my scene of service is over; but I leave those behind me, who will appear for God in my stead, and act, perhaps, with greater fidelity and zeal, for the support of religion in a degenerate age. I leave my poor children destitute indeed of my counsel and help, perhaps in no abundant affluence of worldly enjoyments; but I leave them under the guardian care of my Father and their Father, of my God and their God. I must soon be separated from them, and the distance between us must soon be as great as between earth and heaven; but, as I leave them under the best guidance in the wilderness, so I have a joyful persuasion they will soon follow me into the celestial Canaan. In a little while, I and my dear offspring shall appear before the throne of God; and I shall stand forth with transport and say, 'Behold, here am I, and the children which my God has graciously given me.' Then will the blessedness on which I now enter be multiplied upon me by the sight of every child that has a share in it. Now, Lord, sufferest Thou Thy servant to depart in peace, since Thou hast directed not only mine eyes, but theirs, to Thy salvation."

But, if you see these dear little ones grow up for the destroyer, if you see those whose infant days gave you so many tender pleasures and so many fond hopes deviating from the paths of duty and happiness, how deeply will it pierce you! You now look upon them with a soft complacency and say, "These are they that shall comfort us under our labors and sorrows." But alas! my friends, if this is the case, "These are they that will increase your labors and aggravate your sorrows; that will hasten upon you the infirmities of age or crush you the faster under the weight of them, till they have brought down your hoary hairs with anguish to the grave." Little do they or you think how much agony and distress you may endure from what you will see and what you will fear concerning them. How many slighted admonitions, how many deluded hopes, how many anxious days, how many restless nights, will concur to make the evening of life gloomy! And, at length, when God gives you a dismissal from a world, which the folly and wickedness of your children has so long embittered, how painful will the separation be; when you have a prospect of seeing them but once more, and that at the tribunal of God, where the best you can expect, in their present circumstances, is to rise up in judgment against them, and to bear an awful testimony, which shall draw down upon them aggravated damnation!

And let me plainly tell you that if, in these last moments, conscience should also accuse you of the neglect of duty, and testify that your own sorrow and your children's ruin is in part chargeable upon that, it will be a dreadful ingredient in this bitter cup, and will greatly darken, if not entirely suppress, those hopes with regard to yourselves which alone could support you in the mournful scene. I am fully persuaded that, if you knew the weight with which these things will sit upon your mind in the immediate views of the eternal world, you would not suffer every trifling difficulty, or little care, to deter you from the discharge of those duties which are so necessary to prevent these galling reflections.

To conclude, let me entreat you seriously to weigh the united force of these arguments which I have now been urging, to excite your diligence in this momentous care of training up your children in the way in which they should go. Consider how pleasant the attempt is. Consider how fair a probability there is that it may prosper, as it is in itself a very rational method, as it is a method God has appointed, and a method which He has crowned with singular success. Consider how important that success is to the honor of God and interest of religion, to the temporal and eternal happiness of your children and, finally, to your own comfort both in life and death.

On the whole, I well know, and I am persuaded, sirs, that you yourselves are convinced that whatever can be opposed to such considerations as these, when laid in an impartial balance, is altogether lighter than vanity. I, therefore, seriously appeal to those convictions of your consciences as in the sight of God; and if, from this time at least, the education of children among you is neglected, or regarded only as a light care, God is witness, and you yourselves are witnesses, that it is not for lack of being plainly instructed in your duty, or seriously urged to the performance of it.

11

Sermon 3

"Train up a child in the way he should go, and when he is old, he will not depart from it." Proverbs 22:6

Those of you who have made any observations on human life must certainly know that, if we desire to be agreeable and useful in it, we must regard not only the quality, but the manner, of our actions; and that, while we are in the pursuit of any important end, we must not only attend to those actions which immediately refer to it, but must watch over the whole of our conduct that we may preserve a consistency in the several parts of it. Otherwise, we shall spoil the beauty and acceptance of many an honest and, perhaps, in the main, prudent attempt; or, by a train of unthought-of consequences, shall demolish with the one hand what we are laboring to build up with the other.

This is a remark which we shall have frequent occasion to recollect; and it is of peculiar importance in the business of education. It is, therefore, necessary that, having before described the way in which children are to be trained up, and urged you to a diligent application to the duty, I now proceed:

III. To offer some advice for your assistance in this attempt of leading children into, and conducting

them in, this way.

These will relate partly to the manner in which the attempt is to be made, and partly to the precautions necessary for rendering it effectual: which are, as you see, matters of distinct consideration, though comprehended under the general head of directions.

THE MANNER IN WHICH THE ATTEMPT IS TO BE MADE.

And here it is evident it should be done plainly, seriously, tenderly, and patiently.

1. *Children are to be instructed plainly: in the plainest things and by the plainest words.*

They are to be taught the plainest things in religion in the first place. And it is a pleasing reflection on this occasion that, according to the abundant goodness and condescension of the great God, those things which are the most necessary are the plainest. Just as in the world of nature, those kinds of food which are the most wholesome and nourishing are also the most common. We should show our grateful sense of the divine goodness in this particular by our care to imitate it; and should see to it that, when the necessities of our children require bread, we do not give them a stone or chaff, as we should do if we were to distract their feeble minds with a variety of human schemes and doubtful disputations. The more abstruse and mysterious truths of the gospel are gradually to be unfolded as they are exhibited in the oracles of God, and to be taught in the language of the Spirit; according to the excellent advice of the great Dr. Owen, "making Scripture phraseology our rule and pattern in the declaration of spiritual things." But we must not begin here. We must feed them with milk while they are babes and reserve the strong meat for a maturer age. Take the most obvious and vital truths of Christianity. Tell them that they are creatures, and sinful creatures; that, by sin, they have displeased a holy God, and that they must be pardoned, sanctified, and accepted in Christ, or must perish forever. Show them the difference between sin and holiness, between a state of nature and of grace. Show them that they are hastening on to death and judgment, and so must enter on heaven or hell, and dwell forever in the one or other. Such kind of lessons will probably turn to the best account both to them and you. I know it is a very easy thing to enflame the warm, ignorant minds of children with an eager zeal for distinguishing forms or distinguishing phrases, and to make them violent in the interest of a party, before they know anything of common Christianity. But, if we thus sow the wind, we shall probably reap the whirlwind; venting ourselves and transforming into them a wrath of man which never works, but often greatly obstructs, the righteousness of God. Blessed be God, this is not the fault of you, my friends of this congregation. I would mention it with great thankfulness, as both your happiness and mind, that, as far as I can judge, it is the sincere milk of the Word that you desire. Let it be your care to draw it out for the nourishment of your children's souls, as their understandings and capacities will permit them to take it in.

And while you are teaching them the plainest things, endeavor to do it in the plainest words. It is the gracious method which God uses with us, who speaks to us of heavenly things in language, not fully expressive of the sublimity and grandeur of the subject, but rather suited to our feeble apprehensions. Thus our Lord taught His disciples, as they were able to bear it; and used easy and familiar similitudes, taken from the most obvious occurrences in life, to illustrate matters of the highest importance. A most instructive example! Such condescension should we use in training up those committed to our care, and should examine whether we take their understandings along with us as we go on; otherwise we are speaking in an unknown tongue and, as the Apostle expresses it, are barbarians unto them, be our language ever so graceful, elegant, or pathetic.

Give me leave to add for the conclusion of this head that, though it is to be taken for granted that children in their earliest infancy are to be engaged to what is good and to be restrained from evil, chiefly, by a view to rewards and punishments, more immediate or remote, or by some natural workings of a benevolent affection, which are by all means to be cherished and cultivated; yet, as they might grow up to greater ripeness of understanding, something further is to be attempted. It must then be our care to set before them, in the strongest light, the beauties of holiness and deformities of sin; and, likewise, to propose, in the easiest and most familiar way, the evidences of the truth of Christianity that they may be fortified against those temptations to infidelity with which the present age so unhappily abounds. The external evidences of it are by no means to be slighted, such as the credibility of the gospel history, the accomplishment of prophecies, the unity of design carried on by so many different persons in distant ages and countries, its amazing and even miraculous propagation in the world; all which, with many other considerations to the same purpose, are very judiciously handled in a variety of excellent writings of our own age, of which I know not any more suited to your use than Mr. Bennet's *Discourses on the Inspiration of Scripture,* which I therefore recommend to your attentive perusal; and, with them, Dr. Watts's Sermons on *The Inward Witness to the Truth of Christianity,* from its efficacious tendency to promote holiness. This appears to me the noblest evidence of all, and will, to those who have actually experienced it, be an anchor of the soul both sure and steadfast.

2. *Children should be instructed in a very serious manner.*
There is an unhappy proneness in our degenerate nature to trifle with the things of God, and the giddiness of children is peculiarly subject to it. Great care should therefore be taken that we do not encourage such a humor, nor teach them by our levity or indolence in the manner of instruction, to take the awful name of God in vain while they are speaking of Him or to Him. For this purpose, we must labor with our own hearts to work them to a deep and serious sense of the truth and importance of what we say. This will give us an unaffected

solemnity in speaking which will probably command the attention and impress the hearts of our children. Endeavor to preserve on your own spirit a habitual awe of the great and blessed God, the Lord of heaven and earth, so that, when you speak of Him to those little creatures, they may evidently see the indications of the most humble veneration and reverence, and so may learn to fear Him from their youth. When you speak of Christ, let your souls be bowing to Him as the Son of God, through whom alone you and yours can obtain pardon and life; and let them be overflowing with love to Him for His unutterable and inconceivable grace. And, when you remind them of death, judgment, and eternity, consider yourselves and them as dying creatures; think in how few months, weeks, or days, your lips may be silent in the dust, or they may be forever removed beyond the reach of your instructions; and plead with them in as earnest and importunate a manner, as if the salvation of their immortal souls depended on the effect of the present address. Again:

3. *Children should be instructed in a very tender and affectionate manner.*

We should take care to let them see that we do not desire to terrify and amaze them, to lead them into unnecessary severities, or to deprive them of any innocent pleasures; that what we say is not dictated by an ostentation of our own wisdom and authority; but that it all proceeds from a hearty love to them and an earnest desire of their happiness. Study, therefore, to address them in the most endearing language, as well as with the softest and sweetest arguments. Endeavor, according to the practice of Solomon, to find out acceptable words. And if tears should rise while you are speaking, do not suppress them. There is a language in them which may, perhaps, affect beyond words. A weeping parent is both an awful and a melting sight.

Endeavor, therefore, to look upon your children in such a view as may be most likely to awaken these tender sentiments. Consider them as creatures whom you, as instruments, have brought into being, tainted with innate corruption, surrounded with snares, and, on the whole, in such apparent danger that, if not snatched as brands out of the burning, they must perish forever. And that your hearts may be further mollified, and you may be formed to the most gentle and moving manner of address, let me entreat you to study the Scripture in this view, and to observe the condescending and endearing forms in which the blessed God speaks to us there. Observe them for yourselves and point them out to your children. Tell them how kindly He has demanded, how graciously He has encouraged their services; while He says, "Remember now Thy Creator in the days of thy youth;" and elsewhere, "I love them that love Me, and those that seek Me early shall find Me." Tell them that the Lord Jesus Christ has invited them to come to Him; for He has said, "Come unto Me all ye that labor, and are heavy laden, and I will give you rest; Him that comes unto Me, I will in no wise cast out:" And "whosoever will, let him take of the water of life freely." Such Scriptures as these should be often repeated to them, and should be early inculcated on their memory, with an attempt,

as far as possible, to let them into the spirit and
force of them.

Nor will it be improper, sometimes, to set before
them how much you have done or how much you
are ready to do for them; how many anxious
thoughts you entertain, how many fervent prayers
you offer, on their account. Thus Lemmuel's mother
addressed him, "What, my son? and what, the son of
my womb? and what, the son of my vows?" As if she
had said, "My dear child, for whom I have borne so
much, for whom I have prayed so earnestly; in what
words shall I address you, to express what my heart
feels on your account? How shall I speak my affectionate overflowing concern for your happiness
both in time and eternity?" So Solomon pleads, "My
son, if thine heart be wise, my heart shall rejoice,
even mine;" as if he should have said, "Think how
much is comprehended in that argument, that a
parent's happiness is, in a great measure, to be determined by the character and conduct of their
children." And the Apostle Paul lays open his heart
to the Galatians in those pathetic words, "My little
children, of whom I travail in birth again, till Christ
be formed in you." Yet these were, comparatively,
strangers to him. And should not you, my friends,
feel, should not you express, an equal tenderness for
those who are so nearly allied to you in the bonds of
nature, for those who are indeed parts of yourselves?
But further:

4. *Children should also be instructed patiently.*

You know, when the husbandman has committed the seed to the ground, he patiently expects the

fruit of his labors. So must ministers do when instructing their people. So much parents do when instructing their children. You must not imagine, my friends, that a plentiful harvest will spring up in a day. The growth of nature is slow, and by insensible degrees; nor are you to wonder if advances in knowledge and grace are still slower. Be upon your guard, therefore, against fretfulness and impatience. Your children will forget what you have once taught them; repeat it a second time and, if they forget it the second time, repeat it the third. It is thus that the great God deals with you; and you have daily reason to rejoice that He does. He knows the frailty and weakness of your minds and, therefore, acts by a rule which seems to be laid down with peculiar regard to the very point I am urging. Whom shall He teach knowledge, and whom shall He make to understand doctrine? Them that are weaned from the milk and drawn from the breasts. For precept must be upon precept, precept upon precept; and line upon line, line upon line; here a little, and there a little. As if the prophet should have said, "God has treated you like little children, who must have the same short easy lesson repeated again and again." And is it not indeed thus with regard to you? Does not the patience and condescension of your heavenly Father send to you His ministers sabbath after sabbath, frequently inculcating the same things that what you have forgot may be brought to mind again? Thus should you do by those committed to your care.

Be teaching them every sabbath; that is remarkably a good day for the purpose. Then you have leisure for it; then you have peculiar advantage to pursue the work; then you are furnished with some new matter by what you have heard in public; and, I would hope, your spirits are then quickened by it so that you can speak out of the abundance of the heart: and you may, by discoursing with them on what has been addressed to you, revive the impression on your own souls.

I add, be teaching them every day by occasional discourses when you do not have an opportunity of doing it by stated addresses. Drop a word for God every day, and often in a day. You will probably find your account in it and your children theirs. A sudden glance or thought towards God in the midst of the world is often a great refreshment to the Christian; and a sudden turn to something serious and spiritual in conversation is frequently very edifying to others. It strikes the memory and the heart, and is, perhaps, as a nail fixed in a sure place when many a solemn admonition, and many an elaborate sermon, is lost. It is with pleasure that I frequently hear good Christians speaking of such occasional hints which have been dropped by saints of the former generation. Those transient passages which the pious parents might forget in a few moments, their children have distinctly remembered for many future years, and repeated for their own edification, and, I might add, for mine. Let this, therefore, be an encouragement to you; and, in this respect, in the morning sow this precious seed, and in the evening withhold not your hand, since you do not know whether it shall prosper, or whether both shall be equally good.

Once more, let me entreat you to repeat your pious instructions and admonitions, even though your children should grow up to years of maturity without appearing to profit by them. Say not that you can teach them no more than they already know; or that you can try no new methods which you have not already attempted. You see that, in our assemblies, God often brings back souls to Himself by setting home on the conscience truths which, with regard to the speculative part of them, they know as well as their teachers; and adds a divine efficacy to those institutions which, for a long succession of years, they had attended in vain. "Be not therefore weary in well doing;" but let patience in this instance have its perfect work.

Thus, let your children be instructed plainly, seriously, tenderly, and patiently. I waive some other particulars which I might have added to these, concerning the manner of instructing them, because I apprehend they will more properly fall under the second branch of these directions, when I am further to advise you:

PRECAUTIONS NECESSARY FOR SUCCESS

As to the precautions you must use, if you desire that these attempts in the religious education of your children may be attended with success.

Here I would particularly advise that a prudent care be taken to keep up your authority over them and, at the same time, to engage their affections to you; that you be solicitous to keep them out of the way of temptation; that you confirm your admonitions by a suitable example; that you cheerfully accept proper assistance in this important attempt; and that you humbly and constantly look up to God for His blessing on all.

1. *If we desire to succeed in our attempts for the religious education of our children, we must take care to keep up our authority over them.*

To this purpose, we must avoid not only what is grossly vicious and criminal (which will be more properly mentioned under a following head), but also those little levities and follies which might make us appear contemptible to them. Whatever liberties we may take with those who are our equals in age and station, a more exact decorum is to be preserved before our children. Thus we are to reverence them, if we desire they should reverence us; for, as Dr. Tillotson very justly observed, "There is a certain freedom of conversation which is only proper among equals in age and quality, which, if we use before our superiors, we seem to despise them, and, if we do it before our inferiors, we teach them to despise us."

I will not insist on this hint, which your own prudence must accommodate to particular circumstances, but shall here introduce the mention of correction which, in some cases, may be absolutely necessary to the support of parental authority, especially where admonitions and counsels are slighted.

You know that the Scriptures expressly require it on proper occasions; and Solomon, in particular, enlarges on the head and suggests some important thoughts with regard to it. "Foolishness," says he, "is bound up in the heart of a child, but the rod of correction shall drive it far from him." Nay, he speaks of it as a matter in which life is concerned, even the life of the soul: "Withhold not correction from a child; for if thou beat him with the rod he shall not die: Thou shalt beat him with the rod, and shalt deliver his soul from hell." And is it kindness or cruelty in a parent to spare the flesh to the hazard of the soul? Parents are, therefore, exhorted to an early care in this respect, lest vicious habits growing inveterate should render the attempt vain or hurtful; and they are cautioned against that foolish tenderness which would lead them to regard the tears of a child rather than his truest and highest interest. "Correct thy son while there is hope, and let not thy soul spare for his crying: He that spareth the rod, hateth his son; but he that loveth him, chasteneth him betimes."

Nor can we imagine a more lively commentary on the words than the melancholy story of Eli who, though he was a very eminent saint in a degenerate age, yet erred here and, by a fatal indulgence, brought ruin as well as infamy on himself and his family. He reproved the abominable wickedness of his sons, but did not make use of those severe methods which, in such a case, the authority of a parent might have warranted and the office of a judge undoubtedly required.

Observe the sentence which God pronounced against him for it, and which he executed upon him in a very awful manner. The Lord said unto Samuel, "Behold I will do a thing in Israel, at which both the ears of every one that heareth it shall tingle. In that day I will perform against Eli all the things which I

have spoken concerning his house; when I begin, I
will also make an end. For I have told him, that I will
judge his house forever, for the iniquity which he
knoweth; because his sons made themselves vile,
and he restrained them not. And therefore I have
sworn unto the house of Eli, that the iniquity of Eli's
house shall not be purged with sacrifice nor offering forever." Take heed, I entreat you, as you love
your children, as you love yourselves, that it may not
be said of you that yours have made themselves vile,
and you have neglected to restrain them. Let mothers, in particular, take heed that they do not, as it
were, "smother their children in their embraces," as
a French author smartly expresses it. And let me remind you all to be particularly cautious that the
arms of one parent are not a refuge to the children
from the resentment of the other. Both should appear to act in concert or the authority of the one will
be despised and, probably, the indulgence of the
other abused, and the mutual affection of both en-
dangered.

I cannot say that I enlarge on this subject with
pleasure, but how could I have answered for the
omission of what is so copiously and so pathetically
inculcated in the sacred writings? It is indeed probable that the rugged and servile temper of the generality of the Jewish nation might render a severe
discipline peculiarly necessary for their children; yet
I fear there are few of our families where every thing
of this kind can safely be neglected. But, after all, I
would by no means drive matters to extremities and,
therefore, cannot persuade myself to dismiss the
head without a caution or two. Take heed that your

corrections are not too frequent or too severe and that they are not given in an unbecoming manner.

If your corrections are too frequent, it will probably spoil much of the success. Your children, like iron, will harden under repeated strokes, and that ingenuous shame will be gradually worn off which adds the greatest sting to what they suffer from a parent's hand. And there will be this further inconvenience attending it, that there will not be a due difference made between great and small faults. The laws of Draco the Athenian were justly rejected because they punished all crimes alike, and made the stealing of an apple capital as well as the murder of a citizen. You, on the contrary, should let your children see that you know how to distinguish between indiscretion and wickedness, and should yourselves appear most displeased when you think God is so.

Nor should your corrections at any time be too severe. It is very prettily said by Dr. Tillotson on this occasion that "whips are not the cords of a man." They should be used in a family only as the sword in the republic, as the last remedy, when all others have been tried in vain; and then should be so used that we may appear to imitate the compassion of our heavenly Father, who does not afflict willingly, nor grieve the children of men.

Which leads me to add that we should be greatly cautious that correction is not inflicted in an unbecoming manner, and it always is so when it is given in a passion. A parent's correcting his child should be regarded as an act of domestic justice which, therefore, should be administered with a due solemnity and decorum; and to behave otherwise on the occasion is almost as great an indecency as for a judge to pass sentence in a rage. It is injurious to ourselves, as it tends to spoil our own temper; for peevishness and passion will grow upon us, being indulged towards those who dare not oppose them. And it is, on many accounts, injurious to our children. Solomon intimates that correction and instruction should be joined when he says, "The rod and reproof give wisdom." But what room is there for the still voice of wisdom to be heard in a storm of fury? If your children see that you act calmly and mildly; if they read parental tenderness in your heart, through an awful frown on your brows; if they perceive that correction is your strange work, a violence which you offer to yourselves from a principle of duty to God and affection to them; they must be stubborn indeed if they do not receive it with reverence and love, for this is both a venerable and an amiable character. But, if once they imagine that you chastise them merely to vent your passion and gratify your resentments, they will secretly despise and, perhaps, hate you for it. In that instance, at least, they will look upon you as their enemies, and may, by a continued course of such severities, contract an aversion not only to you, but to all that you recommend to them. Thus, you may lose your authority and your influence by the very method you take to support it, and may turn a wholesome, though bitter, medicine into poison. But I hope and trust that your humanity and your prudence will concur to prevent so fatal an abuse.

2. *If you desire success in your attempts for the education*

of your children, you must be careful to secure their affection to you.

Our Lord observes that, if any man loves Him, he will keep His Word, and the assertion is applicable to the present case. The more your children love you, the more will they regard your instructions and admonitions. God has indeed made it their duty to love you, and the most indispensable laws of gratitude require it; yet, since so many children are evidently lacking in filial affection, it is certain that all this may not secure it in you, unless you add a tender, obliging behavior to all the other benefits you have conferred upon them. I observed under a former head that you should address them in a affectionate manner when discoursing on religious subjects; but now I add that you should carry the temper through life, and be daily endeavoring to render yourselves amiable to them. The Apostle cautions parents that they should not provoke their children to wrath, if they would bring them up in the nurture and admonition of the Lord. On the contrary, you should put on the kindest looks; you should use the most endearing and condescending language; you should overlook many little failings, and express a high complacency in what is really regular and laudable in their behavior. And, though you must sometimes overrule their desires when impatiently eager, yet, far from delighting generally to cross them, you should rather study their inclinations that you may surprise them with unexpected favors. Thus will they learn quietly to refer themselves to your care, and will more easily submit to mortification and denial when it is not made necessary by clamorous and impetuous demands. On the whole, you should endeavor to behave so that your children may love your company and, of choice, be much in it, which will preserve them from innumerable snares, and may furnish you with many opportunities of forming their temper and behavior by imperceptible degrees to what may be decent, amiable, and excellent.

If you manage these things with prudence, you need not fear that such condescensions as I have now recommended will impair your authority; far from that, they will rather establish it. The superiority of your parental character may be maintained in the midst of these indulgences and, when it is thus tempered, it is most likely to produce that mixture of reverence and love by which the obedience of a child is to be distinguished from that of a slave.

3. You must be solicitous to keep your children out of the way of temptation, if you would see the success of your care in their education.

If you are not on your guard here, you will probably throw down what you have built, and build up that which you have been endeavoring to destroy. An early care must be taken to keep them from the occasions, and the very appearances of evil. We should not venture their infant steps on the brink of a precipice on which grown persons, who know how to adjust the poise of their bodies, may walk without extreme danger. More hazardous might it be, to allow them to trifle with temptations and boldly venture to the utmost limits of that which is lawful. An early tenderness of conscience may be a great preservative; and the excess of strictness, though no excess is desirable, may prove much safer than an excess of liberty.

Bad company is, undoubtedly, one of the most formidable and pernicious entanglements. By forming friendships with persons of vicious character, many a hopeful youth has learned their ways and found a fatal snare to his soul. You should be very watchful to prevent their contracting such dangerous friendships; and, where you discover anything of that kind, should endeavor, by all gentle and endearing methods, to draw them off from them; but, if they still persist, you must resolve to cut the knot you cannot untie, and let your children know that they must either renounce their associates or their parents. One resolute step of this kind might have prevented the ruin of multitudes who have fallen a sacrifice to the importunities of wicked companions, and the weak indulgence of imprudent parents who have contented themselves with blaming what they ought strenuously to have redressed.

All bad company is, in this respect, formidable; but that is most evidently so which is to be found at home. Great care ought, therefore, to be taken that you admit none into your families who may debauch the tender minds of your children by pernicious opinions or by vicious practices. This is a caution which should be particularly remembered in the case of servants. Take heed you do not bring into your families such as may diffuse infection through the souls of your dear offspring. It is a thousands times better to put up with some inconveniences and disadvantages, when you have reason to believe

a servant fears God, and will, from a principle of
conscience, be faithful in watching over your children, and in seconding your religious care in their
education, than to prefer such as while they are,
perhaps, managing your temporal affairs something
better, may pervert your children to the service of
the devil. I fear some parents little think how much
secret mischief these base creatures are doing. And
it is very possible that if some of you recollect what
you may have observed among the companions of
your childhood, you may find instances of this nature which riper years have not since given you opportunity to discover. See to it, therefore, that you
are diligently on your guard here.

Again, if you send your children to places of education, be greatly cautious in your choice of them.
Dearly will you purchase the greatest advantages for
learning at the expense of those of a religious nature. And I will turn out of my way to add that
schoolmasters and tutors will have a dreadful account to give if they are not faithfully and tenderly
solicitous for the souls of those committed to their
care. The Lord pardon our many defects here, and
quicken us to greater diligence and zeal! But to return:

Give me leave only to add that it is of the highest
importance, if you would not have all your labor in
the education of your children lost, that you should
be greatly cautious with regard to their settlement in
the world. Apprenticeships and marriages into irreligious families have been the known sources of innumerable evils. They who have exposed the souls of
their children to apparent danger for the sake of

some secular advantages have often lived to see them drawn aside to practices ruinous to their temporal, as well as their eternal interests. Thus, their own iniquity has remarkably corrected them; and I heartily pray that the god of this world may never be permitted thus to blind your eyes, but that you, my friends, may learn from the calamities of other families that wholesome lesson which, if you neglect it, others may, perhaps, hereafter learn from the ruin of yours.

4. *See to it that you confirm your admonitions by a suitable example, if you desire on the whole that they should prove useful to your children.*

A consciousness of the irregularity of your own behavior, in any remarkable instances which may fall under their observation, will probably abate much of that force and authority with which we might otherwise address them. When we know they may justly retort upon us, at least in their minds, those words of the Apostle, "Thou that teachest another, teachest thou not thyself?" Surely, a sense of guilt and of shame must either entirely silence us, or at least impair that freedom and confidence, with which we might otherwise have exhorted or rebuked.

Or had we so much composure and assurance as to put on all the forms of innocence and virtue, could we expect regard when our actions contradicted our discourses, or hope they should reverence instructions which their teachers themselves appear to despise? It is generally true that there is a silent but powerful oratory in example beyond the force of the most elegant and expressive words; and the example of parents has often a peculiar weight with their children, which seems to be alluded to in that exhortation of St. Paul, "Be ye followers (or imitators) of God, as dear children." So that, on the whole, as a very celebrated writer well expresses it, "To give children good instruction and a bad example is but beckoning to them with the head to show them the way to heaven, while we take them by the hand and lead them in the way to hell." We should, therefore, most heartily concur in David's resolution, as ever we hope our families should be religious and happy, "I will behave myself wisely in a perfect way; I will walk within my house with a perfect heart."

5. *Cheerfully accept all proper assistance in the education of your children, if you desire that it may succeed well.*

It will be your wisdom to accept of the assistance which may be offered either from books or friends.

Books may, in this respect, be very useful to you; the Book of God, above all, both to furnish you with materials for this great work and to instruct you in the manner of performing it. Other writings may be subservient to this purpose. Wise and pious treatises on the subject of education may be read with great pleasure and advantage; and you may receive singular assistance from those catechisms, prayers, and songs for children, with which most of your families are now furnished through the condescension of one valuable friend in writing them, and the generosity of another in bestowing them upon us. I hope you will express your thankfulness to both by a diligent care to use them; and I persuade myself that you and yours may abundantly find your account in them; for, while the language is so plain and easy that even an infant may understand it, you will often find not only a propriety, but a strength and sublimity, in the sentiments which may be improving to persons of advanced capacities. There is much of that milk by which strong men may be entertained and nourished.

I add that, in this important work, you should gladly embrace the assistance of pious and prudent friends. I can, by no means, approve that Lacedemonian law, which gave every citizen the power of correcting his neighbor's children, and made it infamous for the parent to complain of it: yet we must all allow that, considering the great importance of education, a concern for the happiness of families and the public will require a mutual watchfulness over each other in this respect; nor is there any imaginable reason to exclude this from the number of those heads on which we are to admonish one another, and to consider each other to provoke unto good works.

Nothing seems more evident than this, and one would suppose that persons who are acquainted with human nature should suspect that self-love might work under this form, and that they might be a little blinded by a partial affection to their offspring. Such a reflection might engage them at least patiently, or rather thankfully, to hear the sentiments and receive the admonitions of their friends of this head. But, instead of this, there is in many people a kind of parental pride (if I may be allowed the expression) which seldom fails to exert itself on such an occasion. They are so confident in their own way, and so magisterially despise the opinion of others, that one would almost imagine they took it for granted that, with every child, nature had given to the parent a certain stock of infallible wisdom for the management of it; or that, if they thought otherwise, they rather chose their children should be ruined by their own conduct than saved by any foreign advice. If this arrogance only rendered the parents ridiculous, one should not need to be greatly concerned about it; especially as their high complacency in themselves would make them easy, whatever others might think or say of them; but, when we consider the unhappy consequences it may produce with regard to the temper and conduct of the rising generation, it will appear a very serious evil, well worth a particular mention, and a particular care to guard against it.

As for the assistance of ministers in this work of education, I persuade myself you will be so wise as thankfully to embrace it, both in public and private; and let me urge you to improve it to the utmost. Accustom your children to an early constancy and seriousness in attending divine ordinances, and be often yourselves inquiring, and give us leave sometimes to inquire, how they advance in acquaintance with religion and in love to it. And, more particularly, let them attend on our catechetical lectures which are peculiarly intended for their service.

I bless God that I have seen the happy effects of this exercise, both in the places where I was educated while a child, and in those where I was for-

merly fixed; and as I am now introducing it among
you with an intent to continue it as long as I am capable of public service, I promise myself your most
hearty concurrence in it. I will not at large insist on
the advantages which may attend it. You easily see
that it will be an engagement to the children to
learn those excellent summaries of divine truth
when their progress in them is so often examined.
By repeating it themselves, and hearing it rehearsed
by others, it will be more deeply fixed upon their
memories. The exposition of it in a plain and familiar manner may much improve their understandings in the doctrines and duties of religion, and, I
will add, you that are parents may, by attending on
these occasions, possibly learn something as to the
way of opening and explaining things which you
may successfully practice at home. In consequence
of all, we may hope that, by the divine blessing,
some good impressions may be made on the minds
of children. And, when they find a minister willing
to take pains to instruct them, when they hear him
seriously and tenderly pleading with them, and
pleading with God for them, it may much engage
their affections to him, and so promote his usefulness among them in other ordinances, and in future years. And give me leave to say, upon this head,
that as no wise, good minister will think it beneath
him to desire the affection of the children of his
congregation, so it is the duty of parents to cherish
in their offspring sentiments of respect and love to
all the faithful ministers of Christ, and especially
towards those who stately labor among them.
Whatever mistakes you may discover in our conduct,

or whatever deficiencies in our public ministrations, you should study to conceal them from the notice of your children, lest they should grow up in a contempt of those whose services might, otherwise, be highly advantageous to them.

6. *Last, be earnest in prayer to God for His blessing on your attempts in the education of your children, if you desire to see them successful.*

This I would leave with you as my last advice; and, though I have had frequent occasion to hint at it before, I would now more particularly urge it on your attentive regard. God is the Author of every good and perfect gift; it is He who has formed the mind and tongue, and who teaches man knowledge and address. On Him, therefore, must you fix your dependence, to teach you so to conceive of divine things, and so to express your conceptions of them, as may be most suited to the capacities, the dispositions, and the circumstances of your children. And to Him you must look to teach them to profit by all, by His almighty grace to open their ear unto discipline, and to bow their heart unto understanding.

A heathen poet could teach the Romans, in a form of public and solemn devotion, to look up to heaven for influences from thence, to form their youth to the love and practice of virtue. Surely you, my friends, are under much greater obligations to do it, and that in a Christian manner; earnestly entreating the God of grace to send down on your rising offspring the effusions of that blessed Spirit which was purchased by the blood of Christ, and is deposited in His compassionate hand. If you have tasted that the Lord is gracious, you are daily living on those supplies; let it be your constant errand at the throne of grace to plead for your children there. Wrestle with God in secret for the life of their souls, and for those regenerating influences on which it depends; and in those family devotions which, I hope you dare not neglect, let the little ones, from their earliest infancy, have a share in your remembrance. You may humbly hope that He, by whose encouragement and command you pray, will not suffer these supplications to be like water spilt upon the ground. And, in the nature of things, it may tend to make serious impressions on the minds of your children to hear their own case mentioned in prayer; and may dispose them with greater regard to attend on what you say to them when they find you so frequently, so solemnly, and so tenderly, pleading with God for them.

Doubt not that every faithful minister of Christ will most heartily concur with you in so great and necessary a request. May God return to our united addresses an answer of peace! May He pour out His Spirit on our seed, and His blessing on our offspring, that they may grow up before Him as willows by the water-courses; that they may be to their parents for a comfort, to the church for a support, and to our God for a name and a praise! Amen.

12

Sermon 4

"Train up a child in the way he should go, and when he is old, he will not depart from it." Proverbs 22:6

In treating this subject of education, I have all along endeavored, according to my usual manner, to make my discourses as practical as I could. While I was describing and recommending the way, and offering my advices with regard to the manner of conducting children into it, most of what I said under those general headings was an application to you. I have, therefore, left myself the less to do here; yet I was not willing to conclude my discourses on a subject which it is probable I shall never so largely resume without:

IV. A particular address to my hearers according to your different relations and characters in life.

This I promised as my fourth and last general heading, and I enter on it without further preface, humbly begging that God, who has so intimate an access to all our hearts, would enable me to speak in the most awakening and edifying manner, and that He would, by His blessed Spirit, apply it to your consciences that it may be as a nail fastened in a sure place; that, hearing and knowing these things for yourselves, you may hear and know them for your good.

I would particularly address myself, first, to parents, then to children, and, in the last place, to those young persons who are grown up to years of maturity, but not yet fixed in families of their own.

1. *Let me address my discourse to those of you that are parents, whether you have been negligent of the duties I have now been urging or, through grace, have been careful in the discharge of them.*

To those who have been grossly negligent in this important care:

I have here one advantage not common to every subject; I mean, that the guilty will immediately know themselves. When we apply ourselves in general to unconverted sinners, ignorance of the nature of true religion, a neglect of conversing with your own souls, or the insinuating prejudices of self-love, may disguise the true state of the case and teach people to speak peace to themselves under the most awful denunciations of wrath and vengeance. But here, one would imagine that the recollection of a few moments might be sufficient to determine the case; because the question relates to past fact, and that not merely to one particular action, but to a long train and succession of labors and attempts.

Now, let your consciences witness whether I am guilty of a breach of charity when I take it for granted that there are some among you who have been, and are, very negligent of the duty I have now been enforcing. You have probably contented yourselves with teaching your children to read, and setting them to learn, like parrots, a prayer and, per-

haps, too a catechism and a creed. But I appeal to
your consciences, have you, from the very day of
their birth to this time, ever spent one hour in seriously instructing them in the knowledge of God,
and endeavoring to form them to His fear and service in setting before them the misery of their natural condition, and urging them to apply to Christ
for life and salvation; in representing the solemnities of death, judgment, and the eternal world, and
urging an immediate and diligent preparation for
them? Where is the time, where is the place, that
can witness that you have been pouring out your
souls before God on their account, and wrestling
with Him for their lives, knowing they must perish
forever without the righteousness of His Son and
the grace of His Spirit? Where or when have you
thus prayed with them or for them? What sermon
have you heard, what Scripture have you read, with
this thought, "This I will carry to my children and
communicate to them as the food of their souls."? I
fear there are several of you that have been so far
from doing it that you have hardly ever seriously
thought of it as a thing to be done.

And, I would ask, why have you not thought of it,
and why have you not done it? Are these creatures
that you have produced like the other animals of
your houses of your field, mere animated systems of
flesh and blood made to take a turn in life for a few
days and months, and then to sink into everlasting
forgetfulness? Or are they rational and immortal
creatures that must exist forever in heaven or in
hell? This is not a matter of doubt with you; and yet
you behave as if the very contrary to what you believe

were evident, certain truth. In short, it is the most barbarous part you act, and more like that of an enemy than a parent.

It is not that you are insensible of the workings of parental tenderness. No, far from that, it may sometimes rise to a weak and criminal dotage; yet I repeat it again, you are acting a hostile and barbarous part. You are greatly solicitous for their temporal happiness. For this you labor and watch; for this you deny yourselves many an enjoyment, and subject yourselves to many an uneasy circumstance; but, alas! Sirs, where is the real friendship of all this, while the precious soul is neglected? Your children are born with a corrupted nature, perverted by sinful examples, ignorant of God, in a state of growing enmity to Him, and, in consequence of all, exposed to His wrath and curse, and in the way to everlasting ruin. In the meantime, it is your great care that they may pass through this precarious, momentary life in ease and pleasure, perhaps in abundance and grandeur; that is, in such circumstances as will probably lull them into a forgetfulness of their danger, till there is no more hope. How cruel a kindness!

It brings to my mind the account which an ancient writer gives of the old Carthaginians, which I can never recollect without great emotion. He is speaking of that diabolical custom which so long prevailed among them of offering their children to a detestable idol, which was formed in such a manner that an infant put into his hands, which were stretched out to receive it, would immediately fall into a gulf of fire. He adds a circumstance, which one cannot mention without horror, that the mothers who, with their own hands, presented the little innocents thought it an unfortunate omen that the victim should be offered weeping; and, therefore, used a great many fond artifices to divert it that, soothed by the kisses and caresses of a parent, it might smile in the dreadful moment in which it was to be given up to the idol. Pardon me, my friends; such is your parental care and love, such your concern for the present case and prosperity of your children, while their souls are neglected: a fond solicitude, that they may pass smiling into the hands of the destroyer!

You know with what just severity God reckons with the Israelites for their abominable wickedness in taking his sons and his daughters, for so He calls the children of His professing people, and sacrificing them to be devoured; and can you suppose He will take no notice of the unnatural neglect of yours. Not to endeavor to save is to destroy; and is it a little guilt when an immortal soul is in question? You probably remember those terrible words in Ezekiel; (may they be deeply inscribed on the hearts of all whom they concern!) "Son of man, I have made thee a watchman to the house of Israel, therefore hear thou the word from My mouth, and give them warning from Me; and if thou speakest not to warn the wicked from his wicked way, to save his life, the same wicked man shall die in his iniquity, but his blood will I require at thine hand." If ever you read this passage with attention, you must own it is exceedingly awful, and must be ready to say, "The Lord be merciful to ministers; they have a solemn account to give." Indeed they have, and we thank you, if you ever bestow a compassionate thought and prayer upon us. But permit me to remind you that, though it is our case, it is not ours alone; you have, likewise, your share in it. Your children are much more immediately committed to your care than you and they are committed to ours; and, by all parity of reason, if they perish in their iniquities while you neglect to give them warning, their blood will be required at your hand.

And when God comes to make inquisition for that blood, how will you be able to endure it? That awful day will open upon you, and the tribunal of God, in all its terrors will stand unveiled before you. Give me leave to direct your eyes to it in this distant prospect while there is yet room to mitigate those terrors. If you go on in this cruel negligence of the souls of your children, how will you dare to meet them at the judgment seat? How will you be able to answer the great Father of spirits when expostulating with you on account of His offspring, as well as yours, who have been betrayed and ruined by your neglect? "Inhuman creatures," may He justly say, "to whom should I have committed the care of them rather than to you? Did they not, by My appointment, derive their being from you? Did I not implant in your hearts the natural affections of parents towards them? And, to increase the obligation, did they not pass through the tender scenes of infancy and childhood in your arms and under your eye? If you had no compassion for their perishing souls, if you would exert no efforts for their deliverance and salvation, from whom could those compassions, those efforts, have been expected? But wherein did they appear? Behold the book of My remembrance, the records of your life, thrown open before you. Where is the memorial of one hour spent in holy instruction, or in fervent prayer with them, or for them? Can I approve, can I acquit, you on such a review? Or shall I not rather visit for these things? And shall not My soul be avenged for such a conduct as this?"

And your children, will they be silent on the occasion? Did Adam, in the distress and amazement of his soul, when in the presence of his Judge, accuse Eve, his wife, so lately taken from his side and committed to his protection, and still, no doubt, appearing lovely in the midst of sorrow? And will your children in that terrible day spare you? You may rather expect they will labor to the utmost to aggravate a crime which costs them so dear, that so they may, if possible, alleviate their own guilt, or, if not, indulge their revenge. "O God," may they perhaps then cry out, in the most piercing accents of indignation and despair, "Thou art righteous in the sentence Thou passest upon us, and we justly die for our own iniquity. We have destroyed ourselves. But wilt Thou not remember that our ruin is in part chargeable here? Had these our parents been faithful to Thee and to us, it would, perhaps, have been prevented. Had our infancy been formed by religious instruction, we might not have grown up to wickedness; we might not, in the advance of life, have despised Thy word and trampled on Thy Son, but might this day have been owned by Thee as Thy children, and have risen to that inheritance of light and glory which we now behold at this unapproachable distance. Oh! Cursed be the fathers that begat us; cursed the womb that bare us; cursed the breasts that gave us suck! Remember us, O Lord, whilst Thou art judging them; and let us have this one wretched comfort, in the midst of all our agonies, that it is not with impunity that they have betrayed our souls!"

This is indeed shocking and diabolical language; and, for that very reason, it is so much the more probable on so dreadful an occasion. And give me leave to ask you one question, my friends, and I will conclude this head. If your children were thus crying out against you in the bitterness of their souls, could you attempt to silence them by reminding them of the care which you took of their temporal affairs, or of the riches and grandeur in which you left them on earth? Nay, could you have the heart so much as to mention such a trifle? And, if you could not then, in the name of God, sirs, how do you satisfy yourselves to confine all your thoughts and labors to that which, by your own confession, will neither secure your children from everlasting destruction nor give them one moment's relief in the review, when they are falling into it?

I will make no apology for the plainness and earnestness which I have used. Eternal interests are at stake, and the whole tenor of Scripture supports me in what I say. I would rather you should be alarmed with hearing these things from me now than tormented with hearing them in another manner from your children, and from God, at last. If you please to take proper measures for preventing the danger, I have told you the way at large; if you do not, I hope I may say, "I am, in this respect, clear from your blood, and the blood of yours, who may perish by your means. Look you to it."

But it is high time that I proceed in my address, and apply myself to those parents who have been careful to discharge the duty we have so copiously described and enforced.

I cannot suppose that any of us would pretend to maintain that in this, or any other branch of duty, we have acted up to the utmost extent and perfection of our rule. I hope a humble sense of the deficiencies of all the best of our services is frequently leading us to the believing views of a better righteousness than our own, in which alone we can dare to appear before a holy God and answer the demands of His perfect law. Nevertheless, it is surely allowable to rejoice in the testimony of our conscience, with regard to the regularity of our own behavior, so far as it is conformable to reason and Scripture; and it is an important duty thankfully to own those influences of sanctifying and strengthening grace by which we are what we are.

It is with great pleasure I recollect the reason I have to believe that many of you Christians who hear me this day are, in the main, conscientiously practicing these duties; and that some of you were doing it long before I was capable of exhorting and directing you. Acknowledge the singular goodness of God by which you have been excited to them and furnished for them.

More especially have you reason to adore it if,

through grace, you can say, with regard to the present success, what you may certainly say as to the future recompense, that your labor in the Lord is not in vain. Let God have the glory of His own work. I persuade myself that you understand the gospel too well to ascribe it to the prudence of your own conduct, to the strength of your reasoning, or to the warmth and tenderness of your address. Whatever of these advantages you have possessed were derived from God; and your very care for your offspring is, as the Apostle expresses it in a like case, the earnest care which God has put into your hearts. But it was not this care, or these advantages alone, that produced so happy an effect. In vain had your doctrines from day to day dropped as the rain and distilled as the dew in the most gentle and insinuating manner; in vain had the precious seed of the Word been sown with unwearied diligence, and watered with tears too, had not God commanded the operations of His blessed Spirit to come down as a more efficacious rain, as more fruitful showers, to water their hearts. O be not insensible to the favor! Your own souls might, to this very day, have been a barren wilderness, a land of drought, a habitation of devils; and behold, not only they, but your families too, are like a field, like a garden, which the Lord has blessed. God might have cut you off many years ago for your neglect of His covenant or your breaches of it; and behold, He is establishing it not only with you, but your seed after you, for an everlasting covenant. I think your hearts should overflow with gratitude and holy joy while you dwell on such reflections as these. This should add a relish to all the pleasure you find in conversing with your children; this should quicken you to further diligence in cultivating these graces which you have the satisfaction to see already implanted; this should reconcile you to all the afflictions with which Providence may exercise you or them; this should support you in the views of a separation, either by your own death or by theirs, since you have so comfortable a hope that, if they are removed, they will go to a heavenly Father, and that, if they are left behind you, they will be safe and happy under His care till you meet in a better world where you will be forever to each other a mutual glory and joy.

But I cannot congratulate you on such an occasion without the danger of adding affliction to the afflicted parents whose circumstances, alas! are far different from yours. I fear, my friends, that there are some among you who look round you, and look forwards, with far different prospects; some who are, with bleeding hearts, borrowing the complaint which we who are ministers of the gospel so frequently breathe forth, "We have labored in vain, and spent our strength for nought."

"O" you may, perhaps, add, "that it were only in vain! Those dear children which we early devoted to God in baptism, which we endeavored to educate in the knowledge and fear of the Lord, the children of our hopes, the children of our prayers, are unfruitful under all our cultivation; or, it may be, visibly turned aside from the good ways in which they were trained up; as if they had known them only to reject and affront them. So that we have reason to fear that all we have already done, as it is as aggravation of their guilt, will be a proportionable aggravation of their ruin."

It is indeed a very pitiable case. We owe you our compassions and we owe you our prayers; but permit us to intermix our consolations and our admonitions. You have, at least, delivered your own souls; and, as you participate in the sorrows of faithful ministers, you may share in their comforts too, and say with them, "Though the objects of our compassionate care are not gathered, yet shall we be glorious, for our work is with the Lord, and our reward with our God." Go on, therefore, in the midst of all your discouragements and, in this respect, be not weary in well-doing. Take heed of such a despair as would cut the sinews of future endeavors. If your child were laboring under any bodily distemper, you would be very unwilling that the physicians should quite give him over, and try no further medicines. You would follow them and say, "Can nothing more be done? Is there not the least glimmering of hope?" Alas! my friends, a child given up by a pious parent is, to a believing eye, a much more melancholy sight than a patient given over by the physicians. Excuse me, then, if I follow you with the question, "Can nothing now be done? Is there not the least glimmering of hope?" Who told you that the sentence of condemnation is sealed while you are sure it is not executed? Is the danger extreme? Let your efforts be so much the more zealous, your admonitions so much the more frequent and serious, your prayers so much the more earnest and importunate. And, on the whole (to allude to the words of David on a much lower occasion), who can tell

whether God will be gracious to you that the child
may live? And the sad apprehensions which you now
entertain may serve to increase the joy with which
you shall then say, "This my son was dead, and is
alive again; he was lost, and is found."

2. *I would address myself to children, to you, the dear
lambs of the flock, whom I look upon as no contemptible part
of my charge.* I have been speaking *for* you a great
while, and now give me leave to speak *to* you; and,
pray, endeavor for a few minutes to mind every word
that I say.

You see, it is your parents' duty to bring you up
for God. The great God of heaven and earth has
been pleased to give His express command that you
should be trained up in the way in which you should
go, even in the nurture and admonition of the Lord.
It is the wonderful goodness of God to give such a
charge; and I think you should be affected with it,
and should be inquiring what you should do in return.

THREE THINGS I WOULD ASK OF YOU

Now, there are three things which I would ask of
every one of you in return for this gracious notice
which the great God has taken of you children; and,
I am sure, if you love your own souls, you will not
deny me any of them.

1. Be willing to learn the things of God.
2. Pray for them that teach you.
3. See to it you do not learn them in vain. Listen
diligently that you may understand and remember

each of these.

1. Be willing to learn the things of God.

The things of God are very delightful and they are very useful; and, whatever you may think of it, your life depends on your acquaintance with them. So Christ Himself says, "This is life eternal, that they may know Thee, the only true God, and Jesus Christ, whom Thou hast sent." Therefore, you children should not think much of the labor of learning these things. Oh! far from that, you should be every day upon your knees begging God that you may be taught to know Him and to know Christ. God has done a great deal more for you than He has for many others. You might have been born in a place where you would never have seen a Bible in all your lives; where you would never have heard of the name of Christ, where you might never have been instructed in the nature of duty and sin, nor have been told of the world beyond the grave; and so would probably have fallen into hell before you had known there was such a place. And the great God has ordained matters so that you are born under the light of the gospel, and have such plain and excellent instructions that you may know more of divine things in your infancy than the wise men among the heathens did when they were old and grey-headed, and had spent all their lives in study. And will you be so ungrateful as not to be willing to learn when such provision is made for your instruction? God forbid! Shall God give you His Word, and your parents and ministers employ their time and their pains to teach you the meaning of it, and will you refuse to attend to it? That would be foolish and wicked indeed! I hope much better things of you. This is my first advice: be willing to learn. I add:

2. Pray for those that are to teach you.

I would hope that you little creatures dare not live without prayers. I hope God, who sees in secret, sees many of you on your knees every morning and every evening asking a blessing from Him as your heavenly Father. Now, let me entreat you that, at such times, you would pray for those that instruct you in divine things; pray that God would bless them for it, and pray that He would help them in it. In praying thus for us, you indeed pray for yourselves. There is a gracious promise to the people of God: "And they shall be all taught of God." Pray that it may be fulfilled. Pray that God would teach us to teach you; also we should attempt it to very little purpose. Pray for your parents, and pray for your ministers.

Pray for your parents, that God would help them to instruct you in such a manner as they have now been directed; that they may do it plainly so that you may be able to understand what they say; and seriously, that you may be brought to a holy awe of God; and tenderly, that you may be engaged to love God and His Word, and Christ and His ways; and pray that your parents may be stirred up to do it frequently, to give you line upon line, and precept upon precept, that you may be put in mind of what you are so ready to forget.

And let me desire you, my dear charge, when you pray for your parents, to pray for your minister too. I declare it again, in the most public manner, it is my earnest desire that children would pray for me. And

I verily believe every faithful minister of Christ would join with me in such a request. We do not, we dare not, despise the prayers of one of these little ones. Far from that, I am persuaded it would greatly revive and encourage us, and we should hope that God had some singular mercy in store for us and His people, if we were sure the children of the congregation were every day praying for a blessing on our labors.

3. Take heed that you do not learn in vain.

The great truths which you are taught from the Word of God are not intended merely to fill your heads with notions, but to make your hearts and lives more holy. You know the way to your father's house, every step of it, but that would never carry you home if you would not go in it. No more will it signify to know the way to heaven unless you walk in it. "If you know these things," says the Lord Jesus Christ Himself, "happy are ye if ye do them." And I may add that, if you do them not, it would have been happier for you if you had never known them. Dear children, consider it; it is but a little while, and you must die; and when those active bodies of yours are become cold, moldering clay, the great God of heaven and earth will call your souls to His judgment seat. As surely as you are now in His house, you will shortly, very shortly, be standing before His awful throne. Then He will examine to what purpose you have heard so many religious instructions, so many good lessons. Then He will examine whether you have feared Him, loved Him, served Him, and received the Lord Jesus into your hearts as your Savior and your King; whether you have chosen sin or holiness for your way, earth or heaven for your portion. And if it is found that you have lived without thought and without prayer, without any regard to the eye of God always upon you, and the Word of God always before you, it will be a most lamentable case. You will have reason to wish you had never heard of these things at all; for He has said, "The servant which knew his lord's will and did it not, shall be beaten with many stripes." Even while I am speaking to you, death is coming on; perhaps his scythe may cut you down while you are but coming up as flowers. I speak to you this plainly and earnestly because I do not know but you may be in eternity before another Lord's day. O pray earnestly that God would give you His grace to fit you for glory; and that all you learn may be so blessed that you may be made wise to salvation by it. The Lord grant that it may.

And I have one thing to tell you for your encouragement, and then I have done with you for this time. However young you are, and however broken your prayers may be, the great and glorious Lord of angels and men will be willing to hear what you say. You may be sure to be welcome to the throne of grace. The Lord Jesus Christ, when He was upon earth, was very angry with those who would have hindered little children from coming to Him. He said, "Suffer little children to come unto me, and forbid them not, for of such is the kingdom of God." And Christ is as compassionate now as ever He was. Go to Him and you may humbly hope He will, as it were, take you up in His arms and bless you. He has said it, and I hope you will never forget it; "I love them that love Me, and they that seek Me early shall find Me." O that I were but as sure that every child in this assembly would go and ask a blessing from Christ as I am that our dear Lord is willing to bestow it! But to draw to a conclusion.

3. *I shall address myself to those young persons who are grown up to years of maturity under the advantages of a religious education, and are not yet fixed in families of their own.*

I hope that many of you have been sensible of the value of those opportunities you have enjoyed and, by divine grace, have been enabled to improve them well; yet, I must add that I fear there are others among you who have unhappily neglected and abused them. I must apply myself distinctly to each of you.

To those young persons who have neglected and abused the advantages of a religious education:

I confess, there are hardly any to whom I speak with so little pleasure, because I have seldom less reason to hope I shall succeed. What shall I say to you? What can I say that you have not often heard and often despised? One is almost tempted in such a circumstance to turn reasonings and expostulations into upbraidings, and even to adopt those too passionate words of Moses, "Hear now, you rebels, you that have grown up in the knowledge and, yet, in the contempt, of divine things; you that have disappointed the hopes and slighted the admonitions of your pious parents, and so have broken their spirits and, it may be, their hearts too, and have brought down their hoary hairs with sorrow to the grave. One way or another you have, perhaps, silenced them. But is it a small thing to you that you have

thus wearied men, and will you attempt to weary your
God also? Can you dare to hope that you shall at last
carry those proud thoughtless heads triumphant
over all the terrors of His Word?" You imagine it a
very happy circumstance that you have got loose
from those mortifying lessons and uneasy restraints
you were once under. But, really, when one seriously
considers where these liberties lead you, and when
they will probably end, a just resentment of your ingratitude is almost disarmed, and indignation is
converted into pity.

Alas! sinners, the way of all transgressors is hard;
but yours is peculiarly so. You whom I am now addressing are in the morning of your days, and it is
not to be supposed that the impressions of a good
education are yet entirely effaced. What future years
may do I know not; but, hitherto, I persuade myself
that you have frequently your reflections and your
convictions; convictions which have force enough
to torment you, though not to reform you; to plant
thorns in the paths of sin, though not to reduce you
to those of duty. But, if you feel nothing of this remorse and anxiety, such a dead calm is then more
dreadful than the fiercest storm and tumult of
thought, a sad indication that your course in
wickedness has been exceeding swift; indeed, so
swift that it is probable it may not be long. Oh, that
it might immediately be stopped by divine grace
rather than by the vengeance you have so much reason to fear!

At least be engaged to pause in it for a few moments, and let reason and conscience be permitted
to speak. How is it that you make yourselves, I will

not say entirely, but tolerably, easy? Is it by the disbe-
lief of Christianity? Do you secretly suspect that the
gospel is but a cunningly devised fable? Yet even
that suspicion is not enough. Let me rather ask, are
you so confident it is so that you will venture to stake
even the life of your souls upon its falsehood? If you
were to come to such a confidence, yet it is amazing
to me how, even on the principles of natural religion alone, persons in your circumstances can
make themselves easy. Can any of the libertines of
the present age, that believe in a God, imagine that
He is altogether such a one as themselves? Can they
flatter themselves so far as to hope that they, in the
ways of negligence, profaneness, and debauchery,
are likely to meet with a more favorable treatment
from Him than those pious parents whose principles they deride? Or that this loose and irregular
course will end better than that life of prayer and
self-denial, sober-mindedness, which they discerned
in them? Few are so abandoned even of common
sense as to think this.

But these are more distant concerns. I bless God
that this kind of infidelity is not in fashion here.
You assent to the gospel as true and, therefore, must
know that God, who observes and records your conduct now, will bring you into judgment for it another day. And, if you go on thus, how will you stand
in that judgment? What will you plead? On what will
you repose the confidence of your souls that will not
prove a broken reed which will go up into your hand
and pierce you deep, in proportion to the stress you
lay upon it? While you behave like a generation of
vipers, think not to say within yourselves, "We have

Abraham for our father." Think not to plead an early dedication to him in the baptismal covenant which you have broken, despised and, in fact, renounced. Think not to plead that external profession which you have so shamefully contradicted and even, by wearing it, dishonored. You will see the weakness of such pleas as these and will not dare to trifle with that awful tribunal so far as to mention them there. And when you are yourselves thus silent and confounded, who will appear as an advocate in your favor? Your parents were often presenting their supplications and intercessions for you before the throne of grace, but there will be no room to present them before the throne of justice; nor will they have any inclination to do it. All the springs of natural fondness will be dried up; they will no longer regard you as their children when they see you in the accursed number of the enemies of their God.

And when you are thus disowned by your parents, and disowned by God, where will you cause your shame and your terror to go? You who have had so many privileges, so many opportunities and, perhaps I may add, so many fond presumptuous hopes too, how will you bear to see multitudes coming from carnal and profane families to share with your parents in the inheritance of glory from which you are excluded? You who were the children of the kingdom, whose remorse, therefore, must be the more cutting; whose condemnation, therefore, must be the more weighty! Observe in how strong and lively a view our Lord has represented this awful thought, in words which, though immediately addressed to the unbelieving Jews, are remarkably ap-

plicable to you: "There shall be weeping and gnash-
ing of teeth, when ye shall see Abraham, Isaac, and
Jacob (your pious ancestors), in the kingdom of
God, and you yourselves thrust out: and many shall
come from the north, and the south, and the east,
and the west, and shall sit down with them in the
kingdom of God, but the children of the kingdom
shall be cast out into utter darkness."

But, through the divine forbearance, you are not
yet shut out. There is still hope even for you, if you
will now return to the God of your fathers from
whom, by these aggravated transgressions, you have
so deeply revolted. Let me, then, once more tenderly
entreat you, and solemnly charge you, by the consolations of the living and by the memory of the pious
dead, by your present comforts, by your future hopes,
by the nearly-approaching solemnities of death and
judgment, by the mercies of God, and by the blood
of a Redeemer, that you consider and show yourselves men; that you set yourselves, as it were, attentively to read over the characters inscribed on your
memories and understandings in the course of a religious education; that you hearken to the voice of
conscience repeating those admonitions, and to the
voice of the blessed God as speaking in His Word to
confirm them; and, finally, that you apply to Him, in
a most importunate manner, for those victorious influences of His Spirit which are able to mollify and
transform these hearts of stone, and to raise even
you from so low a depth of degeneracy and danger
to the character and happiness of the genuine children of Abraham. God forbid that I should sin
against your souls, and my own, in ceasing to pray

that it may be so!

And now, I shall conclude all with an address to those young persons who have been, through grace, engaged to a becoming improvement of the religious education they have enjoyed.

I have the pleasure of being well assured that there are many such among you, many who are now the joy of ministers and parents, and the hope of the church for succeeding years. Let me entreat you, my dear brethren and friends, that you daily acknowledge the divine goodness in favoring you with such advantages, and, what is still more valuable, in giving you a heart to prize and to improve them.

Think how different your circumstances might have been. Providence might have cast your lot in some distant age or country where the true God has been unknown, where your early steps would have been guided to the groves and temples of detestable idols, and you might possibly have been taught to consecrate lust or murder by the name of devotion. Or you might have been educated in popish darkness, where the Scripture would have been to you as a sealed book, and you would have seen Christianity polluted with idolatrous rites, on some accounts more inexcusable than those of the heathen, and adulterated with the most absurd and pernicious errors. There the mistaken piety of your parents might have proved a dangerous snare, while it would have infused a blind and, perhaps, a cruel zeal, and a proud furious opposition to all the methods of better information.

Nay, even here, in a protestant country, is it not

too evident that there are many families in which, had you been born and educated, you would have sat as in darkness and the shadow of death, though in the land of light and the valley of vision? Your infant tongue would have been formed to the language of hell, and exercised in cursed and oaths rather than in prayer. You would have early been taught to deride every appearance of serious godliness; and all the irregular propensities of nature would have been strengthened by examples of wickedness, which might have been sufficient to corrupt innocence itself. When you consider the wide difference between these circumstances and your own, surely whatever your portion of worldly possessions may be, you have reason to lift up your hands to heaven with wonder and gratitude, and to say, "The lines are fallen to us in pleasant places, yea, we have a goodly heritage."

Nor is this all. There are many around you who have shared in such advantages as these, and have sinfully abused them to the dishonor of God, to the grief of their parents, to their own danger and, perhaps, their ruin. And why are not you in that wretched number? Or who makes you to differ from them? Why are not your hearts barred against the entrance of a Redeemer, but because the Lord has opened them? Why were not all the good instructions which have been given to you like seed sown upon a rock, but because God gave the increase? Adore the riches of this distinguishing grace.

And let me earnestly exhort you that you be careful still further to improve it. Give me leave to say that these fair openings of early seriousness naturally raise a very high expectation of eminent advances in religion. Let it be your humble and diligent care that these expectations be answered; that your goodness may not be like the morning cloud, or the early dew, which soon goes away, but rather like the dawning light which shines brighter and brighter till the perfect day.

While Providence continues these holy parents to whom you have been so highly indebted, let it be your constant care, by all the most cheerful returns of duty and gratitude, to express your regards to them, and your sense of so great an obligation. And, I will add, let it be your care to hand down to future ages those important advantages you have received from them.

One generation passes away and another generation comes. It is highly probable that, in a few years, numbers of you will be conducted into new relations; and we please ourselves with the hope that you will carry religion and happiness into rising families. Let not those hopes be disappointed. When God fixes you in houses of your own, let it be your first concern to erect there such domestic altars as those at which you have worshipped with such holy pleasure and sensible tokens of divine acceptance. Let the sacred treasure of divine knowledge which has been deposited with you be faithfully delivered down to your descendants, that they, in their turn, may arise with the same pious zeal to transmit it to another generation that shall be born of them.

And may divine grace, that inexhaustible spring of the most valuable blessings, sweetly flow on to add efficacy to all so that real vital religion may be the glory and joy of every succeeding age till this earth, which is but a place of education for the children of God during their minority, shall pass away to make room for a far nobler scene and state of existence; where pious parents and their religious offspring shall forever enjoy the most delightful society, inhabiting the palace of our heavenly Father, and surrounding the throne of our glorified Redeemer! Amen.

13

Blessings Consequent Upon Parental Fidelity

by Thomas Houston

While parents may expect, and shall assuredly obtain, good to themselves in the faithful performance of duty, they are chiefly to look for a full reward in the blessing upon children and upon children's children in their usefulness in this world, and in their felicity in the world to come. They live and labor for posterity. Enough for them if their work is owned by Him who sits upon the throne, and through the Divine acceptance of their designs and labors, if it is said, "It shall be done in thy son's days." We observe, concerning this blessing:

THE CONVERSION OF CHILDREN IS FREQUENTLY THE FRUIT OF FAITHFUL PARENTAL INSTRUCTION.

A principal object of a Christian parent's concern, we have seen, is the spiritual welfare of the children that God has given him; and their early conversion to God, as the first great step in securing it, must appear to him a matter of no ordinary importance. The conversion of the soul is its passing from death to life - the entrance upon the path that leads to glory - the great change which contains the germ of all that is excellent in character, and carries with it the guarantee of safety and ultimate felicity. The sinner's conversion being this momentous and important, the Christian parent cannot but seek it for his children. All his first duties towards his household will have this as a principal design. Their deliverance from the wrath to come - their introduction into the kingdom of Christ, will be a primary object in the early surrender which he makes of them to God, and in his daily prayers, instructions, and example. The Christian parent has frequently brought his child to Jesus, and his most solemn desires have been presented to God that he might be numbered among the lambs of his flock.

The compassionate Savior often grants to His people in this matter the desire of their hearts. What they commit to Him in believing dedication, He receives and will keep till the day of His future coming and glory. The promise is to believers and their children; and the terms in which it is expressed, all-comprehensive and gracious, encourage parents to expect the blessing which they earnestly seek for their children. "I will be a God to thee, and to thy seed." The same covenant offer which forms their warrant to plead for mercy, and to expect it with humble confidence for themselves, is presented in relation to their offspring. When there is eminent parently piety and faithful training, children frequently afford hopeful evidences of early conversion. God graciously gives to godly parents the soul of a child as a prey in answer to their fervent prayers. He confers upon them thus a first installment of their "wages" for nursing their offspring for Him.

We do not deny that the God of the families of
Israel acts as a Sovereign here, as He does in the ministry of the Word and in the government of providence; nor would we absolutely affirm that children
never depart from the way in which godly parents have
trained them with all fidelity. But we are warranted,
from the whole testimony of Scripture, as well as from
the observation of Divine providence on the subject, to
declare that there is a special blessing annexed to
parental faithfulness in the education of children. In
cases of failure, some neglect on the part of parents is
frequently observable. Undue indulgence on the one
hand, or harshness and severity on the other; one parent thwarting the plans of the other, and irregularity in
parental training; or inconsistency in conduct, will mar
the best instructions and render designs for the benefit
of children abortive. Yet, even where success follows,
no ground is left to any to glory. It is sovereign grace
alone that disposes and enables to be faithful in
domestic as in other duties; and they who received that
for which they travailed as in birth - their children's
souls as a prey - will be most ready to disclaim all idea
of merit and to exclaim, "Not unto us, Lord, not unto
us, but to Thy name give glory, even for Thy truth and
mercy's sake."

The conversion and early piety of children is an object worthy of the earnest desires and devoted painstak-
ing of parents. There seems no reason to doubt the
justness of a valuable expositor (Thomas Scott) that,
where the faithful ministrations of the Word are enjoyed, the conversion of the young may, in most cases,
be traced to parental dedications and prayers, and

their future edifications to the ministry of the gospel. Thus it has been in the history of many who have obtained a good report in the church; and the instances of Timothy, Baxter, Doddridge, and many others whose names are in the book of life, furnish a confirmation of the statement. If this view is correct, with what importance does it invest parental cultivation! How eminent and glorious the reward! The soul of a child given to the prayers and tears of a parent, an immortal spirit delivered from death, and in the dawn of its existence enstamped with the Divine image, or imbued with principles that shall expand to glory, honor, and immortality! How should parents aim at being instrumental in effecting this great change; and beginning early, how should they seek, with all importunity, and labor with all diligence, that Christ may be formed in the hearts of their children, the hope of glory! The happy issue will abundantly repay all their toil, and the joy of children's conversion will far transcend that joy that swelled the bosom when they were born in to the world.

A GODLY RACE IS THUS PERPETUATED.

The promise respecting the continuance of piety among the descendants of faithful parents was repeatedly, and under a great variety of forms, held out to God's ancient people; and, being strictly moral, Christian parents are warranted likewise to claim it as a part of their gracious heritage. They are commanded to instruct their children in God's testimony and law. The result of obedience is that posterity will walk in the way of Divine precepts. The generation to come is brought to know them, even the children that are born, "that they might set their hope in God, and not forget the works of God, but keep His commandments." The covenant with David secured spiritual blessings to posterity in connection with the faithful performance of parental vows: "If thy children will keep My covenant and My testimony that I shall teach them, their children shall also sit upon thy throne for evermore," Psalm 132:12. And this being an exhibition of the covenant of grace, the promise pertains to all believers, and is realized in the way of parental piety and fidelity.

The heads of Christian families ought to be sensible that they live not to themselves. Nursing those who are the future hopes of the church, and training them for the service of God and the enjoyment of heaven, they become the benefactors not only of their own country and time, but also of coming ages. One generation rises to praise God's works to another, and to declare His mighty acts, Psalm 145:4. God has established a connection between parental fidelity and extensive blessing to the church; and it would not be going too far to affirm that the piety of the household is a means more honored than any other for raising up and continuing on the earth a holy race. We do not deny that God, in His sovereign grace, brings others to inherit the blessing, and that even from families where neither precept nor example was on the side of true religion. He is found of them that sought Him not. They "come from the east and west," and "sit down with Abraham, and Isaac, and Jacob in the kingdom of heaven," while the "children of the kingdom" are "cast out." The young of a neglected and degraded population, collected in the Sabbath school, or arrested by the aggressive ministrations of devoted men, and the youthful converts from heathenism frequently present examples of shining piety; and thus at times is the church revived and her membership renewed.

But whatever accessions may occasionally arise from this source, and however great may be the future increase when the isles shall wait for the Redeemer's law, the fulness of Jew and Gentile shall be brought in - the spiritual seed of the Church, in ordinary cases, arises from parental piety and faithfulness. Children are dedicated to God; they are trained early to the Redeemer's service; the seeds of Divine truth, which the hands of godly parents sow, are watered by their prayers and tears, and a holy example continually exhibited before their eyes attracts them to wisdom's ways. The blessing from on high owns this instrumentally and renders it effectual. Children trained to regard the Redeemer's service as honorable and delightful emulate, and sometimes excel, the piety of their parents. Their children enjoy similar advantages; the blessing not only extends from one generation to another, but it enlarges and multiplies as it descends. And long after the humble and devoted parent has rested from all earthly labors, the fruits of his instruction and example are reaped by the church and the nation.

The view of the Divine character, and the encouraging promise presented in the second commandment, exhibit the rewards of parental obedience. God visits the inquities of the fathers upon the children unto the third and fourth generation; while to show that He has more pleasure in blessing than in punish-

ing, and especially to declare the blessings that flow to
posterity through the practical piety of parents, he is
represented as "showing mercy unto thousands of
them that love Him and keep His commandments." A
judicious and pleasing writer has justly observed, in
reference to this part of the Divine dispensation:

> A good man not only leaveth an inheritance to
> his children's children, but to the most distant
> period, the influence of his piety, and of the care
> of that God whom he worshipped as his God, and
> the God of his seed, may be traced. It is like the
> root of the tree which gives life and beauty to ev-
> erything that sprouts from it however remote, or
> the fountain which sends the salutary influence
> of its waters to the farthest extent of its course.
> We are told that when Gideon was dead, the
> Israelites showed no kindness to his house, ac-
> cording to all the goodness which he had showed
> unto Israel; but while public benefactors are for-
> gotten, and the children of the good are often
> neglected, and even oppressed by those whom
> their fathers served, the precious ointment of the
> Almighty's blessing not only refreshes the head of
> a good man, but descends to the skirts of his
> garments, and is felt by his latest posterity.

(Belfrage's Exposition of the Assembly's Shorter
Catechism, p.224.)

Sometimes, in the same family, distinguished piety
continues to flourish through a number of succeeding
generations. The "unfeigned faith" that characterized
the youthful Timothy had dwelt before in his grand-
mother Lois and in his mother Eunice, 2 Timothy 1:5,
and was at once the fruit and the reward of the devotedness of these eminent females. The descendants of

those who have witnessed a good confession of Christ frequently form the preserving and purifying salt of a country for ages; and the testimony of the church is upheld, and her purity maintained, by the posterity of godly men who accounted the reproach of Christ greater riches than all earthly treasures. Sometimes this reward of parental piety is immediate and sometimes more remote. It is related of Dr. Milne, the excellent Chinese missionary, that on the last day of his life, he was overheard by a person who stole softly to his bed ejaculating, "Lord, grant that my children may arise and fill their father's place." The prayer of the dying servant of God was heard and answered for, although he left to his children no earthly inheritance, God put it in to the heart of a benevolent individual in the East to send them to Scotland to be educated with his own children; and after a distinguished course at the University, they have tendered their service as missionaries to the heathen in the land where a parent labored and died.

Christian parents should consider themselves thus placed in a position honorable and highly important. On the faithful performance of the duties towards their children, to which their vows and affections should constantly prompt them, depends in a great measure the perpetuation of the seed of the righteous in the earth; and on their instrumentality it rests whether their offspring are to be numbered among those who are to the Lord a praise and a name in this world, and who are accounted His "peculiar treasure," or to have their place with those children of the kingdom who are doomed to final rejection. Let them lay to heart their obligation and contribute their influence that a holy race may be continued. Thus shall their children and children's children dwell in the land that God promised to their fathers; they shall beome the first fruits of a harvest of blessing, and ages to come shall reap the multiplied benefits that result from parental godliness. "The seed of the wicked shall be cut off. The righteous shall inherit the land, and dwell therein forever," Psalm 37:28-29.

POSTERITY OFTEN BECOME EMINENTLY USEFUL, AND ARE PECULIARLY BLESSED IN THEIR LOT AND LABORS.

The children of faithful parents not only become frequently the subjects of converting grace, and a godly seed is continued, but they are rendered eminently useful to others. A secret blessing is connected with early dedication and religious training. Blessed themselves, the children of pious parents become a blessing to those with whom they are connected; and, while the church enjoys the benefits of their consecrated zeal, even the irreligious of the world are constrained, at times, to behold and acknowledge the excellency of their character, and the peculiar favor with which they are encompassed. A selfish and unnatural kinsman was compelled to testify of Jacob, "I have learned by experience that the Lord hath blessed me for thy sake," Genesis 30:27. The house of Potiphar was blessed for Joseph's sake and, even in prison when the word of the Lord was sent and tried him, he obtained favor with men because the Lord was with him.

Who have been the most eminently useful individuals in every age? Who are they who have advanced the truth, benefitted the church, and performed services of the most profitable and enduring character? With few exceptions, they have been the children or descendants of godly parents. The Scriptures record the character and labors of Moses, Samuel, David, John the Baptist, and Timothy. They declare their distinguished usefulness and distinctly connect it with parental devotedness. The annals of the church, since the canon of inspiration was closed, exhibit a similar connection. Some of the most illustrious reformers - the worthies of Scotland - and those whose writings have been signally blessed to the church, owed much of their usefulness to the prayers and examples of parents who preferred Zion's good to their chief earthly joy. The mother of the late distinguished historian of Knox and Melville, after accompanying her son some part of the way, when he was about to enter the university, kneeled with him by the wayside and commended him to the protection and blessing of the God of Jacob. This was but a single expression of the pious concern which a godly mother had all along cherished about him. And it is impossible to say how much of his future eminent usefulness in the church is to be ascribed to the instrumentality of maternal piety.

It is a matter of painful observation that many of the young live only to themselves. They are trained for the world, and they follow the path of pleasure, or profit, or ambition. Though acquainted with the principles of religion, they make no religious profession; or if, in compliance with custom or the solicitation of friends, they enter the fellowship of the church, they become unfruitful professors and, instead of exercising an influence to win others to the ways of wisdom, their character and conduct operate as an obstacle and stumbling block. Through them, the ways of religion are evil-spoken of and the name of Christ is reproached.

In a great many instances, the young who act thus are the children of parents who are themselves formalists or at ease in Zion; whose example was a constant contradiction to their instructions, and who, unmindful of their solemn vows, nursed their offspring for themselves and for the world rather than for God.

On the other hand, there are some of the youth of the church who, from early life, give evidence of a distinguished, devoted spirit and are singularly useful in their day. They engage early in the service of religion; the dew of their youth is given to God; they consecrate their talents to the Master whom they love and, whatever their hand finds to do, they do it with their might. They do not live to themselves, but to Him who died and rose again. They become benefactors to the world and, through them, the church is increased, edified, and refreshed. They are the sons that "grow up in youth as plants," and "daughters" that are as "cornerstones, polished after the similtude of a palace," Psalm 144:12. Whence arises this remarkable difference? It is owing to the blessing that rests upon those who command their children and household to know the Lord, but it is denied to others.

What they themselves earnestly desire to do for the house of the Lord is often done by their children; and what they are incompetent to effect, the little ones whom they nursed for God are afterwards qualified and honored to perform. Parental dedication is accepted, and parents enjoy a double honor in the object of their affections being the selected instruments for building up the sanctuary and diffusing the savour of the Redeemer's name throughout the earth.

Designed for usefulness in the church, the children of godly parents are blessed in their persons. They are preserved in life and, by strange and gracious providences, obtain the qualifications that fit them for their work, and are conducted forward to their appointed sphere of labor. Amidst dangers they are kept - through temptations they are led in safety - and difficulties that seemed insurmountable are removed. With fewer natural advantages than are enjoyed by others; and, it may be, even without any mental superiority, they are rendered polished shafts in the Divine quiver, and become the instruments of accomplishing works of extensive and lasting benefit in their generation. Even when parents are gone, the Lord takes them up. The blessing of parental prayers and dedications rests upon them when the breasts that nursed them and the arms that fondled them are laid in the grave. They are preserved, provided for, and prospered. A special gracious providence is round about their paths and their footsteps are ordered aright.

A blessing descends too on the works of their hands. Satisfied early with God's mercy and adorned with the beauty of the Lord, their labor of love is owned and accepted, and the work of their hands is established, Psalm 90:14-17. While others of more eminent talent are rejected, and their work, although commanding human applause, are accounted as nothing, the prayerful efforts of humble and devoted servants contribute greatly to advance the Divine glory in the earth.

Of those public servants of God whose works praise them in the gates and who speak by their labors when they are dead, not a few have been the children of godly parents; and they themselves have been ever ready to acknowledge with gratitude that they inherited an unspeakable blessing from parental prayers and example, and that hence too they derived much of their public usefulness. Incalculable is the good which a single individual may thus be the means of conferring upon society. While he lives, it will issue forth like a purifying and refreshing stream. It will continue to flow on while he is gone and, for ages to come, it will go forward in the diffusive blessings of a high and holy benevolence. Christian parents standing at the fountain-head of these healing waters should feel their solemn responsibility and, as the dispensers of blessings to the world, they should consider it alike their honor and their duty to engage their children in a service that brings with it its own reward, and that is doubly blessed: blessing them that labor and those who enjoy the fruit of that labor.

THE CHILDREN OF PIOUS PARENTS THAT ARE LED ASTRAY ARE THUS SOMETIMES RESTRAINED AND RECOVERED.

The fruits of parental instruction do not always come to maturity all of a sudden. As with other laborers in the Redeemer's vineyard, parents are required to sow in hope and, sometimes, to wait amidst disappointments and trials for the expected harvest. To show the power of innate depravity, to evidence the weakness of all instrumentality, and to stir up parents to a constant sense of the necessity of Divine influence, the children even of godly parents sometimes give painful evidences that they are hardened through the deceitfulness of sin, and that they despise all good instruction. Such instances should incite to greater diligence and lead to more fervent prayer and supplication. They should induce parents to consider seriously the manner in which they have discharged their obligations to their offspring, and speedily work to rectify whatever is amiss; but they should not cause them to sink down in discouragement or to relinquish their work in despair. The instances are not few in which the conversion of children takes place after a time of wandering as the fruit of that seed that had been previously sown by parental hands and watered by parental tears.

Christian parents, it is true, should never rest satisfied with distant prospects of future piety in their children. The spiritual interests of those whom God has given them are too momentous and absorbing to be left to uncertainty, and they should continue to travail as in birth till they have some comfortable evidence that the objects of their tender solicitude have been plucked as brands out of the burning, and have been numbered in the family of heaven. But while the blessing desired may be delayed, the hopes of future fruits of their labor should raise them above discouragement. God is not unfaithful to forget a "work of faith and labor of love," however weak may be the instrument that performs it, however lengthened may be the period of hope deferred. The prayers and counsels of godly parents are often a check to thoughtless and wayward children. Even in the season of folly, they are thereby held back as by an unseen hand from courses that would harden them forever, or would lay a grave-stone upon their future repentance.

Augustine was reclaimed from error and profligacy and became a burning and shining light in the church as the fruit of the prayerful and anxious concern of an eminently pious mother. The reproof tendered to her by a Christian minister, when she gave way to despair in the prospect of her son being lost, may still supply encouragement to parents to labor and hope to the end. Said he, "Woman, it is impossible that a child of so many prayers and tears should be lost."

Nor are the children for whom many believing prayers and tears are offered often left to wander in sin unchecked or given over to final impenitency. When early instructions appear unavailing, subsequent amendment sometimes gives evidence that backslid-ings have been healed, and parents, while they live, are called to rejoice over children that appeared lost being found again, and over those that were dead being made alive. And even should this joyful discovery not be made to them in time, the tidings of their children's conversion may be carried to them in glory; and their felicity will be enhanced as they join the angelic choir in rejoicing over a repenting sinner when that restored one is the child for whom they prayed, and for whose welfare in life and death they were intensely con-cerned.

14

The Duties of Children to Their Parents

by Samuel Stennet

"Children, obey your parents in the Lord: for this is right. Honor thy father and mother, which is the first commandment with promise, that it may be well with thee, and thou mayest live long on the earth." Ephesians 6:1-3

PART 1

The artless simplicity and commanding authority with which the moral precepts of the Bible are enjoined upon us must, I think, strike the mind of every attentive reader with pleasure. Nothing could be more natural than for the Apostle, after he had held up to the view of the Ephesians the exceeding riches of the grace of God in Christ, to persuade them to the duties of benevolence. A gospel that originates in supreme love cannot surely be believed, felt, and enjoyed without impelling men to every office of kindness which the light of nature teaches and enjoins. Upon these grounds, he had recommended not only the more general and public duties of social life, but those particularly of husbands and wives. And, as families arise out of the conjugal relation which give existence to another species of duties essentially important to the welfare of society, these duties too he explains and enforces. Parents he exhorts to bring up their children in the nurture and admonition of the Lord; and children, in our text, to behave themselves with all becoming reverence and duty towards their parents.

It is to children the admonition in the text is addressed, in which denomination are included both males and females of every rank and condition of life: sons and daughters-in-law, adopted children, and even illegitimate children, too; for there is a duty owing from them to their parents, however unworthy and dishonorable a part such parents may have acted. And by parents are meant both father and mother, as it is particularly expressed in the commandment which the Apostle quotes. "Honor thy father and thy mother," which shows that parental authority is not confined to the father only. Be the paternal rights what they may, there are maternal rights also, and these draw after them duties and respects from children to the mother as well as the former to the father. And it is further to be observed that obedience and reverence are due not to immediate parents only, but to their parents also; that is, grand-fathers and grand-mothers, and indeed to all in the ascending line, that is, uncles and aunts.

Now the duties enjoined on children to their parents in our text are all comprehended in the two ideas of obedience and reverence.

First, obedience. "Children, obey your parents."

That is, listen to their instruction and be obedient to their commands. In the early part of life, when children are totally incapable of governing themselves, absolute and unlimited obedience is required. When reason opens, and they can discern good and evil, they are still to be obedient in all things so far as is consistent with a good conscience. And ever after, on the liberal grounds of friendship, they are to accommodate themselves to the wishes and views of their parents, provided these do not clash with the duty they owe to superior authority. This limitation some think is expressed in the words immediately subjoined, "Obey your parents in the Lord;" that is, so far as is consistent with the regard you owe to the authority of God. Or, perhaps, the Apostle's intention may be to point out the piety which should mingle itself with their duty. "Obey them in obedience to the divine command; have regard to Christ in your obedience, and to them as His disciples and servants." And so all the pleasing qualifications of affection, cordiality, and cheerfulness, are included in the admonition.

Second, reverence. "Honor thy father and mother." That is, cherish in your breasts the most affectionate esteem for their persons and characters; behave yourselves towards them in the most respectful and dutiful manner; and speak of them with all possible honor and reverence. But some think by honoring our parents is meant providing for their comfortable support, when advanced in life and incapable of subsisting themselves; this, however, is most certainly included in the phrase: "Make the latter part of their days as easy and happy to them as you can."

The duties thus enjoined on children to their parents the Apostle enforces by various considerations.

The first he mentions is their fitness. "Obey your parents in the Lord: for this is right." It is just; it is fit and reasonable in itself, what the light of nature teaches, and all nations and ages have acknowledged it to be expedient. It is most decent and becoming to obey and reverence those to whom, under God, we are indebted for our existence. It is on the grounds of equity and gratitude, most naturally to be expected, that we should make every return in our power to those who have shown us all imaginable care and kindness. And a due regard to their instructions and authority will, in its consequences, be greatly beneficial to us, as they are far better able on many accounts to direct and govern us, especially in our minority, than we are ourselves.

The next argument is taken from the express will of God, signified in the fifth commandment. This is one of those precepts of the moral law which the great God so solemnly pronounced on Mount Sinai, and which He wrote with His own finger on the tablets of stone. With an audible voice He said, "Honor thy father and thy mother," and it is His pleasure that voice should be heard through all the world and to the end of time. Wherefore, children are to obey their parents "in the Lord," that is, in obedience to the authority of the great God.

Here the Apostle, as he passes on, observes, that "this is the first commandment with promise." From hence, the church of Rome would insinuate that the

second commandment, which is so directly opposed
to their doctrine and practice of worshipping images, is not obligatory under the gospel. "For," say
they, "that commandment has a promise annexed to
it; but the Apostle tells us this is the first with
promise, wherefore he hereby plainly annihilates
that." But the reply is extremely natural. The
promise added to the second command (which indeed is rather an assertion than a promise) is no
other than a general declaration of God's merciful
disposition to all who love Him and keep His commandments, and evidently relates to the whole law.
Whereas the precept of which the Apostle is here
speaking is the first and only one that has a promise
annexed to it peculiar to itself. It should here also be
observed that the language of the text establishes
the authority of the decalogue or moral law with respect to us Christians as well as the Jews, teaching us
not only that we should make it the rule of our lives,
but that we may and ought to be influenced in our
obedience by a regard to the blessings it promises.
And, in respect to the precept before us, the Apostle
evidently meant by calling it the first commandment with promise, to draw an argument from
thence to persuade children to a dutiful behavior
towards their parents. This, as if he had said, is a
duty of the greatest consequence, the ground-work
of all other social duties and, therefore, distinguished from the rest by a particular mark of the divine favor.

And what is the promise thus held up to the view
of children? It is this, "Honor thy father and
mother, that it may be well with thee, and thou

mayest live long on the earth." In Exodus it is expressed somewhat differently, "that thy days may be long upon the land which the Lord thy God giveth thee," Exodus 20:12. And in Deuteronomy 5:16 thus, "that thy days may be prolonged, and that it may go well with thee, in the land which the Lord thy God giveth thee." The sense, however, is fully conveyed in the text, excepting the promised land's not being particularly mentioned. This omission, some suppose, was owing to a wish to preclude all occasion of countenancing a vain confidence which, at that time, prevailed much among the Jews that they should not be dispossessed of their country. But, as this epistle was written to the Ephesian church, which consisted of Gentile as well as Jewish converts, it should rather seem the omission, which does not affect the spirit of the promise, was with a view to accommodate it to Christians in general. Now the plain import of it is this, that those who, in obedience to the divine authority, pay due respect to their parents will be likely to enjoy worldly prosperity and long life. I say "likely" because the promise is so worded as to convey an idea of the direct tendency of dutifulness in children to promote their temporal welfare, which we shall largely show hereafter is the case. But, considered as a positive promise, it was remarkably fulfilled in regard of the Jews. And, however temporal rewards and punishments are not now dispensed in the manner they were among that people who subsisted under a peculiar form of government, yet there are not a few instances of dutiful children who have been distinguished by the smiles of Providence; and it is true of them all, in regard of their best interests, that acting thus in the fear of God, it is well with them in this life, and shall be well with them forever in the life to come. Thus, the Apostle enforces this great duty by the law of nature, the express command of God, and the many advantages that attend the right discharge of it. The text thus explained, we proceed more particularly to consider:

First, the various offices required of children towards their parents.

Second, their obligations to these duties.

THE DUTIES WHICH CHILDREN OWE THEIR PARENTS.

These we shall class under the three heads of Obedience, Reverence, and Support. Obedience I mention first because the main expressions of it, especially in the absolute and unlimited sense of the word, are required of children in the early part of life. Reverence is next because that ripens and improves with reason. And support is last of all because the tender offices meant by this term are to be rendered parents in the decline of life, and are, with good reason, understood to be included, as was observed just now, in the word honor.

1. *Obedience.* The duties comprehended in this idea we shall consider in reference to matters civil and religious, keeping in our eye, as we pass on, the different ages, capacities, and circumstances of children.

As to civil matters.

In this description, we include what relates to

food, dress, company, amusements, deportment, learning, discipline, and everything else which the morals of children are conversant about. The will of the parent, in regard of all these matters, under the restrictions which will be hereafter mentioned, should be dutifully complied with.

In the earliest stage of life, obedience is the result of instinct, not reasoning. Cast, as infants are, in this helpless state upon the care of others, they are under a necessity of submitting. But, when they begin to acquire strength, and to become capable of resisting, they should obey upon the general idea of filial duty. For, though they may not be able clearly to comprehend the fitness of what is required of them, they may yet have sense enough to perceive that the age, authority, and affection of their parents gives them a right to demand submission and obedience. And, for children possessing this idea to dispute the point with them in any matter insisted on is to offend against the decision of their own reason. Their reason teaching them submission, their language no doubt should be, "My father knows better than I what is right to be done in this case and, therefore, I ought to comply; I will comply."

Hence, if we may be allowed to digress a moment, appears the importance of taking pains with children at this early age to impress their minds with the general obligations of filial obedience. Parents should now steadily assert their authority and insist that they will, at all events, be obeyed, letting their children know by their words and actions that they have power over them, that God has given them that power, and that they hold it by the consent of all mankind. But, at the same time, they should be alike assiduous to secure their cordial affection by convincing them that they cannot possibly mean to do them any harm, but, on the contrary, all the good in their power. So children will be persuaded that it is their interest, as well as their duty, to obey, even though what is required does not fall in with their inclinations. But, if a child at this early age is froward, obstinate, and unyielding, and a parent, through false tenderness, suffers him wantonly to violate his commands, the latter is as much, yea more to blame than the former; and if such perverseness is not subdued, the consequence will, in all probability, be fatal to them both. But to return:

When reason further opens, and children become capable of clearly perceiving not only the authority their parents have over them, but the difference between good and evil, between justice and injustice, truth and falsehood, humility and pride, meekness and passion, gratitude and ill nature, and the like, then their obligations to obedience increase; for, their parents requiring them to do what their own judgment teaches them ought to be done, authority and conscience, every act of disobedience, in such case, is more criminal than before, for are they not guilty both of acting contrary to a conviction of what is in itself right, and also of treating the authority of their parents with contempt?

Further, when children arrive at mature age, though they are to be justified in disobeying such commands as are directly opposed to the clear dictates of their own reason and judgment, yet they ought to listen respectfully to the counsels of their parents, and in cases of a doubtful nature, on which age and experience are better capable of deciding, it is both their wisdom and duty to yield to their opinion. "My son, hear the instruction of thy father," said Solomon, "and forsake not the law of thy mother. For they shall be an ornament of grace unto thy head, and chains about thy neck," Proverbs 1:8-9. And, most certainly, it should be their assiduous concern to please their parents, even to the latest period of their lives, by conforming to their will not only in matters of importance that are just and right, but in matters perfectly indifferent and which do not affect the rights of conscience.

In fine, it is an argument of good sense and filial duty in children to take pains to impress this important sentiment on their minds, during their minority especially, that their parents consider their interests as their own, and are much better capable of judging, in most cases, what is expedient for them than they are themselves. Under this persuasion, every act of obedience will be easy and pleasant, and will draw after it the happiest consequences to both parties while, on the contrary, ill-humor, discontent, and refractoriness will not fail at once to afflict the injured parent, and to make the undutiful child himself miserable. Let us now proceed:

To matters of religion.

Hitherto we have been speaking of moral duties only, I mean such as are discoverable by the light of nature, and which we owe to our fellow-creatures. Our view is not extended further to discoveries which God is supposed to have made of Himself, and the manner He will be worshipped by a positive revelation. The opinions of mankind differ here, and a great variety of religions obtain in the world. Wherefore the question before us is, how far the religion of parents is binding upon their children; or, what influence the opinion, profession, and authority of parents are to have upon filial obedience.

Here we are to proceed by steps, as we did under the former particular. When children are in the earliest stage of life, and incapable of judging of these matters, it is no doubt their indispensable duty to treat the religion of their parents with all decent respect and to conform regularly to the externals of divine worship. They are not as yet "in their own right," and if parents, conceiving of this or that mode of religion as of divine authority, are obliged in conscience not only themselves to conform to it, but to enjoin conformity on them, it follows that they ought to comply, there being no dictate of reason or conscience on their part to justify a refusal. It is, therefore, a violation of the law of nature for the children of a Mahometan, a Papist, or any other religious profession, to treat the opinion or worship of their parents with disrespect and contempt. Nature revolts at the idea. A Christian cannot bear to see his creed or his devotion laughed at by any, much less by his children. And why should we suppose those who differ from us have not the same feelings on this head with ourselves? When Moses says "Thou shalt not revile the gods," Exodus 22:28, he perhaps means to forbid an indecent and opprobrious treatment of the religion of the country

where we happen to be, however contrary it may be
to our own views. And, if so, this precept of his, in effect, still more strongly forbids a similar behavior in
children towards the religion of their parents.

But that absolute obedience in matters of religion, which parents have a right to exact of their
children during their minority, becomes more and
more limited or conditional as they approach to
years of discretion. As soon as they are at all capable
of perceiving the grounds on which the religion of
their parents stands, it is their unquestionable duty
to enquire into those grounds. Enquiry is what parents ought to enjoin, and it is one part of filial obedience to comply with such injunctions. And, while
reason teaches that they should not take their religion absolutely on trust, it teaches also that they are
under the strongest obligations to listen seriously to
what is offered in favor of it. A child ought to suppose, unless he has glaring proof to the contrary,
that his father is sincere and in earnest in pressing
these matters upon him. And, if this persuasion
does not awaken his attention and put him upon
the most diligent enquiry, he is chargeable with
manifest undutifulness and disaffection. So far
parental authority should influence children.

And its use thus far, be their parents religion
true or false, is very considerable. If it is false, filial
attachment, thus exciting them to enquiry is an advantage, as it becomes an occasion of their detect-
ing the mistaken grounds of such religion, and so
of dissenting for just reasons from it. And, if it is
true, the same filial attachment is of use as it thus
becomes the occasion of their possessing a satisfac-

tory evidence of the truth of what they before only presumed to be true. And, more than this, that filial affection which thus magnifies in their eye the father's sincerity and zeal, and gives the most pleasing aspect to his pious and holy example, by so doing, possesses them of a further collateral and confirming evidence of the truth of the religion they have thus examined and approved. But, when filial attachment precludes enquiry, and has no other effect than to beget a mere implicit faith, the obedience which results from such faith is reprehensible and criminal. Conformity to the religion of our parents, on this ground, is disobedience to the voice of reason and of God.

The amount of the whole is in short this: filial duty demands, on the part of children when they become capable of reasoning, the most sober and diligent attention to the instruction of their parents in matters of religion; but it does not require implicit assent and obedience yielded to parental authority without enquiry, and, more especially in contradiction to the sense and dictate of conscience, is a violation of the allegiance due to God only.

When the woman of Samaria had listened to our Savior's discourse, and was persuaded on the fullest conviction of His being the Messiah, she immediately informed her relations, neighbors, and acquaintances of what had happened, and entreated them to come and see the man who had told her all she ever did and judge for themselves whether He was not the Christ. The conduct of the Samaritans on this occasion is precisely such as filial duty requires of children towards their parents in matters of religion when they are capable of judging of them. The Samaritans did not absolutely refuse their assent to the woman's report. That would have been both unreasonable and indecent. It might or it might not be true. She was evidently in earnest; their good she consulted, the story, upon the face of it, carried the air of probability and importance, and to have treated it with contempt would have been highly unbecoming. The proper use, therefore, of his influence and authority was to excite their attention and enquiry. This effect it had. They went out of the city to Christ, heard Him themselves, and then declared that they believed not merely because of her saying (that was only the occasion of their coming at the desired evidence), but because, having heard Him, they were persuaded, upon the same grounds which had convinced her, that He was indeed the Christ, the Savior of the world.

It is here further to be observed that however children may see reason, upon calm and serious enquiry, to dissent from the religion of their parents; they are, nevertheless, obliged to treat both them and their profession with all decent respect. Instead of contumeliously affronting the one or the other, it is rather their duty decently to throw a veil over them, as Shem and Japheth did over their father's nakedness.

2. *Reverence is the next branch of filial duty to be considered.*

Little needs to be said here by way of explanation. Both the persons and characters of parents should be held in the highest esteem and veneration. As to the former, the language and deportment of children should be decent and respectful. The familiarities indeed of early life, and of hours of recreation and pleasantry, are very properly to be allowed. A haughty, distant, morose carriage on the part of parents tends to break the spirits of children, and to beget a disguise in their breasts which, however it may assume the appearance of reverence, will in the end weaken, if not totally destroy, the springs of ingenuous and affectionate obedience. Yet a too-great freedom in discourse and behavior should be checked not only as it is a breach of good manners, but as it will be apt, in a course of time, to degenerate into a contempt of parental authority. A meek, submissive, respectful demeanor in children towards their parents is lovely in the eyes of all, and is ever deemed by prudent people an argument of good sense as well as filial piety. The behavior of Joseph to his father Jacob, and of Solomon to his mother Bathsheba, fails not to give pleasure to every reader. The former we see, though next in authority to Pharaoh, "presenting himself to his father and bowing before him with his face to the earth," and the latter, though a mighty prince, "rising up from his throne to meet his mother, bowing himself to her, and causing a seat to be set for her at his right hand," 1 Kings 2:19. The ancient laws of the Romans carried the matter so far as to oblige children to call their parents gods.

But such a deportment in children will not be natural and easy unless they cherish in their breasts a partiality in favor of their parents' character for good sense, integrity, and piety. Where these qualities really reside, they demand a greater degree of respect from children, in whose eyes they may be supposed to magnify, than from others. Where they really are not, natural affection should at least create a doubt on the matter, if not wholly veil the contrary imperfections from their view. And, where they are found in a degree only, it is the tender office of filial imagination to heighten and exaggerate them. Credulity here is an argument of good sense, and partiality a virtue rather than a vice. What son, unless he is a brute, can willingly admit the idea that his parents are fools, or that they are void of all principle and piety? On the contrary, what ingenuous dutiful child is there but feels himself disposed to believe that they possess every natural and moral excellence in a greater perfection than others? This persuasion, I say, should be cultivated as far as it can anyway consist with truth.

The effect will be highly beneficial in many instances. It will be so to children themselves to conciliate their regards to the counsels and precepts of their parents, for that obedience which is the result of a strong prejudice in favor of the wisdom, experience, and good-will of those who govern is always more easy and pleasant than that which is extorted by a mere dread of authority. This partiality, too, will be highly pleasing to parents and add greatly to their happiness; and, as it will cement the union between both parties, so it will contribute not a little to domestic felicity. Besides, this reverence for their parents will interest children in the defense of their characters on all occasions, which is a very important branch of filial duty. Some of the noblest actions recorded in profane and sacred history are those which have sprung from the warm and undignified zeal of persons of distinguished virtue for the just reputation of their ancestors.

3. *Support is another office due from children to their parents.*

In this idea is included every kind of assistance that can be afforded them, to render their last days easy and comfortable. It is sad indeed to see old age, which should have nothing but its own infirmities to struggle with, sinking under the pressures of penury and want; and especially when this is the effect of the imprudent arrangement of their affairs in favor of unnatural children. For surely nothing can be more foolish than for parents, whom Providence has blessed with an affluence of the things of this life, to throw themselves into a state of absolute dependence on their children. If this is at any time done, through an excess of fondness on the one part, and in compliance with avaricious views on the other, very slender returns of filial reverence and affection are to be expected. Such unhappy parents have, in too many instances, lived to see their imprudent confidence abused, and their incautious generosity rewarded with neglect, if not contempt. The idea, however, of securing the homage and obedience of children by parsimoniously withholding from them the necessary means of improving their fortunes in life is as mistaken a conduct on the other hand. A competency is all a prudent and good parent would wish to reserve to himself when ease and retirement are his only objects as to this world, except it is the gratification of a benevolent disposition in the little circle of declining life. "I would not," says a sprightly writer, "in the evening of my days, strip myself to my very shirt; a warm nightgown I may be allowed to provide myself."

But, possessed of such an uncontrolled competency, there are yet many offices of kindness requisite on the part of children to render the closing scene of life comfortable. Attention, reverence, sympathy, and an assiduous wish to please are the proper cordials to be administered to old age by the tender hands of filial affection. And these are cordials which dutiful children will account it their highest honor and happiness to administer to the latest period. To that moment, they will look forward with painful anxiety; its approach they will dread, and use every means in their power to protract it to the utmost length. And, when it does arrive, they will meet it with tears of genuine sorrow and regret. And how pleasing the sight to see dutiful and affectionate children, after having cheerfully devoted the vigor of youth to the service of their parents, surrounding their dying beds with unfeigned grief, following their dear remains to the grave with the most passionate lamentations, and recording in their faithful memory the debt of gratitude they owe to parental care and love! Affecting examples of this kind I might here cite, but they shall be referred to the following sermon; in which we mean to hold up to the view of children the various considerations which humanity and religion suggest, to move the springs of filial duty and affection.

PART 2

We have laid before children the duties they owe to their parents, all which are comprehended in the ideas of obedience, reverence, and support.

And now we proceed, second, to persuade them by suitable motives to the cheerful discharge of these duties. Our arguments we shall class under three heads:

1. The law of nature.
2. The express command of God.
3. The examples of persons eminent for their virtue and piety. And how happy will it be if these reasonings, accompanied with a divine energy, produce the desired effect!

1. *The law of nature.* This law operates two ways: by instinct and by reason. Instinct is a strong bias to actions, which produces its effect without any previous reasoning or consideration. It is common to men and brutes, and cannot be counteracted without a violent force put on nature. Of this kind, as we have observed before, is that excessive fondness which parents, particularly mothers, feel for their offspring. And of this kind, too, is that regard which children feel for their parents, especially in the earlier part of life. During that period, it supplies the place of reason and urges them to the reverence and obedience which they, afterwards, come clearly to perceive is their duty. And from this principle, the force of which all children feel, we may be allowed to argue with them as they are advancing to years of discretion. Cast your eyes back, children, to the ear-

liest moment you can recollect; call to mind the ea-
gerness and attention with which you looked up to
your parents for support and protection, and the
reverence, submission and obedience which this attachment to them drew after it; and say whether you
can avoid inferring from thence, now that you are
capable of reasoning, your obligation to the duties
we have been recommending. It is the voice of nature, and will you, can you, eradicate from your
breasts a propensity that is coeval with your existence? If you could, what would be the effect but to
sink you beneath the level of the brute creation?
Horrid degradation!

But it is reason that enables us to perceive what
are the true grounds upon which the law of nature
stands. And, if we can clearly make it appear, that
equity, gratitude, and interest require a cheerful
compliance with the duties we have been recommending, it will follow that whoever withholds such
compliance stands chargeable with complicated
guilt and shameful absurdity.

First, the law of equity demands filial obedience.

It is a truth, acknowledged on all hands, that respect and submission are due from inferiors to their
superiors. The authority which the latter acquire
over the former is founded in age, wisdom, experience, property, benefits conferred, and the consent
of the community; and these obligations, saving the
just rights of conscience, are not to be disputed
without manifest injustice. Now, upon this ground,
how equitable are the claims of parents upon their
children! They have the advantage of age, experience, and property, to which must be added the con-

sideration of their having done more for their children than any others could possibly do for them; yea, that of their being, under God, the instruments of their existence. Should it be objected, "You have done no more for me than natural affection obliged you to do," it is replied, "That is not, in every instance, true; and, if it were, it does not, in justice, vacate their claim of obedience." But the best reply to such unnatural disingenuity is, "Let your children, when you have them, object this to you, and then tell us how you like such treatment." Indeed, the common sense and feelings of mankind reprobate such language. All wise and good men agree in the reasonableness of filial obedience, and nothing but the most horrid depravity can extort from the human breast an objection to it.

Here I cannot help taking notice of the unexampled absurdity and profligacy of the leaders among the Jews in our Savior's time who, under a specious pretence of regard to positive, sapped the foundation of moral duties. In no instance was it more flagrant than in their decision on a question relative to what is now before us. A man wishes to be free from his obligation to this great command, "Honor thy father and mother." He comes to these men for advice upon the matter. And what say they? "Oh! bring a gift to the altar, do some work of supererogation and you shall be free." Thus did these hypocrites make the commandment of God of none effect by their tradition. What sober man but shudders at such impiety as this! And how does this monstrous perversion, of the grounds of morality, tend directly to the dissolution of all the bands of civil society and the introduction of every kind of iniquity! Obey your parents then, children, for this is right; it is just. But to the demands of justice we will add these:

Second, the demands of gratitude. And here, if there is in any the least ingenuous sentiment in the human breast, we have an opportunity of addressing it by motives that are irresistible. You children that are just rising into life, cast your eyes backward to the first moment of your existence, and realize the innumerable expressions of parental affection with which you have been followed to the present time. What pangs did not your tender mother endure when she brought you into life! With how fond a heart did she clasp you in her arms, lay you to her breast, and pour her very soul upon you! With what painful anxiety did she anticipate your wants! With what unwearied attention did she provide for them! And from how many evils did she hourly protect you, gathering you as a hen gathers her chicks! What a variety of comforts have your parents, each of them, denied themselves, and what a variety of labors have they incessantly undergone in order to procure for you a thousand enjoyments! Your happiness, your usefulness, your honor, your final salvation, were their grand objects through the term, the long and tedious term, as it seemed to you, of non-age. How often, shook with alternate hopes and fears, have they stood trembling by your cradle and your bed, watching the event of threatening disorders! With what solicitude have they led you on every step, through the devious paths of childhood and youth, holding you back from this and that insidious

snare, and shielding you against this and that violent assault of temptation! What various reasonings,
apprehensions, and cares have agitated their minds
respecting your education, the manner in which
they should conduct themselves towards you, and
the hands to whose guidance they should entrust
you! How often have their hearts bled within them
when regard to your real interests obliged them to
sacrifice fond indulgence to the demands of rigor-
ous correction! How have they restrained your impetuous passions, borne with your childish prejudices, gratified your innocent wishes, pleaded with
you on your best interests, and poured out their cries
and tears to heaven on your behalf! And with what
painful anxiety, mingled with eager hope, have they
looked forward to the event of all those measures
they have taken with you, to prepare you for the station of life you are perhaps now just entering upon!

And now are there not returns due to all these
expressions of parental kindness? Shall inattention
and neglect on your part draw tears of sadness from
those eyes which have so often looked on you with
tender pity? Shall harsh and disrespectful language
grate on those ears which have been ever open to
your cries? Shall unnatural disobedience pierce the
bosom that has so passionately loved you? Shall
sullen ingratitude crush the heart that has doted
upon you? Shall folly and sin, in a word, bring down
those grey hairs with sorrow to the grave which affection for you, as well as old age, has rendered truly
venerable? God forbid! On the contrary, does not
every ingenuous sentiment, and every pious feeling
of the heart, call loudly on you to exert your utmost

efforts towards discharging a debt which, after all, it
will never be in your power to repay? Ought you not
to revere their persons, and hold their characters
sacred? Ought you not to approach them with respect and to kindle into a shame at every insult offered them? Ought not their commands to be a law
with you and every deviation from them a force put
upon your nature? Ought you not religiously to regard their admonitions and patiently submit to
their censures? Ought you not to consult their happiness in every step you take and accommodate
yourselves even to their humors? Ought you not,
when they are in the decline of life, to afford them
all the assistance in your power? To watch their
looks with assiduity and attention, to bear their
pains with them, to soothe their ruffled passions,
support their feeble steps, make their bed in their
sickness, and, if you cannot hold back death from
them, yet by your sympathy and prayers disarm him
at least of some of his terrors? Gratitude for a thousand kind offices you have received demands all this
at your hands. Once more:

Third, interest holds the same language. To resist instinct, to oppose reason, to deny the claims of
justice, and to stifle the entreaties of gratitude, one
should suppose, must be a painful business. Yet the
momentary pleasure resulting from the gratification
of depraved passions does, in some instances, get
the better of all these considerations; shame, however, and remorse must be the consequence. On the
contrary, a ready compliance with the dictates of nature and reason seldom fails to afford pleasure; or, if
some sacrifice must be made of present ease and

pleasure, yet the solid advantages that result thence are more than an equivalent. Such is the case here.

When frowardness in early life prevails over parental authority, children are themselves the sufferers as well as their parents and, indeed, in a greater degree than they. They not only lose all the real benefits which would result to them from submission, but a foundation is laid for miseries of the most fatal kind in this world and in another. Not to speak of the absolute necessity of submission, in order to their present support and protection; how great is its importance in order to their escaping future evils, and in order to the forming them for the duties and pleasures of mature age! Children, accustomed to violate the laws of filial obedience, seldom, when grown up, make good members of society. Impatient, self-willed, proud, fierce, and void of natural affection, they are a disgrace to their species, shunned of all good men, and abandoned to contempt and misery while they who obediently submit to the yoke nature kindly imposes are hereby fitted for honor, prosperity, and all the social enjoyments of life.

Here let us consider a little more attentively the influence which a dutiful deportment towards their parents has upon the reputation, fortune, comfort, and, with the blessing of God, final happiness of youth. What young person of a liberal mind but would be glad to be on a respectable footing in the circle of a virtuous acquaintance! And what is there that tends so directly to secure to him this felicity as the character of being a dutiful son? In this idea are comprehended all the social and friendly virtues.

Thus described, he is understood to be just, humane, and benevolent, and so is respected, confided in, and beloved, has an early admission to the acquaintance of men of character, and a natural introduction to business. Religiously regarding the admonitions and cautions of prudent and affectionate parents, he escapes a thousand evils into which conceit, perverseness, and ill education precipitate multitudes around him; and, paying a due attention to their maxims and counsels, he acquires a thousand enjoyments which he would otherwise miss. Led by the skillful hand of age and experience, faithfully and cordially held forth to his assistance, he is guided safely through the dangerous path of youth and temptation, happiness and usefulness. How many have gratefully acknowledged themselves indebted under Providence to parental wisdom for the extraordinary success they have met with in worldly business, the distinguished situations in life to which they have attained, and the reputation in which they have been held by all around them! Had it been their unhappiness, as it has of too many young people, to turn with disgust from the sage advice of their fathers, to trust to their own understandings, and to fall in with the flattering counsels of youthful companions, the reverse would have been their fortune, and they would have sunk into disgrace, misery, and oblivion. But, besides the consideration of the many advantages which result directly, and in the natural course of things, from a dutiful attention to the instructions of virtuous and prudent parents, it is to be remembered that such conduct is pleasing to God and usually followed with the smiles of Providence. But of this we shall have occasion to speak more largely hereafter.

The pleasure, too, which an ingenuous mind must feel in the idea of making parents happy by rendering them that reverence, obedience, and support, which is their just due clearly shows it to be the interest of children so to do. Benevolence is its own reward and, if this is true in regard of offices of kindness in general, with how much greater force may this sentiment be applied to the matter before us! Where justice, gratitude, affection, and instinct all unite to persuade us to make others happy, what pain must it give us to resist! What pleasure to comply! Can I then see a parent, to whom I owe ten thousand obligations, unhappy, and not be myself unhappy? Especially if I have ground to apprehend that a jealousy of my being deficient in point of tenderness is the cause of it? On the contrary, what satisfaction, what refined satisfaction, must I feel from contributing the utmost in my power to his or her repose and comfort, especially in the closing scene of life! Every such exertion, though painful in itself, must be pleasant, infinitely pleasant, in the reflection. O the joy! To smooth the brow of parental adversity, to assist the infirmities of declining nature, to wipe away the falling tear, to lift up the palsied hand, convert languor into smiles, and make the dying bed of old age easy!

But the most important consideration of all is the influence which filial obedience has upon the religious character of children and, of consequence, on their noblest interests here and hereafter. If our parents fear God, our final salvation is their grand

object. With a view to this, they teach, counsel, restrain, and correct us, weep over us, expostulate with
us, and pray incessantly for us. Now, what are we doing, when we turn a deaf ear to all they say, but de-
priving ourselves of the greatest advantages and laying violent hands on our immortal souls? A religious education is a singular blessing. Happy are
they who improve it! How many perverse, undutiful
children have lamented their abuse of it with the
sharpest accents upon their dying beds! And how
many of the contrary character, whose dutiful carriage has furnished one among many other proofs
of their piety, have acknowledged this great benefit
with their latest breath, thanking God that they were
not left to the folly and madness of treating parental
counsel and authority with contempt! It is your interest, then, children, to obey your parents. Your
reputation, your health, your worldly prosperity, your
comfort, your happiness, your happiness in this
world and in that to come, all, under God, depend
upon it.

2. *From the law of nature, we proceed now to urge upon
you the express command of God.*

"Honor thy father and thy mother" was one of
those commands pronounced by the blessed God
Himself on Mount Sinai amidst the solemnities of
thunder, lightning, fire and smoke. It is the next in
order to those which respect our duty to God, and
takes the precedence of all the other duties required
of us towards our neighbor. It is put in immediate
connection with divine worship: "Ye shall fear every
man his mother and his father, and keep my sab-

baths: I am the Lord your God," Leviticus 19:3. And, indeed, it is not imaginable that such children as are not disposed to honor their parents, can be in a disposition to worship God. The most tremendous judgments are denounced on those who violate this law. Under the Jewish economy, he that cursed his father or mother was to be put to death. And the stubborn, disobedient, and rebellious son, having been convicted of these offenses before the elders of his city, was to be stoned with stones so that he died. Among the curses to be pronounced on Mount Gerizim, this was one, "Cursed be he that setteth light by his father or his mother: and all the people shall say, amen," Deuteronomy 27:16. Solomon, in the book of Proverbs, holds the same language. "Whoso curseth his father or his mother, his lamp shall be put out in obscure darkness," Proverbs 20:20. "Whoso robbeth his father or his mother, and saith, it is no transgression; the same is the companion of a destroyer," Proverbs 38:24. And again, "The eye that mocketh at his father, and despiseth to obey his mother, the ravens of the valley shall pick it out, and the young eagles shall eat it," Proverbs 30:17 The prophet Ezekiel exhibits this, among many other heavy charges, against the Jews, that "they set light by father and mother," Ezekiel 22:7, and threatens them with very sore calamities on account of it. And, with these remarkable words, the canon of the Old Testament Scriptures is closed, "Behold, I will send you Elijah the prophet, before the coming of the great and dreadful day of the Lord. And he shall turn the heart of the father to the children, and the heart of the children to their fathers, lest I come and smite the earth with a curse," Malachi 4:5-6.

What the moral law, by the lips of Moses and the prophets, thus enjoins, the New Testament confirms. Our Lord recognizes the duties of filial obedience in His discourse with the Scribes and Pharisees, whom He severely reprehends for having mutilated the commandment of God respecting this matter, and made it of none effect by their tradition. "God commanded, saying, Honor thy father and mother: and he that curseth father or mother, let him die the death. But ye say, Whosoever shall say to his father or his mother, It is a gift by whatsoever thou mightest be profited by me, and honor not his father or his mother, he shall be free. Thus have ye made the commandment of God of none effect by your tradition," Matthew 15:4-6. And as He thus establishes the authority of the divine command, so He makes that affection which nature has implanted in the breasts of children to their parents, and on which the duties of filial obedience are grounded, a measure by which every disciple of His is to estimate the genuineness and transcendency of his love to Him: "He that loveth father or mother more than Me, is not worthy of Me," Matthew 10:37.

The Apostles, too, particularly enjoin this precept on children, "Obey your parents, say they, in all things, for this is well pleasing unto the Lord," Colossians 3:20. "If any widow have children or nephews, let them learn first to shew piety at home, and to requite their parents; for that is good and acceptable before God," 1 Timothy 5:4. And among the many striking characters by which the degeneracy of the last times is strongly marked, those of disobedience to parents, and the want of natural affection, are not the least.

But, without citing any further authorities from Scripture, we shall content ourselves with recalling your attention to the words of the text, "Children, obey your parents in the Lord: for this is right. Honor thy father and mother, which is the first command with promise, that it may be well with thee, and thou mayest live long on the earth." The law of nature is the law of God. God requires whatever is fit and right. Obedience to parents is fit and right; therefore, God requires it. Thus, you see, the Apostle refers us back to the decalogue, telling us that this is binding on Gentiles as well as Jews, upon us under the Christian as well as those under the Mosaic dispensation. It is God's command now as much as when He spoke those words Himself on Mount Sinai, "Honor thy father and mother." Wilfully, therefore, to violate this law, is to offend against the express authority of God, and cursed is he who thus dares to affront his Creator. What, then, are they doing who trifle with the obligations they owe their parents? To all such impenitent sinners, the Jew first and the Gentile also, he will render indignation and wrath, tribulation and anguish.

But, in order yet further to enforce obedience to this command, the Apostle holds up to our view the promise originally annexed to it, "It is," he reminds us, "the first commandment with promise," distinguished by a particular mark of the divine regard, and designed to be considered by us as the ground of all the other duties we owe to society. He that wilfully violates this precept is in the direct road to the open violation of all the precepts that follow. And, indeed, it would be easy to show, both from the reason and nature of the thing and from the history of mankind, that all those tremendous evils which shake the foundations of civil society such as theft, murder, adultery, perjury, and the like, originate from the want of natural affection, and a failure in filial obedience. And, on the contrary, it would be as easy to show that all the social virtues comprehended in the general idea of love to our neighbor naturally flow from this first and most important of them, dutifulness to parents. There scarcely ever was an affectionate, obedient child who did not make a useful member in society.

And how much it is the will of God, that a universal attention should be paid to this precept, may be further argued from the promise itself of temporal blessings annexed to it. "Honor thy father and mother, that it may be well with thee, and thou mayest live long on the earth." I do not mean here to show how filial obedience tends to promote worldly prosperity (that has been done already), but to consider worldly prosperity as actually promised to filial obedience. That the promise was so to be understood in reference to the Jews, none, I suppose doubt. It was by temporal rewards and punishments chiefly that they were governed. And he who carefully examines their history will find not a few instances of the fulfillment of this promise to persons eminent for filial piety. Some of them we shall have occasion to mention under the next head of discourse. But the promise, as appears by the use the

Apostle here makes of it, extends further than to the Jews. And, if we will understand the phrases of its being well with us and our living long on the earth, in a qualified sense, as we certainly should, the state of Christians in civil society being different from that of the Jews, it will not be difficult to prove that God is mindful of His promise now as well as formerly.

There are few ages and few countries which do not furnish some remarkable instances directly in point to the matter before us. We ourselves have known persons whose tender regards to their parents have been tried by very peculiar circumstances, and who have acquitted themselves in a manner as extraordinary; these persons, I say, we have seen emerge from low and obscure stations in life to situations of affluence and eminence in which they have flourished to a good old age. So that it might be said of them, in the strictest sense of the expression, that it has been well with them and that they have lived long on the earth. But admitting, with respect to many dutiful children, that an abundance of wealth, honor, and years does not fall to their share; yet if so much of this world's good is allotted them as it is for their real advantage to have, and if, having been useful and happy in life, they die in honor and peace, the words of our text may be said, in the general and substantial import of them, to be made good to them. And that this is a fact in regard of those who obey their parents in the Lord, that is, obey them from a sense of duty to God, is capable of clear proof. Such persons may be called pious or godly, and we are assured that "godliness hath the promise of the life that now is, and of that which is to come," 1 Timothy 4:8.

It is the will of God then, children, that you obey
your parents. Be persuaded, therefore, to your duty.
You believe that there is a God, that He governs the
world, that prosperity and adversity are at His disposal, that you must die, and that your happiness in
a future state depends upon His favor. Will you then,
dare you, be wilfully disobedient to so great a Being
who can make you miserable in this world, and who
can destroy both soul and body in hell? But rather
let me entreat you, by the mercies of God, to render
a cheerful obedience to His will by the mercies of a
God, who, in the character of a tender and indulgent Father, deigns to pardon the numerous offenses of us His undutiful but penitent children for
the sake of the obedience and death of Christ, His
only begotten and well-beloved Son. And now, to all
the arguments we have drawn from the law of nature, and the express command of God, I have only
to add those which result,

3. *From example.* Here, to illustrate is to persuade;
to hold up to your view instances of filial piety is, at
once, to instruct you in your duty and to allure you
to it. And thanks be to God! Degenerate as the world
is, history, both profane and sacred, furnishes examples enough to our purpose. We will content ourselves here with citing a few from Scripture.

The reverence which Shem and Japhet expressed
for their father's honor did not fail to draw a blessing upon them, as did the contrary behavior of Ham
a curse upon his family. The entire confidence
which Isaac placed in his father Abraham, and the

ready submission he yielded to his will on the most
trying occasions, were tempers truly admirable, and
signally rewarded by heaven. Jacob acted as became
one who had received the blessing at the hand of
his venerable parent when he paid so dutiful a regard to his commands in the alliance he contracted
with the family of Laban. And it was commendable
in Esau, whatever might be his character in other
respects, to forbear marrying the daughters of
Canaan, because he saw they pleased not Isaac his
father.

The many expressions of filial duty and affection
which occur in the story of Joseph must strike every
attentive reader with admiration and pleasure: nor
can we see him distinguished in so extraordinary a
manner as he was by the smiles of providence without concluding that his piety to his father was
highly pleasing to God. The love which good old
Jacob bare to him in his tender years was, no doubt,
heightened by the son's assiduous attention to conform to the will of so indulgent a parent. And, as he
learned obedience by suffering, for he was trained
in the school of affliction, so he gave the most affecting proofs of it when elevated to the highest station next to Pharaoh in Egypt. How earnestly did he
enquire of his brethren, when they came to buy corn
of him, after the welfare of his father! "Is your father
well, the old man of whom ye spake? Is he yet alive?"
Genesis 43:27. What a tender message did he send to
him by his brethren, entreating him to come down
to Egypt, and assuring him that he should be near
him, and he would nourish him lest he should
come to poverty! What respect did he show him by

meeting him in his chariot with his proper attendants at Gothen! And what ardent affection, by falling on his neck and weeping on it for a considerable time! How did he pride himself in the honor of presenting his aged parent to Pharaoh! In short, filial affection, reverence, and obedience stamped his whole conduct to the end of life. When he presented his children to their grandfather to receive his dying blessing, "he bowed himself with his face to the earth," Genesis 48:12. When he had performed the last tender office of closing his eyes in death, "he fell upon his face, and wept upon him, and kissed him," Genesis 50:1. And the dear remains of his venerable parent he failed not to attend to the land of Canaan, and to deposit them in the sepulchre of his ancestors with every possible expression of genuine sorrow and affectionate respect.

So extraordinary a character as Moses is not to be passed over in silence, and the rather as a remarkable circumstance occurs in his story to justify the inference that he was particularly attentive to the duties we have been recommending. The circumstance I refer to was the respect he paid to Jethro, his father-in-law, when he made him a visit in the wilderness. "Moses went out to meet him, and did obesciance, and kissed him," Exodus 18:7. Nor did he content himself with rendering him these external expressions of regard; he listened to the prudent advice which Jethro gave him, "and did all that he had said," Exodus 18:24. And thus were the duties of filial obedience, which he so solemnly enjoined on the Israelites, exemplified in his own conduct.

The generous attention, too, of Ruth to her

mother, Naomi, amidst all that sad reverse of fortune which she suffered in a strange land, is not admired enough. Naomi was her husband's mother, a widow, childless, and reduced to poverty. In this destitute state, she resolves to return to her own country. It might naturally be expected, considering what is the manner of the world, that Ruth, having lost her husband, Naomi's son, should have no great objection to the parting with his mother. But such is her attachment that she will, on no account, leave her. And how God rewarded her duty and piety in the story at large related; she married into a wealthy family, became the mother of numerous offspring, and had the great honor of standing on the list of those from whom the Messiah descended.

David was as eminent for his magnanimity and generosity as for his sincere and fervent piety, and his attention to the safety and repose of his venerable parents during the cruel persecution he suffered from the house of Saul affords a striking proof of the one as well as the other. Driven as he was by that infatuated prince into the wilderness, he presented an address on their behalf to the king of Moab, entreating him to grant them an asylum at Mizpeh, "Let my father and my mother," says he. "I pray thee, come forth and be with you till I know what God will do for me. And he brought them, it is added, before the king of Moab: and they dwelt with him all the time that David was in the hold," 1 Samuel 22:3-4.

The next instance to be mentioned, and which we have already adverted to, is Solomon. From the great respect he paid to his mother when he was grown to man's estate and had ascended the throne

of Israel, it may be fairly concluded that he held all
that duty we have been explaining and enforcing in
the greatest reverence. And his dutiful carriage to
his parents was one striking proof of the wisdom for
which he is so much celebrated in sacred writ. The
particular I refer to was his behavior to his mother
when she demanded an audience of him. It is said,
"the king rose up to meet her, and bowed himself
unto her, and sat down on his throne, and caused a
seat to be set for the king's mother; and she sat on
his right hand," 1 Kings 2:19.

The obedience of the Rechabites to the commands of Jonadab, their father, and in instances too
of a very self-denial nature, is held up by the prophet
Jeremiah to the view of the Jews in order to expose
the exceeding great undutifulness of their carriage
towards them. Jonadab had solemnly forbidden
their drinking wine all their days, and building
houses, and cultivating vineyards and fields, for reasons too particular to be here explained. They were
obedient; no temptation could prevail on them to
violate their father's commands. Wherefore this
message is sent them by the prophet, in the hearing
of the Jews. "Because ye have obeyed the commandment of Jonadab your father, and kept all his precepts, and done according unto all that he hath
commanded you; therefore thus saith the Lord of
hosts, the God of Israel, Jonadab the son of Rachab
shall not want a man to stand before me for ever,"
Jeremiah 35:18-19.

We might mention other striking examples,
both in the Old and New Testaments, but that of our
Lord Jesus Christ shall suffice. It is said of Him,

when He was twelve years old, that "He went down with his parents from Jerusalem to Nazareth, and was subject unto them. And He increased in wisdom and stature, and in favor with God and man," Luke 2:51-52. And the affectionate attention He paid to them through the whole of His life may be easily imagined from the tender words which dropped from His lips in the very article of death. Seeing His mother and the disciple whom He loved, standing by the cross on which He was expiring, He said to her, "Woman, behold thy son!" and then to the disciple, "Behold thy mother!" meaning thereby to commend them to each other's cordial regards. And the sacred historian immediately adds, "From that hour that disciple took her unto his own house," John 19:25-27. How admirable an example is this! And what a deep sense must our Savior have had upon His mind of the importance of filial duty, thus solemnly to enjoin it, in effect upon us all, with His expiring breath!

Thus have we urged upon children the duties they owe their parents by arguments drawn from the light of nature, the express command of God, and the examples of persons eminent for wisdom, virtue, and piety. Weigh these arguments, children, we beseech you, and resist the force of them if you can. Should you, however, be insensible to them, you will forfeit all claim to humanity and good sense, as well as religion. On the contrary, should you feel their force, and be disposed cordially to obey your parents in the Lord, we are authorized by the Word of God to assure you that it shall be well with you in this world, and in that which is to come.

15

The Duties of Children
by Henry Venn

1. *The duty of children towards their parents is to honor them by respectful language, by abstaining from everything that may reasonably give them the least offense or disquiet.* All young people who receive the Scripture as the rule of their behavior will esteem it their duty to be exact and conscientious in this respect because, in the Scripture, God requires children to honor their father and mother, promising His blessing to all who do so. This homage is expressly said to be "well pleasing unto the Lord," Colossians 3:20. The crime of disobedience to parents is marked as the just object of the curse and judgments of God, for you read that immediately after the prohibition of idolatry, a sin levelled directly against the glory of God Himself, and after appointing all Israel to pronounce the idolater accursed, the very next offense which, at the same time, is held forth as the object of universal execration is the neglect of paying a dutiful regard to parents: "Cursed be he that setteth light by his father or mother, and all the people shall say Amen," Deuteronomy 27:16. And, in case any child was "stubborn and rebellious," refusing to obey the voice of his father or of his mother after correction, it was the special appointment of the Most High

God that his father and his mother should "lay hold on him, and bring him out unto the elders of his city, and unto the gate of his place; and they were to say unto the elders of his city, This our son is stubborn and rebellious, he will not obey our voice; he is a glutton and a drunkard. And all the men of his city shall stone him with stones, that he die: so shalt thou put evil away from among you; and all Israel shall hear and fear," Deuteronomy 21:18-21.

What strong conceptions of the great guilt of disobedience to parents must this ordinance raise in the minds of all who regard the Word of God? For, though this civil and political law is not now in force against rebellious children, it remains still a sufficient proof of the detestation with which God regards the disobedience of children towards their parents.

2. *It is the duty of children to conceal and extenuate the imperfections of their parents, so far as truth and justice will admit.* This is but a small return for the great benefits which they have received; and if, instead of thus acting tenderly, they join in reproaching their parents, in exposing voluntarily either their sins or their indiscretions, they are very criminal in the sight of God. It was the sin of publishing and ridiculing, instead of covering, his father's shame, which brought down a signal judgment upon Ham, the son of the righteous Noah.

3. *It is the duty of children to requite their parents, as far as lies in their power, for all the comforts and benefits by their means bestowed upon them.* Ingratitude is the only sin which never found one single advocate; yet, of all ingratitude, the negligence of children in supporting and comforting their parents is by far the most black and abominable that can be practiced by man towards

man. For what care and expense, what solicitude and labor for the welfare of their offspring, are not parents usually wont cheerfully to bear? Now when, in the course of God's providence, parents stand in need of some returns of the same tender disposition towards themselves, when the infirmities of age or the burden of affliction comes upon them, what child that is not without feeling, as well as without any tincture of Christianity, but must rejoice to be as helpful to them, now going out of the world, as his parents were to himself when he first came into it? This exercise of gratitude is marked in Scripture as the bound duty of children towards their parents, and a neglect of it is considered not only as a renunciation of the Gospel, whatever zealous professions of love for it may be pretended, but as a crime which even pagans, void of the light and advantage of God's Word, would many of them abhor. "If any provide not for his own (his own near relations and, especially, his own aged parents), he hath denied the faith, and is worse than an infidel," 1 Timothy 5:8.

The exact proportion, indeed, which a child ought to set apart for the discharge of this duty to his parents, must be various according to the condition of life. But if it is inadequate to the income of the child, God will regard it as a vile and despicable offering. And this rule may always be observed, that if a child can be lavish in the pursuit of pleasure, and live in expensive splendor, while he is satisfied with assigning to his parents a strait and bare subsistence, a sense of duty is certainly not felt; and what is given is given rather from a fear of scandal or from dread of remorse than from love to God or affection to his own parents.

4. *The last duty I shall mention due from children to their parents is obedience.* Obedience in all cases which lie within the proper scope and influence of the authority of parents; where their commands do not lead their children to oppose what God had required, to do violence in matters of conscience to their own minds, or to transgress the laws of their country.

These are the duties which children are bound, from their relation to their parents, to observe. And those children who obey the Scripture will be found dutiful and affectionate, and very observant of these things. Indeed, those parents who are neglected or despised by their children may generally impute it to themselves. It is the effect and punishment of their own sin. They fostered when they should have corrected wicked tempers in their children's earliest years; they shamefully sacrificed parental authority to a froward mind, and abjectly submitted to be governed by those over whom they were appointed governors in the order of nature, and by the command of God. Or where this most foolish and cruel fondness has not been the cause of undutifulness to parents, a profane education, in ignorance of Christian principles, often had; for this encourages a proud, independent spirit, which, as it fears not God, will not pay reverence to man, neither feeling obligation nor bearing restraint. Excepting, therefore, a few cases, Christian parents, through the grace of God prospering their endeavors, will reap as they have sown, and enjoy, even before they leave this world, the fruit of those cares and pains with which they have studied to promote the salvation of their children, and will often die in the pleasing expectation of meeting them in endless glory.

16

Heaven Considered as a Family
by Samuel Stennett

"In my Father's house are many mansions; if it were not so, I would have told you: I go to prepare a place for you." John 14:2

PART 1

Among the many figures used in Scripture to represent the blessedness of heaven, none is more instructive and pleasing than that of a family. Domestic connections are the first in nature and, if the duties resulting from them were rightly discharged, they would be productive of the noblest enjoyments. With the assistance, therefore, of this figure, we propose now to lead you into a contemplation on the joys of heaven; and, from thence, to derive an argument in favor of those tempers and duties which have been so largely explained and recommended in the preceding discourses. Now, it will be necessary at our entrance on this delightful subject to present you with the picture of a family that approaches as near to perfection as possible. Such a picture we shall draw. Excuse me if the coloring is too high. We mean it should glow on the bosom of the beholder and kindle there all the passions of admiration, delight, and rapture.

The family we have in our eye, and I flatter myself more than one such family has existed in our world, were in affluent circumstances. Their habitation was neat, convenient, and elegant; it did honor to the skill of the architect without offending the simplicity of nature. The father was a wise, affectionate, good man; a sincere disciple of the meek and lowly Jesus, whose doctrine he professed and whose example he followed. A rich treasure of knowledge he had acquired and, with it, the happy art of communicating that knowledge to others in a plain, easy, and pleasant manner. The welfare of those entrusted to his care lay near his heart, and the schemes he daily planned for promoting it, which originated in prudence and benevolence, succeeded to his wish. His fervent piety, like the precious ointment that ran down from the head of Aaron to the skirts of his garment, diffused its sacred fragrance through all the house. The counsels of divine wisdom which flowed like a silver stream from his lips were sweetly mingled with the most pleasing expressions of paternal tenderness and love; and how was the felicity to persuade with greater energy by his example than his words.

The partner of his life, inexpressibly dear to him, had all the charm which virtue and religion could add to a form that commanded admiration and love. She was modest, prudent, and kind. Her happiness consisted in attaching the affections of her family to herself, and so disposing the affairs of it that harmony and cheerfulness should prevail through the

house; and the measures she took to this end were
followed with the same success that crowned the
generous offices of her husband. Now, was she less
attentive than he to the duties she owed to God; her
devotion was as sincere, though perhaps more rapturous than his. Such being the character of these
amiable people, it is not to be wondered that they
reigned securely in the affections of their domestics,
and possessed an authority over them, on all occasions cordially acknowledged, without their seeming to assert it.

Their children, for they had a numerous family,
inherited the virtues of their parents, as well as a
striking resemblance of their persons. While young,
they fondly hung on the bosom of their mother,
amply rewarding maternal attention and care with
the playful and endearing smiles of infant simplicity. Beauty bloomed in their countenances; and, as
the power of reason expanded, the seeds of religion,
which had been carefully sown in their breasts,
sprung up under a divine influence, and promised a
fair and joyful harvest. They knew, they felt, they acknowledged their ignorance, guilt, and depravity,
and looked for pardon and eternal life through the
mediation and grace of the Lord Jesus Christ. Each
step they advanced towards manhood furnished
some pleasing proof of their progress in knowledge,
purity, and benevolence. Filial obedience was their
delight and, when a temptation to undutifulness at
any time found access to their imagination, it was
quickly opposed by the warm resentments of un-
conquerable attachment. The social commerce daily
carried on between their parents and them, in a

most soft and easy manner, was a continual source of growing pleasure to them both, as was also the commerce that subsisted among themselves. Friendship, that balm of human life, was here enjoyed with little or no interruption. A mutual exchange of sentiments and passions, accompanied with a thousand offices of generous love, confirmed the union nature had created. And so they were happy, in a degree, beyond what is usual in the present life. They tenderly bore each other's griefs and sincerely shared in each other's joys. How good, how pleasant must it have been, to behold brethren thus dwelling together in unity!

The characters, too, and deportment of the servants were such as entitled them not only to the good-will, but the affection of the family. They were modest, faithful, diligent, and cheerful; contented and happy in their stations, and ever disposed to do their duty from motives of love as well as interest. The golden rule of doing to others as we would have them do unto us was deeply imprinted on their breasts, and it was their aim not only to escape the reproaches of a self-accusing conscience, but to enjoy the commendations of those they served and, more especially, the approbation of the great God.

In a house composed of such members, it may be easily imagined, peace and pleasure must have abounded. The welfare of the whole was the object of every individual, and each one partook liberally of the general stock of happiness which their mutual labors produced. One office of kindness succeeded another. Business and relaxation had their proper hours assigned them. Now they were in action, then at rest; now employed in their several departments, and then enjoying the pleasures of social intercourse. Their table was richly spread with the bounties of providence and their cup ran over. Strangers to sickening intemperance and guilty mirth, they ate their food with relish and drank their wine with cheerfulness. The friends of virtue and religion met a hearty welcome at their board and indigence was liberally relieved by their hospitality. Their eyes pitied the distressed and their hands clothed the naked; the widow, the fatherless, and stranger blessed them. The stated seasons of devotion they considered as the most usual and improving portions of time. With pleasure they assembled, with attention they listened to the doctrines and precepts of God's Word and, animated by one Spirit, they addressed their prayers and praises to the great Author of all their enjoyments.

Thus happily they passed their days, distributed in prudent proportions between actions, study, recreation, and devotion. Following the simple dictates of nature, they acquired and preserved health; living on good terms with their neighbors, they secured to themselves peace; cultivating domestic affections, they enjoyed a flow of innocent and enlivening pleasure; improving their opportunities for contemplation and discourse, they grew in wisdom and virtue; and, conversing daily with heaven in the duties of religion, they were gradually prepared for the sublime services and joys of that better world.

Such was the family we mean to describe, and whose story, in many interesting particulars of it, it would have been both edifying and pleasing to re-

late. But we forbear. Enough, I think, has been said
to kindle in our breasts an ardent desire to copy
their amiable example, and to partake of the rich
pleasures they enjoyed. Would to God there were
many such families as these! But we have another
object in view by holding up this picture to our
imagination; it is to assist us in our attempts to
frame some conception of the blessedness of the future state. This figure, you see, our Savior adopts in
the text, and upon this figure we mean to ground
the present discourse.

The Apostles, to whom the words were more immediately addressed, may be considered as compos-
ing one family. Over this family, our Savior, in the
character of an indulgent parent, presided. With
them He, from day to day, associated in all the
habits of the most tender and familiar friendship;
defending their persons, supplying their wants, as-
sisting their labors and, by His instructive and animating discourse, at once enlightening their understandings and diffusing heavenly joy through
their hearts. But He was now at the eve of His final
departure from them. The tidings of this sad event,
with which He had just acquainted them, filled their
breasts with the deepest anxiety and sorrow. With all
the tenderness, therefore, of a dying parent, He ad-
ministers seasonable consolation to them. He says,
"Let not your heart be troubled: ye believe in God,
believe also in Me." So He leads their views forward
to the world whither He is going, assuring them
that they should, by and by, follow Him to that bliss-
ful state, and there enjoy in the highest perfection
those domestic pleasures of which they had here

had some taste. "In My Father's house are many
mansions; if it were not so I would have told you: I
go to prepare a place for you." These are words
which I need take no pains to prove to you may, with
truth, be considered as addressed to all His faithful
disciples in every age and country, as well as the
Apostles.

Heaven He compares to a house, to convey an
idea of its beauty, convenience, and stability. The
house, He tells them, was His Father's, that great
Being to whom He stood related after a manner infinitely more glorious than any other, as He was His
own, His only begotten, and well-beloved Son. A
house built by His Father in which He constantly re-
sides, and where He displays His glories in the most
perfect manner. In this house, there are mansions,
abiding places, apartments for every one of the family, suited to their several capacities and conditions.
Of these mansions He tells them there are many, to
intimate that the members of this family are numerous, and that provision is made for them all.
And to prepare this happy place for them, and for all
who stood related to Him, was His object in going
there, as well as to receive Himself the just reward of
His sufferings. To all which He kindly adds that, if it
were not so, He would have told them. They had, before this, heard of heaven, framed some idea of it,
and been firmly persuaded of its reality. And they
might rest assured that such was His affection for
them, and such the convincing proofs He had given
them of it, that, if they had been imposed upon in
this manner, He would not have failed to undeceive
them.

Now, upon all these expressive circumstances in our Savior's figurative description of heaven, assisted by a variety of other passages of Scripture, we might ground many positions respecting the nature, perfection, extent, and continuance of the heavenly blessedness. And, from thence, we might proceed to a particular examination of the evidence of a future state of happiness to which that peculiar mode of language our Lord uses naturally leads us, a mode of language admirably expressive of His native simplicity and ingeniousness, and of the affectionate regards He bore to those with whom He was thus familiarly discoursing. On these things we might, I say, with great profit and pleasure, insist. But, waving the particular and accurate investigation of these important points, we will content ourselves with a general illustration of the metaphor before us, and the rather as this treatment of our text best comports with our intention in the choice of it. And so we will proceed to improve the subject.

Let us then consider the state of the blessed under the idea of a family.

To this figure, there are allusions in other passages of Scripture besides our text. The people of God, you need not be told, are often described as His children and servants; and "of Him, the Father of our Lord Jesus Christ, the whole family in heaven and in earth is named," Ephesians 3:14-15. Now, the ideas which this pleasing emblem suggests, we shall class under the following particulars:

I.   The house in which this family dwells.
II. The members of which it is composed.
III. Their employment and pleasures.

IV. The continuation of their existence and happiness.

I. Heaven is the house in which this family dwells.

Beauty, convenience, and stability, as we intimated before, are the ideas which first strike our minds when we speak of a house. And, when we attentively consider the fair mansions of the great, while we are pleased and delighted with the proportion, elegance, and grandeur of these noble structures, we fail not to admire the skill of the architect. The effect leads us back to the cause, and we presume that a builder who had so happily succeeded, were he to exert his powers on a larger scale, a plan of still wider extent, he would give further proofs of his ability. So, palaces the most superb, like those of which we read in ancient history, rise to our view and we are struck with wonder and veneration.

In such manner, we may proceed in our attempts to frame some idea of that august edifice which the great Parent of the universe has erected, at an infinite expense, for the entertainment of His family above. A sample He has given of His power and skill in the creation of this world, the mansion He had built for the residence of mankind during their abode on earth. What a pleasing employment to a contemplative mind to survey the wonderful building in all its parts, and the several parts in the relation they bear to the whole! When we go down to the foundations of this house, consider the superstructure raised thereon; examine the materials of which it is framed, and the manner they are arranged in which it is framed, and the manner they are arranged. Enter into its several apartments, measure its prodigious extend, dwell on the innumerable beauties with which it is adorned, and then gaze on the magnificent covering cast over it. When we thus contemplate, I say, this house built for the residence of man, how are our minds overwhelmed with the most stupendous ideas of the power and skill of the great Architect!

Hence, then, we may conclude with unquestionable truth that the house He has erected for the everlasting reception and entertainment of His own proper family, the family He most tenderly loves, the family He has redeemed with the blood of His own Son, must be commodious, beautiful and splendid beyond imagination. It is the house of God, the greatest of all beings! When infinite greatness and goodness unite to prepare a mansion for the residence of favorites, that mansion can lack nothing to make it glorious in the highest degree.

II. The members of which this family is composed.

The head of the family is the ever-blessed God, the fountain, centre and essence of excellence, perfection and happiness. What tongue can describe, what mind conceive, His peerless glories? The most exalted seraph cannot comprehend them. When our imagination has wandered through the universe, collected every possible excellence, and attributed them to one immense, omnipotent, and eternal Being, we shall even then have acquired but a faint idea of God. Such, however, is the character of Him who deigns to be the Master of this august house, the Father of this illustrious family! To a mortal eye He is invisible, but not so to the happy spirits who compose His household above. Their intellectual sight is too refined, strengthened, and enlarged, as not to be hurt or dazzled by the full blaze of glories poured upon it from the Sun of righteousness. They see God; they know Him; they converse with Him after a manner most pleasing, delightful, and rapturous.

As Master of this great family, He presides over their affairs with consummate wisdom and prudence, takes effectual care of their interests, prepares their table for them, and causes their cup to run over; He assigns to every one His proper service, accepts their offices of duty and love, and rewards their obedience with infinite liberality and goodness. And, as a Father, He is ever among them in all the habits of the most endearing familiarity, unbosoms His soul to them, assures them of His favor, enriches them with His bounty, and makes them happy beyond expressions and imagination. The most perfect picture that can be drawn of an earthly parent exhibits but a shadowy resemblance of His paternal wisdom, faithfulness and love. These qualities, in whatever degree they may be supposed to exist among any of His intelligent creatures, originate from Him; when He, therefore, in the character of a Father, assembles His children about Him, they will, no doubt, be displayed in all their transcendent perfection.

Christ is the Son of the living God, Matthew 16:16, His own, His only begotten Son, Romans 8:32 and John 1:14, the brightness of the Father's glory,

and the express image of His person, Hebrews 1:3.
But it is in the relation He bears to the children of
this family as their elder brother that we here consider Him. Such was His compassion for them, such
His love to them, that He voluntarily became a man,
and wept and bled and died to restore them to their
original innocence, and entitle them to the joys of
heaven. "As the children were partakers of flesh and
blood, He also Himself took part of the same,"
Hebrews 2:14. Although, "being in the form of God,
He thought it not robbery to be equal with God, yet
He took upon Him the form of a servant, was made
in the likeness of men, and being found in fashion
as a man, humbled himself, and became obedient
unto death even the death of the cross," Philippians
2:6-9. "Wherefore God hath highly exalted Him, and
given Him a name above every name," Revelation
5:9. He rose from the dead, ascended in that very nature He had assumed up into heaven, and there displays His mediatorial glories to the view of "ten
thousand times ten thousand, and thousands of
thousands, whom He has redeemed by His blood,"
Revelation 5:11, and who all join in ascribing
"blessing, honor, glory, and power, unto Him that
sitteth upon the throne, and unto the Lamb for ever
and ever," Revelation 5:13. What unutterable joy
must this happy company feel while their wonder-
ing eyes are thus entertained with the lively memorials of their elder-brother's unexampled compassion and love!

There, too, the Holy Spirit, the Comforter, who
proceeds from the Father and the Son, dwells. That
divine Spirit who descended upon the Savior at His

baptism in a bodily shape "like a dove," Luke 3:22, and who poured such a rich variety of gifts and graces upon the Apostles quickly after their Master's triumphant ascent up into heaven. There, I say, He dwells, irradiating the minds of the blessed, uniting their hearts to God and each other, and diffusing the fragrant odors of His grace through all the house. Under His auspicious influence, descending like the precious ointment on the head of Aaron or like the dew on the mountains of Zion, the fruits of knowledge, purity, and friendship are ripened to the noblest perfection and enjoyed with increasing flavor and delight to all eternity.

The children of the family come next to be considered. Angels are thus described in Scripture; but, that we may the better conform to the figure in our text, we will confine the character of children here to the redeemed from among men, and the rather as our Savior had them chiefly in His eye. These not only received, in common with others, their existence from God, the Former of their bodies and the Father of their spirit, but all the rights and privileges, and all the powers and capacities, peculiar to children. They had wandered from their Father's house and spent their substance in a strange land; but, by the mediation of Christ, their elder brother, and the gracious influence of the Holy Spirit, they were brought back to His church here on earth, the nursery or school He has appointed for the purpose of training and preparing His young children for the employments and pleasures of heaven. And, from thence, at the proper time they are removed, and united to the general assembly and church of the first-born above. The family is not, indeed, at present made up, the children are not all collected together. But when that happy period shall arrive, what an immensely numerous and illustrious company will this be! A company consisting of patriarchs, prophets, apostles, martyrs, confessors, and all the excellent of the earth: men of God who had existed in all ages and parts of the world, and under various dispensations, characters, and descriptions; who were once struggling with the incapacities, prejudices, and painful feelings of infancy and childhood, but are now arrived at man's estate, and possessed of abilities equal to the noblest exertions, and the most sublime gratifications. Once immersed in darkness, sin and sorrow, they are now exulting in the enjoyment of light, purity and happiness, all illuminated by the same divine Spirit, and actuated by the same heavenly principle, all of one mind and one heart, united to God their Father, and to each other as brethren, by the indissoluble bands of the most perfect friendship, and the most generous love. Such are the children of the family.

And, if the holy angels, agreeable to the figure we have adopted, may be considered as the servants of this princely household, nothing can be lacking to add dignity and glory to it. Yes, they are the servants of the great King, nor do they look upon it as beneath them to minister, at His command, "to the heirs of salvation," Hebrews 1:14. When He sent them on this errand to our world, they clapped their wings for joy; they instantly took their downward flight and, with rapture, sing "Glory to God in the highest, on earth peace, and good will towards men

below," Luke 2:14. They, friendly spirits! watch
around the tents of good men during their stay on
earth, guard them with their flaming shields from
the powers of darkness, bear them hence at death to
the bosom of their Father, wipe the falling tear of
mortality from their eyes, array them in the princely
robes appointed them, bid them welcome to their
long-wished-for home, and are never weary of rendering them every possible office of kindness and
love through an endless duration of existence. Of
such members is the heavenly family composed.

The next question is, how are they employed and
what are their pleasures? But this enquiry, with what
follows, we must refer to the next sermon.

PART 2

We have considered the house which the blessed
God has built for the reception and entertainment
of His family, and the members of which it consists.
Let us now proceed.

**III. How they are employed and what are their
pleasures?**

Action is necessary to enjoyment. Not exerting
our powers is an occasion of misery as well as abus-
ing them. It is not, therefore, the depraved and profligate only that are unhappy, but the thoughtless
and indolent. We cannot, indeed, in the present life,
exert our faculties to their full extent without feeling, more or less, pain and weariness. God has,
however, wisely so ordered it that the good proposed
shall compensate the fatigue endured in the acqui-

sition of it. And this consideration operates very generally on mankind to rouse them from sloth and stimulate them to action. But in heaven, the powers of nature, restored to their full vigor, exert themselves to the utmost without any fatigue or uneasiness. So the end of our existence will be attained in the most pleasing manner and we will become completely happy.

Now, I will apply this reasoning to that domestic idea of heaven we have adopted. The pleasures of the family are usually contrasted to the hurries and fatigues of business, and so we conceive of our house as a place of rest. But this rest does not consist in a total cessation from action; if it did, we would not be happy. It is true, we here repose ourselves and, by food and sleep, here recruit our animal spirits. But we do not pass all our time in indolence. We have our several employments: this and that active service to render one another, and the business of amusing and improving our minds by meditation, and familiar discourse. The retirement of a house is favorable to study, and the piety, good sense, and friendly dispositions of the several branches of a family are noble incentives to conversation. Occupied with these pleasing ideas of domestic employment, how cheerfully does the man of business in the evening of the day retire to his habitation! What joy does he feel to find himself encircled by his family, partaking with them of the bounties of indulgent Providence, and enjoying with them, in perfect ease and tranquility, the enlivening pleasures of social intercourse!

Thus may we conceive of heaven. At the evening

of the day, the hurrying, fatiguing, troublesome day
of human life, the good man retires to his home, his
Father's house, the mansion which Christ, His elder
brother, has prepared for him. There he ceases from
his labors, rests in the bosom of his God, and has no
other recollection of his past pains, disappointments, and sorrows, than contributes to increase his
happiness and heighten his joys. There he finds
himself instantly surrounded with that blessed
company we have been speaking of, all expressing,
by their cheerful smiles, the satisfaction they feel in
his having joined them, and all with infinite cordiality tendering him offices of love too numerous
to be reckoned, too substantial and glorious to be
described. And there, which is the main thing we
have in view, his intellectual powers are employed,
without embarrassment or weariness, in the contemplation and discussion of the most pleasing,
noble, and improving subjects.

Here, would our time admit, and might imagination be allowed its full scope, with what pleasant
scenes might we feast our eyes, with what ravishing
discourse delight our ears! I think I see this happy
family, assembled in the fair and stately mansion
their Father has erected for their eternal abode, arrayed in the pure and splendid garments of immortality, health, peace, and joy, blooming on their
countenances, their Friend and Savior bidding
them welcome to the richest banquet His love could
prepare, angels waiting on them, and the Master of
the house unveiling His glories to their view. I think
I hear their discourse. The subject is immensely
grand, the glories of the ever-blessed God displayed

in His works. They have powers for increasing delight to it. Every step they advance in their enquiries about it is marked with precision and certainty. The heavenly vision, glorious as it is, oppresses not their mental sight; the ecstatic joy it affords disturbs not their perception of the object. Their ideas and reasonings are interchanged with unimaginable swiftness and facility. And the pleasures which flow in one perpetual stream from the inexhaustible Fountain of knowledge are common to them all.

The theme has infinite varieties, each of which is a new source of admiration, love, and delight. Now they fix their eye on the first great Cause of all things, whose nature the brightest intelligences cannot comprehend, whose essence no created imagination can explore. They gaze on His glories which surprise, but do not confound; inspire reverence, but forbid fear. From Him they turn their attention to the works of His hands. Now the skill of the great Architect in the house built for their residence, its furniture, and entertainment, employs their contemplation; and then it will be the wondrous effects of His wisdom and power in the more remote provinces of His boundless empire. Now they dwell on the nature, capacities, and interests of the various orders of being that hold a different rank in the creation from themselves; and then on their own nature, faculties, laws and ends of existence. Now the scheme of providence respecting the world whence they came, occupies their minds; states, kingdoms, and empires passing in review before their astonished eyes: and then the long, the diversified, the entertaining detail of each other's history holds their attention with growing delight. Now they call over the several events that happened to them from the moment they came into existence to that of their translation there, and all the circumstances that combined, under the controlling influence of heaven, to bring about their final felicity; and then they recollect with rapturous joy the intimate connection of these events with the greatest and most sublime of all, their redemption by the death of the Son of God. On this transporting subject, "wherein He hath abounded towards us in all wisdom and prudence," Ephesians 1:8, they exert the utmost powers of imagination and reason. With every step they take, new light breaks in upon their minds and new joys circulate around their hearts. So a pure flame of ingenuous gratitude and love is kindled in their bosoms to the Father of mercies who laid the plan in the counsels of eternity, to the divine Jesus who carried it into execution, and to the Holy Spirit the Comforter who displays the glories of it to their enraptured sight. Thus employed in contemplating the most glorious objects, discussing the noblest truths, conversing about the most interesting events, and intermingling with their discourse the harmonious melody of the most exalted devotion and praise; thus employed, I say, how pure, substantial, and satisfying must their pleasures be!

Go into a family of piety and love. Some few such families there are in our world. Read the character of each member in his countenance. Be a witness of the tender offices of kindness they render each other. Join their company. Make one with them in their parties of innocent amusement. Listen to their instructive, entertaining, and endearing discourse. Hear their pleasant details of interesting events. Enter into their more serious reasonings. Share with them in the comforts and joys of their undissembled and fervent devotion. You will say with rapture, "Verily this is the house of God, it is the gate of heaven!" Genesis 28:17. But the pleasures enjoyed by this little society, though they may distantly resemble those of the blessed above, fall infinitely short of them.

How commodious is the habitation in which this infinitely large and noble society reside! No convenience is lacking to make it pleasant and delightful in the highest degree. There are apartments in it for everyone of the family, and Christ is gone before to make them ready. How delicious is their food! It is the food of angels. How highly flavored are their joys! They drink of rivers of pleasure that flow from the throne of God and the Lamb. How illustrious the company! They are all wise, holy, and good; free from every possible taint of folly, imperfection, and sin. Each one enjoys health, ease and tranquility without abatement or interruption. They are upon terms of the strictest amity and the most cordial friendship. Their discourse is upon subjects as delightful as they are instructive; subjects that afford the richest pleasure to the imagination and diffuse a sacred glow of divine affection through the heart. The Father of the family is present in the midst of them, pouring upon them the noblest profusion of beneficence and love. Their elder Brother and Friend, who loved not His life unto death, for their sakes, unbosoms His heart to them. The holy Spirit not only irradiates their understandings but, in the character of a Comforter, possesses them of the richest consolations. The innumerable hosts of angels who attend them are happy in contributing all in their power to their happiness. What refined, what exalted, what divine pleasures must this family enjoy!

The great Apostle of the Gentiles, in the midst of his labors here on earth, was admitted for a few moments into their company. And so enraptured was he with the joys he there felt, that whether he was in the body or out of the body he could not tell: it was paradise, and he heard things which it is not lawful for a man to utter, 2 Corinthians 12:1-4. Let us check our imagination then in its flight. We have not senses capable of sustaining the heavenly vision; we have not faculties at present equal to the investigation of this sublime subject. One thing, however, more must be observed of this family, and that is:

IV. The continuation of their blessedness.

When we visit the pious families that have been described, and share with them a few hours in their employments and pleasures, how reluctantly do we take our leave of them! And, when we see death, that cruel enemy of human felicity, breaking up these little societies, or at least ravishing some of the lovely members that compose them from the embraces of the rest, how we mingle our tears with theirs and silently say within ourselves, "Ah! it had been better for them if their pleasures had suffered more allays and interruptions; the event would have been less painful." Sad sight! to see dutiful and affectionate children pouring their unavailing tears over the tomb of a parent whose counsels, company, and love were continual sources of pleasure to them! Or over the graves of brethren and sisters with whom they dwelt in the sweetest harmony and friendship. So, however, it must be: so it is for their real interest that it should be. The several members of these communities on earth are called away in their turn to join the general assembly above. But Oh! how infinitely delightful the thought! That assembly, once met, shall never, never separate. Their habitation, persons, employments, friendships and pleasures shall suffer no change, diminution, interruption or end.

The fairest mansion on earth must, in a course of time, decay. Not a vestige now remains of those dwellings so famed in Scripture for the piety, friendship, and hospitality of their inhabitants. Yes, the time will come, when the vast fabric of this world shall be laid in ruins. But such is not the destiny of this more noble house above. No earthquake shall shake it, no fire consume it, no tempest destroy it. It shall remain for ever a monument of the skill and power of him who hath built it. It is "a building of God, a house not made with hands, eternal in the heavens," 2 Corinthians 5:1.

Here, one generation passes away and another comes. Parents die and their children succeed them; and, after a while, families that have boasted of their ancient extraction, become extinct. But, in this house above, all are immortal. Sickness, pain, and death have no admission there. Health ever blooms in their countenances and not the least declension of spirits, vigor, or strength, disturbs their repose. They feel no change, they dread no change. They are all happily met together and have the comfort of knowing they shall never part. It is the will of the eternal God, the Father of the family, that their existence, like His own, should have no end.

A thousand circumstances arise in this state of vicissitude and sin to dissolve our connections, interrupt our duties, disturb our discourse, and diminish, if not annihilate, our pleasures. Though the family is not broken up, yet, by this or that cross accident, its affairs are deranged, its members for awhile separated, one and another rendered incapable of their proper business, smiling plenty interdicted, pleasant discourse interrupted, the harmony of the house threatened, and all its joys sometimes converted into sorrow and sadness. But, in heaven, the reverse is the case. The order of the family is preserved inviolable; every one fills his proper station without a wish or an occasion of absence; one office of love follows another in perpetual succession, plenty ever abounds, peace reigns undisturbed, social intercourse flows on without interruption, friendships contracted are never dissolved, and pleasures new, various, and refined, are enjoyed without satiety, diminution, or end. The sun, once risen on those pleasant abodes, never goes down; and, when millions of years have rolled round, the happiness of the family is but beginning.

Thus have we attempted some faint description of this illustrious family above. A faint description it indeed is; yet I flatter myself it has made such an impression on our hearts that none of us can forbear asking some questions.

QUESTION. Is there really such a family as this? If there is, may I hope at death to be admitted into it? And, if I may, how shall I, in the meanwhile, express my gratitude to Him who has opened so glorious a prospect to my view?

ANSWER. To these questions, permit me, by way of improvement, to assist you and myself in making a reply. What we have affirmed of a future state of happiness is true.

We have, indeed, adopted a figure to assist us in our description of it; but to that figure our Lord Jesus Christ has directed us. "In my Father's house are many mansions. I go to prepare a place for you." And He who said this "is a faithful witness," Revelation 1:5. He is the truth itself, John 14:6. The Apostles had conceived a hope of this state before He thus expressed Himself: and such was His integrity and benevolence that we may be sure, to use His own language, had there been no such state, He would have told them.

It will scarcely be expected that I should here enter particularly into the evidence of this most cheerful and animating truth, or I might show you, that admitting it involves in it no absurdity or impossibility, that whoever considers the powers of the human soul, the history of Providence, the present state of the world, and many characters that actually exist on our earth, must allow that it is highly probable, and that the positive evidence of Christianity, beaming upon us like the sun in all its meridian glory, to possibility and probability adds certainty.

But on these topics of argument we will not now insist. All I mean is to derive a presumptive or collateral proof of what we cannot but wish to be true from the figure which has assisted us in our conceptions of it. A family, a pious family, especially a family that answers to the description in the beginning of this discourse, is a shadow, of which heaven is the substance. Visit the pleasant mansion wherein the God of grace deigns to dwell and see whether you are not struck at your very entrance with this prophetic inscription written in fair characters upon it. This is the gate of heaven.

Man is an intelligent being. As such, he is made for society. Families are the first social connections that take place among men. These are so constructed by the wise appointment of heaven as to create a union most permanent and endearing. And this union, were the duties of it practiced, would be continual source of truly noble and rational pleasure. But alas! sin has shaken the very foundations of these little societies, defaced their beauty, and spoiled their joys. They, however, still exist and, amidst all the disgrace and injury they have suffered, still exhibit proofs of the wisdom and goodness of the Creator, still reminding us of the happiness we were originally formed to enjoy. If, therefore, instances can be produced of any of these communities emerging out of the general wreck of human apostasy, recovering something of their ancient beauty and glory, and becoming in a degree, at least wise, holy, and happy, one would be apt from thence to derive a probable argument in favor of some further benevolent invention of the great Author of all good. Who knows, one cannot forbear saying, but these domestic pleasures, springing from the pure source of genuine religion, may be previews of more noble pleasures to be enjoyed hereafter? Perhaps the peace, order, friendship, and love restored to this and that dwelling are the early dawn of future and everlasting bliss. This and that house is become a temple of the living God; the Holy Spirit has condescended to take up His abode there, there to shed abroad the sweet perfumes of His grace and to conciliate some, if not all, of the members of it to the dominion of divine love. And would the blessed God thus dwell with men on earth, if He were not disposed to admit them by and by to dwell with Him in heaven! Surely this happy house is a figure, a type, a model of that infinitely more noble mansion, my Bible tells me, He has prepared for the whole family of the redeemed above. Religion would not again have flourished on earth if the glorious prospects which bring it into existence were all to expire in death. But the next question is:

QUESTION. May I hope, when called away from my habitation here below, to be admitted into this blessed family above?

ANSWER. An interesting question it is! It demands our most serious attention. Ah! my friends, to little purpose have we held up to your view the domestic employments and pleasures of heaven, if you should by and by be denied a share in them; if, when you knock at the gate of the house, the Master should say, "I know you not." As, therefore, we regard our present comfort and our everlasting happiness, let us well consider the grounds on which we are to expect admission into this family, and what is necessary to prepare us for associating with such company.

If heaven is our lot, we must acknowledge ourselves indebted to the free grace of God for it. "The gift of God is eternal life, through Jesus Christ our Lord," Romans 6:23. We must receive it with all that humility which a sense of our demerit inspires, and with all that gratitude which the value of the gift itself, and the immense expense at which it is procured, demand. That man considers his guilt, and the punishment it merits, on the one hand, and the infinitely glorious character of the Savior, and His deep humiliation and sufferings, on the other; but feels himself disposed most cheerfully to acknowledge with the Apostle that by grace he is saved through faith, and that not of himself, for it is the gift of God. But a meekness for heaven is as necessary as a right to it. And, since they who are to compose the family above are gradually prepared for it here by the salutary influence of the Holy Spirit, let us examine ourselves carefully on this great question, whether any of the genuine fruits of His operations appear in our tempers and lives. To those fruits, we will confine ourselves at present which are proper to our domestic character; a family of religion being, as we have shown, an emblem of heaven, and the nursery or school wherein men are trained up for the employments and pleasures of that state.

A family destitute of all order, decency, and love, and devoted to pride, sensuality, and contention, we may be sure, can have no connection with the general assembly above. That house, too, bears but little affinity to it, whatever character it may have for sobriety and good manners, which has no altar erected in it to God, and is a total stranger to all acts of piety and devotion. There may be indeed one here and there in these families who is a candidate for heaven, a lonely plant that sheds its sweet fragrance amidst the thorns and briars of these wretched wildernesses. And, on the contrary, in families truly venerable for their regards to religion, there may be here and there a root of bitterness springing up which shall by and by be rejected. But the members that shall compose the family above are chiefly to be looked for in the mansions where religion has set up her lovely banner and diffuses her sweet and balmy influence. Now what is our domestic character? Let us enquire how we have hitherto been used to conduct ourselves towards God, our parents, brethren, wives, children, preceptors, attendants, friends, associates and servants; whether we have treated them unbecomingly either in deed or word.

You masters, have you dedicated your house to God? Have you vowed to heaven that vice shall not enter your dwellings? Have you nobly resolved to exert the authority of kings and priests in these little commonwealths over which you preside? Do you sternly frown upon sin? Do you tenderly cherish every appearance of virtue and religion? Do you devoutly officiate from day to day at the altars you have set up in your tents? And is it your aim to enforce your instructions by your example? Be assured when you lay down your office as kings and priests on earth, you shall instantly resume these characters, but with infinitely greater dignity and splendor in the world above.

You mistresses, do you concur with the partner of your cares and joys in all his active and generous concern for the welfare of your families? Does the happiness of your offspring and your servants in this world, and in that to come, lie near your hearts? Do you bring up your children in the nurture and admonition of the Lord? Do you endeavor to sow the early seed of piety in their breasts? Do you counsel, encourage, and reprove them? Do you weep over them and pray for them? Is it your wish to mingle simplicity with prudence, gentleness and authority, and cheerfulness with seriousness, in all your deportment? Be assured, you shall by and by rest from your labors and your works shall follow you. There are mansions preparing for you above, and therein shall you be everlastingly happy.

You children, do you obey your parents in the Lord? Do you dwell together in unity! Do you meekly bear with one another, tenderly sympathize with one another and cordially assist one another? Is it your wish to make some recompense to those whose anxious care has led you up into life by copying after the holy examples they have set you? And is your filial piety cherished and improved by a prevailing sense in your breasts of the duty you owe to your Father in heaven? Be assured, you shall at death be received again to your parents' embraces and, with them, enjoy domestic pleasures in their highest perfection.

You servants, whom Providence has directed to these pious houses that you might receive a new and divine life, have you from the noblest motives ministered to them who have ministered to you! Have humility, faithfulness, diligence, and cheerfulness marked your conduct, reflected credit on your Christian profession, and entitled you to the friendship of those you have served? Be assured that "of the Lord ye shall receive the reward of the inheritance: for ye serve the Lord Christ," Colossians 3:24.

The public walk of life affords innumerable occasions of self-examination and trial. But would men bring their tempers and conduct to the tests which domestic intercourses furnish, these would, I think, suffice to throw a light upon their real characters. Is all that sweet peace, that smiling content, that tender sympathy, that generous friendship which prevails in a virtuous family congenial to your soul? Do you prefer the instructive and entertaining discourse that perfumes the tabernacles of the righteous above all the boasted joys that abound in the tents of sin? With cordial pleasure do you unite with the excellent of the earth in their returning exercises of devotion? Is a name and a place in such a house as this more envied by you than the most shining stations in the courts of princes? No doubt, then, you are related to the happy family above; mansions are preparing there for your reception, and angels are waiting to conduct you to your long-wished-for home.

To close the whole, let us express our gratitude to the great Author of all these our glorious hopes, in every possible way that duty and love dictate.

How vast, how immense, how inconceivable is

the love of God! He made us reasonable beings. He
formed us for the duties and pleasures of social life.
He established domestic connections. He bound us
to Himself and one another by the most firm and
endearing bands. But ah! pride and rebellion tore
these bands asunder. The Author of our happiness
abandoned the mansion He had built. Sin, with all
her deformed and wretched train, entered. And, in
the dwelling where the opposite graces had sweetly
reigned, strife, envy, discontent, malevolence, and
misery displayed their horrors. But Oh! amazing
grace! The Father of mercies pitied us. He sent His
Son to vindicate the rights of justice, to extirpate
Satan from the seat he had usurped, and to restore
harmony and love to the habitations His Spirit had
deserted. The Prince of peace arrayed Himself in
mortal flesh, and wept and bled and died to compass
these great ends. This object He has attained.
Families emerge from the ruins of human apostasy,
recover in a degree even here their original simplicity, beauty, and glory, and by and by acquire their
utmost height of splendor and perfection in the
world above. What amazing grace is this! Rejoice, O
heavens, and be astonished, O earth! Let every bosom that receives these tidings exult with joy!

But, amidst the joy we feel, let us not lose sight of
those returns of duty which this unexampled grace
demands. There are many ways of expressing our
gratitude, and this of a cheerful persevering attention to domestic duties is not the least. Have we
thrown open the doors of our hearts and hailed the
King of glory to His residence there? Let us consecrate our houses also to His service. Let the fragrant

incense of prayer and praise daily ascend to heaven. Let all our actions, intercourses, and pleasures be regulated by His will. And, to His honor, let our knowledge, substance, influence, example, and all, be devoted. So shall we have the refined, ecstatic, god-like pleasure of forwarding the great and good design the Father of mercies has adopted, even that of rescuing our children, servants, and connections from impending ruin, forming them for the several stations they are to fill in life; and introducing them at length to the unutterable joys of heaven.